BUDDHAFIELD DHARMA

BUDDHAFIELD DHARMA

Practicing Buddhism on the Land

Published by Avalonia

www.avaloniabooks.co.uk

Published by Avalonia
BM Avalonia, London, WC1N 3XX, England, UK
www.avaloniabooks.co.uk

BUDDHAFIELD DHARMA: PRACTICING BUDDHISM ON THE LAND
© Buddhafield, 2016
Individual authors retain the copyright to all their work, as credited.
All rights reserved.

First published by Avalonia, April 2016
ISBN 978-1-905297-94-8

Typesetting and design by Satori
Cover image: Yatra photograph by Lokabandhu
Illustrations as credited in the text.

British Library Cataloguing in Publication Data. A catalogue record for this book is available from the British Library.

DEDICATION

This book is dedicated to Devapriya, Teddy Stones, Fraser Clark and Dayajit: four generous souls who gave so much to Buddhafield in its early days.

ACKNOWLEDGEMENTS

Buddhafield has been the creation of a great many people, many of whom are hardly mentioned, if at all, in this book: it is not, after all, a history of Buddhafield. Over its 25-year life it has had several generations of leaders, plus a very great many stalwart helpers without whom not a single retreat, café, or festival could have been held. Deep thanks to all of them.

This book also is the creation of many people, and at least it's possible to thank a few of them by name: Mumukshu, for her original vision of a 'Buddhafield Dharma book', and Akasati and Shantikara for their gathering and editing of the Dharma talks that make up the body of the book. Alice, for the recipes from the Buddhafield Café, and Satyajit, for his pithy advice on 'Do's and Don'ts' at the Festival. Rupadarshin, that genius of improvisation, for his elegant instructions on how to construct a Buddhafield Hot Tub and Dome. Andy Smith and others at Festival Eye for their great reviews (and occasional criticisms!) of the Buddhafield Festival over the years, and Satyadarshin, for many of the photos. Dayajoti, for her labour of love in gathering together many inspiring Dharma quotes used in Buddhafield over the years, and for the list of Festival themes, and Ratnarashi, for reviewing the final material and making helpful suggestions for improvements. And an especial thank-you to Sorita d'Este from Avalonia, for her help and encouragement in bringing this long-planned work to publication.

Other contributors are acknowledged in the text itself.

Lokabandhu, March 2016, Glastonbury

FOREWORD

For the last twenty years Buddhafield has pioneered a new approach to the practice of Buddhism. It is an approach that emphasises the importance of our being in touch with the natural world. In Buddhafield we live in the open air, meditate in the open air, listen to the Dharma in the open air and communicate with our friends in the open air. In this, we follow the example of the Buddha, who according to tradition gained Enlightenment sitting under a Peepul tree and died lying in a grove of Sal trees that showered him with their blossoms. Some of his most important teachings he gave out of doors.

Buddhafield events are drug-free and alcohol-free, and its annual summer festival - the Buddhafield Festival - provides an ideal venue for those with children, and for young people.

At a Buddhafield event we not only feel in touch with nature but experience ourselves as being part of it. We realise that we have bodies as well as souls. We feel healthier, happier and more integrated. This is to claim quite a lot, but the tens of thousands of people who have attended Buddhafield events over the years can testify to its truth.

sd. Urgyen Sangharakshita
Founder, Triratna Buddhist Order and Community.

TABLE OF CONTENTS

INTRODUCING BUDDHAFIELD'S DHARMA

A FIELD OF LIVING BEINGS

The name 'Buddhafield' is perfect for Buddhafield. It has the obvious connotation of 'Buddhists in a field', but also a more secret, esoteric meaning which comes from the later Buddhist tradition and especially a classic Sutra called the 'Vimalakirti Nirdesa.' In this, a Buddhafield is described as the field of positive influence, of spiritual energy, generated by a Buddha or Bodhisattva – a field which may extend across multiple worlds and many dimensions of existence, and in which beings, having once managed to enter it, are almost spontaneously purified. This is the sort of atmosphere Buddhafield aims to create on its retreats and at the Festival.

Here're a few lines from the Vimalakirti Nirdesa in which the Buddha explains just what it is that makes a Buddhafield so potent. The Buddha is in dialogue with a young nobleman, the Licchavi youth Ratnakara, and his five hundred companions, saying -

THE PURIFICATION OF THE BUDDHA-FIELD

"Noble sons, a buddha-field of bodhisattvas is a field of living beings. Why so? A bodhisattva embraces a buddha-field to the same extent that he causes the development of living beings. He embraces a buddha-field to the same extent that living beings become disciplined. He embraces a buddha-field to the same extent that, through entrance into a buddha-field, living beings are introduced to the buddha-gnosis. He embraces a buddha-field to the same extent that, through entrance into that buddha-field, living beings increase their holy spiritual faculties. Why so? Noble son, a buddha-field of bodhisattvas springs from the aims of living beings.

"Ratnakara, a bodhisattva's buddha-field is a field of positive thought. When he attains enlightenment, living beings free of hypocrisy and deceit will be born in his buddha-field.

"Noble son, a bodhisattva's buddha-field is a field of high resolve. When he attains enlightenment, living beings who have harvested the two stores and have planted the roots of virtue will be born in his buddha-field.

"A bodhisattva's buddha-field is a field of virtuous application. When he attains enlightenment living beings who live by all virtuous principles will be born in his buddha-field.

"A bodhisattva's buddha-field is the magnificence of the conception of the spirit of enlightenment. When he attains enlightenment, living beings who are actually participating in the Mahayana will be born in his buddha-field.

"A bodhisattva's buddha-field is a field of generosity. When he attains enlightenment, living beings who give away all their possessions will be born in his buddha-field.

"A bodhisattva's buddha-field is a field of tolerance. When he attains enlightenment, living beings with the transcendences of tolerance, discipline, and the superior trance - hence beautiful with the thirty-two auspicious signs - will be born in his buddha-field.

"A bodhisattva's buddha-field is a field of meditation. When he attains enlightenment, living beings who are evenly balanced through mindfulness and awareness will be born in his buddha-field.

"A bodhisattva's buddha-field is a field of wisdom. When he attains enlightenment, living beings who are destined for the ultimate will be born in his buddha-field.

"A bodhisattva's buddha-field consists of the four immeasurables. When he attains enlightenment, living beings who live by love, compassion, joy, and impartiality will be born in his buddha-field.

"A bodhisattva's buddha-field consists of the four means of unification. When he attains enlightenment, living beings who are held together by all the liberations will be born in his buddha-field.

"A bodhisattva's buddha-field is skill in liberative technique (upaya-kausala).

When he attains enlightenment, living beings skilled in all liberative techniques and activities will be born in his buddha-field.

"A bodhisattva's buddha-field consists of the thirty-seven aids to enlightenment. Living beings who devote their efforts to the four foci of mindfulness, the four right efforts, the four bases of magical power, the five spiritual faculties, the five strengths, the seven factors of enlightenment, and the eight branches of the holy path will be born in his buddha-field.

"A bodhisattva's buddha-field is his mind of total dedication. When he attains enlightenment, the ornaments of all virtues will appear in his buddha-field.

"A bodhisattva's buddha-field is the doctrine that eradicates the eight adversities. When he attains enlightenment, the three bad migrations will cease, and there will be no such thing as the eight adversities in his buddha-field.

"A bodhisattva's buddha-field consists of his personal observance of the basic precepts and his restraint in blaming others for their transgressions. When he attains enlightenment, even the word 'crime' will never be mentioned in his buddha-field.

"A bodhisattva's buddha-field is the purity of the path of the ten virtues. When he attains enlightenment, living beings who are secure in long life, great in wealth, chaste in conduct, enhanced by true speech, soft-spoken, free of divisive intrigues and adroit in reconciling factions, enlightening in their conversations, free of envy, free of malice, and endowed with perfect views will be born in his buddha-field".

From the VIMALAKIRTI NIRDESA SUTRA, Chapter 1
Translated by Robert A. F. Thurman

BUDDHAFIELD'S VISION

Buddhafield has explored many different ways to talk about itself over the 25 or so years of its existence. Two are presented here: its most current 'Vision Statement', which you'll find on the Buddhafield website, and a much earlier version, from early 1995, before the name 'Buddhafield' had emerged – though it was to do so at the end of that same year, when the first Buddhafield Festival was conceived. No vision or mission statement will ever please everyone, and a simpler, but very popular one simply states *"Buddhafield is."* For those who prefer a few more words, here's the present one:

"Buddhafield is a community of men and women dedicated to following the Buddha's spiritual path. We are part of the wider community of the Triratna Buddhist Community, which is itself part of the wider Buddhist tradition.

"We are drawn to nature as the primary context for our life and practice — to the beauty of the natural world, to the living experience of interconnectedness it gives us, to the ancient sacred sites and landscapes around us. Therefore, we wish to create sanctuaries and shrines, for our own and others' benefit; to live simply and to live lightly on the land, using appropriate technology and exemplifying best practice in all that we do.

"Living in community, we aspire to include all of ourselves — to integrate work, play, practice, and our economic needs; to be receptive to our own and others' experience, to communicate in truth and harmony, and to live as a Sangha, building a Buddhaland for the benefit of ourselves and all beings.

"Because we believe in the universal value of the Dharma, and in our urgent need for a more harmonious relationship with nature, we wish to welcome others into our community and to actively go out to them, teaching the Dharma and sharing our inspiration, experience, and value."

MISSION STATEMENT 1995

Back in 1995, the loose team of Londoners who made up the Buddhafield crew didn't really have an official name, though one was being sought. Two contenders were the unlikely-sounding "FWBO[1] 'benders'" and "FWBO Upaya", the first referring to the canvas structures used for its meditation teaching, known as 'benders'; the second referencing the Buddhist ideal of 'Upaya-Kausala', or 'Skilful Means' – the willingness on the part of the Buddhas and Bodhisattvas to experiment and try new things in their desire to spread the Dharma. At the Glastonbury Festival, however, the project was known just as the 'Buddhist Meditation Marquee' and its café was the 'Green Buddha Café.' Here's the 1995 'Mission Statement', produced for the benefit of others within the FWBO who'd heard of this strange new wildly popular project that was running things in fields and at Festivals and wanted to know more:

"Our aim is to create contexts where members of the Western Buddhist Order can come into contact with people outside the existing FWBO situations, and provide the opportunity for them to become more involved in the Movement.

We aim to introduce people to the practices of Buddhism as understood within the FWBO whilst being open to the organic development of skilful, creative, and imaginative ways of communicating the deeper principles of the Dharma.

This year we will be running the Buddhist Meditation Marquee and the Green Buddha Cafe at the Glastonbury pop festival; probably three camping retreats including one more serious meditation retreat; and hopefully teaching meditation at WOMAD[2] and the Forest Fair festivals. There are also plans to purchase some land to use for other outdoor activities. If all goes to plan, this year we will teach 1,000 people meditation, organise 1,000 retreat-days, and raise £1,000/day every day the cafe is open".

---

1 The FWBO has now changed its name to the Triratna Buddhist Community. Likewise the Western Buddhist Order is now the Triratna Buddhist Order.

2 WOMAD is the 'World of Music, Arts and Dance' festival.

BUDDHAFIELD TODAY

The following pages showcase some of the principal dimensions of the current Buddhafield project – the Café, the Retreats, the Land, the Festival, and Buddhafield's proud tradition of meditation teaching at Glastonbury and other alternative festivals, an important part of its history and one that has enabled it to make contact with many thousands of people over the years.

Many other Buddhafield initiatives have come and gone over the years, or perhaps make an occasional appearance from time to time. For instance, there's Bodhi Nights, Buddhafield in the City, and Buddhacity, three experiments in drug-free dance nights in Bristol, London, and Brighton respectively, which over many years proved a great winter season complement to Buddhafield's main summer schedule.

There's also been Buddhafield/Q, an ambitious though short-lived outreach initiative; the Trevince community, deep in the Devon countryside and home for ten years to most of Buddhafield's core members; the Green Buddha Café, which gave birth to the present Buddhafield café; and last but by no means least the 'Megaproject', a bold attempt to house all people and activities that make up Buddhafield in a large property set in a large piece of land – and to do this, somehow to raise the very substantial sums of money that would be necessary. The Megaproject hasn't happened yet – but there's hopes that it will one day: watch this space!

Most recent, perhaps, is the Buddhafield Arts Collective, which came into being in 2015 through the shared aspirations of artists who had been involved over the years with the Buddhafield Festival's Décor Team to share a year-round creative support network and to expand on the shared experiences and deep connections that have formed over their years of involvement with the Festival.

Buddhafield has also given rise to three sister projects: Buddhafield East, Buddhafield North, and Buddhafield NZ in faraway New Zealand, each of which have their own stories which others will need to tell one day.

BUDDHAFIELD LAND

Buddhafield is the proud owner of Frog Mill and Broadhembury – two beautiful pieces of land in the West Country of England. They make a great pair of sites, complementing and contrasting one another: Frog Mill is relatively flat and easy to use, Broadhembury wild, sloping, wet, and difficult of access. Broadhembury is also home to the Prajnaparamita Sanctuary, a separate project but one that's very closely linked to Buddhafield, not least because of the extraordinary story of how the land came to be Buddhafield's back in the late 1990's.

Here's a few words about each –

BROADHEMBURY

Broadhembury was the first piece of land Buddhafield came to own, and as such will always occupy a very special place in its heart. The story of how it came to Buddhafield is an extraordinary one, and has been well told by Satyajit: you'll find his live talk online on Soundcloud.

On this land (very varied and including wetland and deciduous bluebell woods) Buddhafield is beginning to turn its vision into reality, integrating the magic of its retreats with the challenge of practicing sustainable land use in a real and long term way.

Thanks to the generosity of many, and the hard work of the Buddhafield collective over the last 5 years, Buddhafield's nearly raised enough to buy outright all 25 acres of the Broadhembury site — and is currently having a final push to raise the last £21,000! Please see the Land Appeal page on the Buddhafield website for more information — or find the Land Appeal stall at the Buddhafield Festival.

Stone Buddha guarding the entrance to Broadhembury

FROG MILL

The Buddhafield Stupa at Frog Mill

In 2006, with the help of loans from friends, Buddhafield bought its second piece of land: seventeen acres of land on Dartmoor. It's known as 'Frog Mill,' named after the ruins of an old Domesday-book-era mill found on the land. The site consists of several fields with thick established hedgerows a stream dividing the site and has views of Dartmoor.

Buddhafield describes it thus –

> *"Our aim for this tranquil site is to develop a magical and safe environment, providing the opportunity for adults and children to experience connection with a beautiful piece of land, hopefully for many years into the future. We are looking into various kinds of tree planting, including an organic orchard, and coppice for fuel and wildlife habitat. Taking on this project has been a leap of faith for us: in 2006 we borrowed £85,000 to buy the land and we wish to wholeheartedly thank all who have contributed £65,000 to our Land Appeal so far.*

Owning this land means that Buddhafield's larger retreats have a site that can be developed for their needs, and it has been for some years already the home of the annual 'Village' retreat.

PERMACULTURE AT BROADHEMBURY

We know that many of our current ways of using land are damaging and unsustainable. Permaculture — short for 'permanent agriculture' — is a way of looking at things, looking at the relationships between elements in a situation and how they affect each other, whether that's your back garden, a farm, or a planet. The ethics of permaculture take into consideration both care of the earth and care for people, asking not "What can I get from this land, or person?" but "What does this person, or land have to give if I co-operate with them?"

A good definition comes from Bill Mollison, regarded by many as the 'guru' of permaculture:

> *"Permaculture is the conscious design and maintenance of agriculturally productive ecosystems which have the diversity, stability, and resilience of natural systems. It is the harmonious integration of landscape and people providing their food, energy, shelter, and other material and non-material needs in a sustainable way."*

Some permaculture precepts can be summarised as -

> *Working with nature, rather than against it*
> *Seeing the problem as the solution*
> *Making the least change for the greatest effect*
> *Recognising that the yield of a system is theoretically unlimited*
> *And recognising that everything makes its own garden.*

Buddhafield seeks to embody permaculture design principles in the stewardship of both its pieces of land. In 2004, it employed the permaculturalist Phil Corbett to carry out a survey of Broadhembury, following which Dharmamrta developed a permaculture design for the site. This included planting trees for firewood and for fruit; creating terraces to provide flat land for camping, and planting hedges for shelter and privacy. Work on the design got underway during the winter of 2004, and continues. Work on the land will be an integral part of at least one Buddhafield Retreat each season. In 2009, it held a second Buddhafield Permaculture Design Course/Retreat, again on the Broadhembury land, led by permaculture teachers Steve Reid and Dharmamrta. The design task on that focused on ideas for developing the Permaculture Plan for Broadhembury, and some of these are copied below. The ethos behind the design brief was to provide at least some of the food and fuel we will need in the future by planting trees and edible plants now, and already over 200 trees have been planted on the upper slopes of the land, plus some own-root apple trees.

More recently developments include the creation of a 'forest garden': a planting of fruit, nut and fuel-giving trees and shrubs that will grow naturally like a forest — once planted, the trees are more or less left to get on with it. Buddhafield was awarded £10,000 by the Lottery fund in January 2011 to plant and develop the forest garden. By contrast, the priority for the 'Hearth', a flat area at the bottom of the site, is to make it safer, more accessible and more beautiful. There is plenty of wildness on the site, but the Hearth area needs to be a place where people can relax and be comfortable. All this is encapsulated in the following plan, composed after the 2009 retreat:

YEAR ONE

Start work on Forest Garden. Remove some areas of gorse, plant the trees. The Forest Garden will be established over the next few years.

Fill in various ditches with stone or pipe.

Establish pathways around the Hearth (possibly using woodchip made on site) mainly using existing trackways.

Plant more trees on the ash pasture (creating coppice for firewood).

Planting on the Hearth — particularly on the newly reclaimed area next to the ponds.

Harvest willow for use at the Buddhafield Festival.

Improve the ponds by the entrance to the hearth (year two also) and remove willow and bramble in that area.

General tidy up of earthworks including adding topsoil to the nearside of new terrace, tidy spoil removed from ditch behind.

Flatten terraces with roller.

Establish an area for wood chopping and pallet/gas bottle storage behind hot tub.

Plant hedge for cover around this area.

Create compost bays above the turning circle using festival poo and adding gorse and bracken.

Create trackway from hot tub area to shrine through the carr (woodland terrain).

YEAR TWO

Lay small section of hedge to south of hot tub to let in more light.

Remove some of the Douglas fir.

Further work on the Forest Garden, ponds and beautification of the Hearth.

Create a living willow walkway through the willow connecting Hearth to gorse area.

Remove a few more trees from ash pasture and plant more trees.

Level the back terrace (nearest to willow compound) and solve the waterlogging issue.

Working retreat at Broadhembury: preparing the Forest Garden

BUDDHAFIELD RETREATS

The aim of a Buddhafield retreat is to give the opportunity to have time away from normal everyday life, with all its demands and distractions, to explore who you are and how you are. Perhaps it is also to allow you just to be with "the way things are" for a while. A retreat can be an opportunity for reflecting on your life, exploring the Buddha's teaching, or deepening connection with nature. All Buddhafield retreats are camping retreats held on beautiful sites in the English counties of Devon, Somerset, or Sussex.

Living simply, elegantly and close to nature all go some way to providing the space – the 'supportive conditions' - for positive change to happen within ourselves. We use Buddhist practices such as meditation and ritual to help us engage with different aspects of ourselves.

Buddhafield retreats are open to people with all different levels of experience of Buddhism, though some, especially the annual 'Total Immersion' retreat, are reserved for those with prior experience of Buddhafield's introductory teaching. You don't have to be a Buddhist at all to participate in our 'open' retreats, on which introductory sessions are provided. The general approach to our retreats is that you are free to join in whatever is useful to you.

WHAT HAPPENS ON A BUDDHAFIELD RETREAT?

Most retreats follow a similar daily programme, with meditations first thing in the morning, a work period after breakfast, and then the main morning activity. Depending on the retreat, that could be a talk, workshop, discussion, practical activity or more meditation.

Although each retreat has a different theme or emphasis, participants generally learn and practice two kinds of sitting meditation, the Mindfulness of Breathing and the Metta Bhavana — loving-kindness — meditation practices. There may be periods of walking meditation too. Retreats are usually led by one or two teachers who are ordained members of the Triratna Buddhist Order.

Retreats are a truly communal experience, where everyone's contribution to running the camp is important, whether that involves chopping wood, preparing vegetables or keeping the hot water going for tea.

Afternoons are free for walking, catching up on sleep, chatting, reading, writing, or simply 'being.' There are often yoga or Tai Chi sessions on offer.

In the evenings, there will generally be a Buddhist ritual in the richly decorated shrine tent or in a sacred place under the skies. This is an opportunity to engage the heart and imagination, with chanting, drumming, poetry, and dance. Before bed, you can enjoy a hot drink by the fire or a soak in the hot tubs under the night sky.

All kinds of people come on Buddhafield retreats, of all ages, and from many different backgrounds. We find that the shared experience of elemental living, beauty and practice supports a very warm-hearted and open environment where deep communication can arise, and lasting friendships are forged. Buddhafield retreats are generally one or two weeks long.

The following paragraphs introduce some typical Buddhafield retreats; some held annually, and some 'one-offs.'

TOTAL IMMERSION: MEDITATING WITH THE TREES

The 'Total Immersion' retreat is Buddhafield's very popular annual four-week retreat for lovers of meditation - and for those who want to learn to love meditation. We invite you to join us in creating a silent meditation community in the magical meadows & woods of Easterbrook, a secret valley deep in the Devon countryside. It's a unique opportunity to deepen and practice intimacy with the beauty and teachings of the natural world. Living a life stripped down to its essentials we become sensitive again to the language of the birds; as our inner chatter falls away, our minds and hearts open to each other.

INTRODUCING THE TOTAL IMMERSION RETREAT:
AN INTERVIEW WITH KAMALASHILA

Sarah Boak asks Kamalashila what
Buddhafield's Total Immersion retreat is all about.

Sarah: How did Total Immersion retreats come into being?

K: The original Total immersion retreat was held at Dhanakosa [Retreat Centre in Scotland] led by myself, Vessantara and Viveka in around 2005. I thought it would work in Buddhafield, and we started the following year. I have led them ever since. Some years ago Paramananda got interested, and we started alternating years.

What are the benefits of retreats held in a natural setting?

K: If you live in nature, nature teaches you how to be natural. We come out of a highly artificial world into retreat. There are few straight lines and flat surfaces in nature, and it is not designed for convenience. This means we have to be much more aware even to live a simple life. There is an element of freshness and spontaneity that is unique. All these things generate the very best conditions for meditation reflection and generous behaviour – with the right teaching setup I think retreats in nature can even be better than a dedicated retreat centre.

What effect does spending such a long time in silence have?

K: There will still be verbal teaching, questions, and ritual chanting, so the silence is not absolute. But... Peace. Clarity. Confidence. Love. Silence doesn't mean we don't communicate or look at one another. We get to know one another deeply by relaxing in each other's company.

Are there teaching elements to these retreats? How do the retreat leaders support people's own self-reflection process?

K: There's a main daily teaching and question-answer session, as well as smaller, more off the cuff teachings throughout the day — plus of course one-to-one practice reviews for everyone.

Do you have any advice for people who are considering coming on the retreat but haven't done a silent retreat before or haven't spent such a long time on retreat before?

K: For most practitioners, longer retreats are easier, simply because there is more time to settle in and to relax with everyone in the community. But it's also possible to come for just the first two weeks.

What surprises you the most about the Total Immersion retreat?

K: That every year, Padmapani manages to upgrade even further his already incredible Naga Shrine. When we first started it was a little booth on a plank next to the stream. Last time I was there it was big enough for the entire retreat to do a puja right in the river itself – and the shrine itself was extraordinary. Perhaps not actually surprising (I know Padma very well) but definitely amazing.

Even after all this time leading these retreats, and with so much meditation experience, do you still benefit yourself from the Total Immersion retreat?

K: I always learn new and deep things about the Dharma from being in a fully natural environment over time. Nature is humbling and grounding as well as being incredibly beautiful, and this shifts your whole perspective — first on the elusive 'self', and then on the nature of existence. Getting to that takes time though. You need to be living in one place long enough to be part of the environment — then you start to understand. Usually, we are external observers, and that doesn't teach us much that's useful. What one learns is not information – which we already have plenty of – but about what we are and what our place is.

You've said a little about the difference between Buddhafield retreats and retreats at Centres – can you say any more? i.e. What does Buddhafield do differently and why is it worth people engaging with this different approach?

K: I think the previous answer applies here too. It is about being immersed in nature to the point where you realise you are part of it. And Buddhafield crews know from long deep experience of living on the land how to support everyone to do that. Their expertise and ingenuity are very impressive.

What do people tend to experience moving from the Total Immersion retreat back into daily life? What benefit does an extended period of meditation such as this have on people's day-to-day life in the modern world?

K: People will vary, but most will experience a lasting boost to their clarity and confidence. Leaving the beauty of retreat may be a bit challenging for some, but even that is educative and in the long term will make our lives more authentic, natural and real.

Meditating in the Naga Shrine

An Unexpected Meeting with the Wiseman
by Vessantara

Vessantara's account of his time on the 2012 Total Immersion retreat makes it vividly clear just how deep you can go on such a retreat – and what strange things can happen when you get there. He says -

I recently returned from the Buddhafield Total Immersion retreat in South-West England. The local weather gods are obviously a literal-minded lot, as they took the retreat title at its word and rained on us for all but 3 out of the 31 nights I spent there. So our field gradually turned into a mudbath as the weeks went by. I'm extremely impressed with how the Buddhafield team managed to keep the retreat running so well. Personally, being genetically designed for the wet West of Ireland, I didn't mind the conditions. In fact, from a Dharma point of view, I thought the constant rain was no bad thing. There was no other reason to be in that damp, squelchy field except to practise the Dharma. (To their credit, none of the 60 people left early, though I'm sure some felt like it from time to time.)

For me, it was a real relief after 6 months of setting up my life and renovating a flat, to be back on retreat and out in nature again. I'm in my element in the elements. Having been staying in Vijayamala's mother's house, where even in summer the heating is on at Ghanaian levels, my body sang at walking along lush Devon lanes and sitting by a swollen river.

I enjoyed our team, who all saw very eye-to-eye about how to teach meditation. As I expected, in that situation the fact that we were couples was very secondary to us being Order members guiding a retreat. (In agreeing to be part of the team, I had no intention of making any kind of statement about couples; for my reasons for deciding to do the retreat see my March report.) And, after over four years, I really appreciated the chance to teach on a meditation retreat again.

I found that within 2 or 3 days of arriving and having more time to meditate, I touched into a degree of carefree happiness and connection with the Dharma that I hadn't felt since my time in France. In fact, it was almost as if the whole long retreat experience was still there, just waiting to be unpacked again. My meditation was uneven, but there were times when I felt deeply in touch. I had one wonderful meditation which culminated in a small voice saying 'The blessings are completely present', and it felt like it. Then, on the last morning, I had a dialogue with Tara in which she assured me that everything would be OK at death, in the bardo and thereafter. She would always be there. She said: 'Where else could I ever go? I am you'.

However, difficult psycho-physical processes can go on, seemingly in parallel with deep meditation. During the retreat, I tapped into a feeling of overwhelming hunger, which was both physical and emotional. It related to something that happened to me as a baby. I was born and began to thrive, and then I started losing weight again. Eventually, my worried parents took me to a consultant. He examined me and said with surprise: 'This baby is starving.' It transpired that my mother had an abscess inside her breast. So although I was feeding, I wasn't getting what I needed, in fact, I was being poisoned. All this came flooding back, in waves. Whilst it didn't fully resolve over the month, by turning towards it whenever it came up, the intensity of the feeling diminished quite a bit.

On the last morning of the retreat, after my dialogue with Tara, I volunteered to drive a couple of people to the station. I went up to the car parking area, where there was an old barn, to get my (borrowed) car, only to discover that the brakes had locked. (The extreme wet weather had been too much for them.) I was sitting contemplating the smell of rubber, when suddenly there was someone standing by my offside wing: a middle-aged man, wearing a puffy jacket with 'Robert Wiseman Dairies' on it. I hadn't noticed him walk up, and the car park was empty. He seemed to have come out of nowhere. He said 'Have you tried rocking it?' We tried that, and various other ideas. Finally he said: 'I can fix it for you, but I'll have to take the wheel off.'

How a milkman with no tools was going to fix my brakes was beyond me. But I left him to it, to rush off and find someone else to do the station trip. When I came back ten minutes later, the wheel was indeed off, and he was cleaning rust off the brake assembly. Five minutes later I had a working car. It transpired that he wasn't a milkman but a mechanic, and he had a workshop in the old barn. I was told later that he hardly ever came up to use his workshop, so I was very fortunate that he happened to be there that morning.

However, for me, he was a magical apparition. Lost in what to do about my locked wheel, I hadn't seen him approach. It was as if a bodhisattva milkman with wish-fulfilling powers had appeared out of the earth. The theme of my whole month had been that, despite all the suffering in the world, life is deeply OK, and provides what you need if you entrust yourself deeply enough to the Three Jewels. It seemed as if the universe had decided to give me a small practical demonstration at the end of the retreat.

More than that, it was serendipitous, to put it mildly, that after weeks of going through a deep process all about my mother's milk, this mechanic should just happen to be wearing a milkman's jacket. (He told me that he had no connection with a dairy; he'd just acquired it to keep warm.) And if the universe wanted to add a little pun, to point out that there were deep, intelligent processes at work, then, of course, it would be the Wise/man dairy...

Cambridge, August 2012
Reproduced with permission from Shabda

Sitting around the fire, Broadhembury

BUDDHAFIELD AND THE PATH OF PARENTING:
THE VILLAGE RETREAT

The much-loved and long-running 'Village Retreat', held on Buddhafield's land at Frog Mill in Devon, is by far Buddhafield's largest retreat, with up to 300 men, women, and children of all ages gathering towards the end of the summer holidays for a burst of community before school starts again... Many come every year without fail, meaning that many of its young team members today came throughout their childhood and have quite literally grown up together. It grew out of a series of 'Family-Friendly' and 'Child-Friendly' retreats exploring how best to create conditions for parents to practice meditation, Dharma study and community living while their children were looked after and could themselves have fun while learning something of Buddhism's approach to life. These retreats were pioneered by Devapriya, who sadly died in 2012 but is remembered by a stupa in his honour at Frog Mill.

In 2012, Libby Davy heroically documented the history of the Village Retreat, which had then been going as a practice community for over 14 years. Her material offers some wonderful and inspiring insights into a strong-hearted communal effort to engage fully with the Buddha's teaching in the midst of family life. The archive, originally in audio form and produced in conjunction with the team at FreeBuddhistAudio, contains beautiful material, funny material, and challenging material - yet all speaks clearly of the Dharma and of re-imagining the ancient tradition of 'householder practice' in ways that should be of immediate interest to anyone concerned with finding and opening up new paths to the Buddha in the 21st Century. The project, eight years in conception (ever since Libby first came across the retreat at Glastonbury by reading a flier in the Buddhafields Café), came out of many years of discussion with Devapriya, Amaragita, Vimalaraja and many others on the Retreat and within Buddhafield/Triratna.

Libby writes of her experience in recording the archive, saying: "There were so many highlights for me. The best bit really was listening to people, streams, birds, the wind in the trees when during the 2012 retreat, and then again when we were reviewing the vast amount of material! There was so much of it, from a place I have truly grown to love and see my family and so many others be nourished by. I really appreciated hearing Vijayadipa talk about how the "inner child" can come out to play, about her three generations on the retreat, and so many other interviews. I was also delighted to find a segment on FreeBuddhistAudio of Sangharakshita talking about the hot tubs at Buddhafield, and how much freedom is available to us through such expressions of the Dharma.

"In the interviews we talked about the evolving place of children, young people, families and (by extension) parents and couples within the Buddhist world. There were long conversations about how the retreat community is playing a part in opening up that space, and supporting us all to enter the crucible of parenting - of life - consciously. Our first plan was to write a book, but what we have ended up with seems more relevant for now. Perhaps most poignant was making sure Devapriya's perspective was captured while he entered the last stage of life. The Caravan of Love it was. I would bring the day's recordings into him, so he had the chance to hear nearly everything, and reflect on his visionary, heroic legacy - in between choofs on his cheroot! Many thanks to all who helped make it happen and continue to support us, including Candradasa, Amaragita, Graeme Sutherland and Paul Chauncy".

The archive includes a great conversation with Amaragita, one of the pioneers of the family-friendly retreat, reproduced below, in which she explores questions such as –

"How do you maintain a deep practice of the Dharma when you have a family?" and "How can householders bring the Buddha's teachings to bear on their lives and also feed their own experience into the wider sangha?" It's a fascinating look at aspects of community practice, including single-sex activities, teenager contexts, working with noisy toddlers, developing ritual - and doing 'chocolate meditation'! Throughout it she speaks movingly of "being with her two loves," family and Dharma, rooted in a mythic context and in harmony with nature and the land.

The History and Vision of the Village Retreat
by Amaragita

Amaragita recounts the history of the Buddhafield 'Family-Friendly retreat' and explores a little of what makes it so special for her.

"My involvement with Buddhafield's 'Family-Friendly' retreat started after I'd had my daughter and realised I'd been a bit unrealistic about how often I'd be able to get on retreat once I had children. I already loved – absolutely adored – going to the Buddhafield Festival, and when she was about two I discovered the retreat and thought "right, now I can have an opportunity to be on retreat!" – it was just pragmatic really, wanting to get on retreat, and realising that here was an opportunity to be on retreat and have my children – my family – with me.

But as soon as I got there I realised it completely met a need of mine I didn't even know I had, which was for a sense of community, specifically inter-generational community. When you go to a Buddhist Centre or a retreat you're taking yourself there as an individual, which is fantastic of course. And if you're living in a Buddhist community, working in Right Livelihood, you can feel a sense that your Buddhist life is your home life, your work life, all of it is encompassed in a community. But if you're in a family situation it's harder to feel that, to feel within a context which mirrors what's going on on the inside, as it were. And this particular retreat – being Buddhafield, being on the land, and very arts-based, lots of music, lots of creativity, lots of making of things, was very appealing to me.

But also there were two people who were steering it, master-minding it: Devapriya and Carl Davies, and their ideas were ones that I resonated quite strongly with, especially the way they created a very archetypal, mythic realm on the retreat. They were very open to the idea that householders could practice, very supportive of how the parents there could develop that - it was a very small retreat when I started going on it, which was struggling a bit attracting enough people to be on the team each year.

I had a background in organisational development and working with volunteers, and I gradually saw there were a few structural things about how the retreat was organised, how it could be adjusted a bit and how that would really enhance it. I was chatting to Devapriya, just joking, and said: "wouldn't it be great if there was a waiting list to be on the team of this retreat?!" We had a good laugh about it – but that is, pretty much, what's happened now: there's more people want to be on the team than we have spaces for. Devapriya was very good at spotting people who had something to offer and just giving them space to run with things, so I gradually got involved. It became a bit of a winning team - a combination of him spotting something that I had to offer and me being very comfortable with what was already going on.

Devapriya was definitely the visionary for the retreat, and was always connecting with other people who he could see shared that vision. But at the same time it's odd to say that he led it or even that we led it – it's such a big retreat, it's like the Festival: there are lots of different team leaders, and what we do is create a framework for it. When you're in the midst of it, there's so much going on there's no one at the helm, really. It's got a life of its own really.

There're three key things we want to do each year. One is creating a culture where householder practice is valued and developed and emphasised and awakened, so people don't think they have to wait for 15, 20 years until their kids grow up so they can do the "real thing" in terms of Buddhist practice. So, on the retreat we have lots of different ways of having 10, 15, 20-minute meditations during the day, in lots of different places – so pretty much wherever you go, you get the opportunity for meditation. And we've got different sorts of meditation – for instance; we've got meditation for mothers with toddlers, where the toddlers will just be toddling around and there'll be a led meditation with someone there to keep them from harming themselves. We've got 'chocolate meditation' for children... we've got meditation all around really, and not just meditation, a sense of practice being everywhere. That's not new of course, but really focussing on it, in a setting where there's a real range of ages, is very effective.

So the retreat becomes the same as life is back home, so there's not that sense of disconnect , e.g., "I can't meditate the kids are making too much noise!" – on the retreat we don't shush the kids, you learn to meditate in the noise. Which is very different from other retreats! It's interesting; we've got some people coming from the one-year course at Adhisthana, and we've joked "you think you've got a good practice? – come on the retreat and see how long your patience lasts!" So we're learning to roll with what's actually happening, you know?

Then the second thing is a mythic context. We're following Triratna's system of practice every year through having a mandala of practice, and we go through a set of archetypes as well, so we have the archetypes of Warrior, Lover, Magician, and King/Queen underpinning the different practices, so every year the whole thing becomes a journey. And – just to make it more complicated! – we have a Dharmic topic each year, so we've been doing the Six Paramitas for a few years, one Paramita every year.

And thirdly it's about being in the land, the landscape, the aspect of connecting with the earth, connecting with the environment. These are the three things we do every year.

We've also been working with the 'Single-Sex principle' in a way that I think reflects what it's really about. On the retreat we've now got a 'Men's Lodge' – a men's tipi - , plus a Women's Lodge, with different things going on within them – absolutely lovely rituals and ceremonies, for instance to honour the new mothers, people who've just become mothers, and new fathers, and we're developing what will become full-blown 'Rites of Passage' for young men and women, rituals which are gender-specific, which are about coming into your own womanhood or manhood. For me, it's a way of organising things that's based on common sense, for certain activities it just makes sense. For instance, my daughter's twelve, she's just beginning to get sex education at school, and for that they find it's necessary to separate the girls from the boys because what the girls and the boys want to talk about is just different. And I think in most cultures, in most traditional cultures, there's always been a sense of there needing to be an identification with and a strengthening and a coming into your own in your own gender. And if that is strong and good, it's also a basis on which to have good relationships with the other gender. So we've been having men's and women's tipis, and this year we're starting to have a mixed tipi as well – so we're gradually evolving things which people find helpful. It all comes out of people's experience; it's not that there's a template being applied: "you must do single-sex", or "you must do XYZ".

There's more and more teenagers on the retreat - last year we had 25, aged 14-19; we even had some who wanted to come without a parent – their parents didn't want to come anymore, but they did... That was very beautiful: one of the things they said is that it was the only place where they didn't have to fit in, to be a particular type, like a Goth, or a this or a that or the other, and when they came on the retreat they felt really comfortable just to be themselves, not any particular type, and they found that really refreshing.

So there's a lot going on, and a lot of people there, but it's definitely a retreat rather than a Festival, with a normal retreat programme. There'll be two meditation slots in the morning, 6-7 and 7-8, and all the meals are provided, so you don't need to make your own or search for cafés like on a festival. We have a big Community Circle each morning where we allocate work for the day, and everyone is allocated to a smaller group, or kula, which meets every day. That's a place you can do a bit of meditation, talk about the retreat theme, talk about your experience, your experience of how the retreat is going. And then in the afternoon, there's generally a Dharma talk, and in the evening, we have some kind of ritual or ceremony, which leads into the Puja. There's a lot of other activities as well – yoga, hot tubs, workshops like Bushcraft, singing, things like that.

So it's like a regular retreat, but it's in a field, with everyone camping. And there's a Kids Team of people specifically working with the children, so the children are looked after for a period of about two-and-a-half hours in the mornings, to give the parents space for instance to go to their Kula groups. And the children take part in various ways - they put on plays, they take part in the rituals, they have water fights...

From one point of view it's like a very chilled-out, relaxed family holiday, but one which has a theme of being able to really practice, do meditation, do pujas; and what that means is people find they're really able to connect: a very strong element on the retreat is being able to meet people. Some of us have been coming on the retreat for years, and people tend to come back year after year and get to know each other quite well, so each time they're able to reflect on the year, how it's gone, what you want to take into the next year, that sort of thing...

Over the time I've been involved with it, it's grown a lot; in fact, there was one year we were way over-subscribed, which was to our detriment really. One of Devapriya's ideas to address that was to grow the retreat 'sideways', to have two retreats, so we could keep the numbers on each to a more friendly amount. What we've developed is a kernel of people, an organising team we call the Heart Team, with about 20 people on it, who are committed to it year-round - we go on retreat together twice a year, we study together, we think about next year's event, and so on. And there are loads of people on the retreat who want to be on the Heart Team, more than we have real roles for them – so we're starting to see if there's a second kernel there who want to start developing and organising another retreat. In time, I can imagine there might be small family-friendly Buddhafield retreats East, South, West, North, plus our existing big one where people can come to get more ideas, a sense of what people have done before, and then go back to their more local area and develop those retreats there.

There's also a vague idea – I don't know how many years it will take us to incubate this – to run a Children's Camp, a Buddhist children's camp, perhaps having it running alongside our camp. There's also someone who wants to establish a 'Yogi's Zone' on the retreat, where there would be space for longer meditations, but somehow joined to the Village. So there's various ideas and threads, we try to nudge them along – but we can only do as much as we feel we can all cope with. But it feels like a very strong and successful model.

What's really lovely is that the adults love it. Devapriya always used to say "our job is to keep the kids happy; if the kids are happy the parents can get on with their practice", but I think it works the other way round as well – the adults are so clearly happy to be there, enjoying their connections with each other, enjoying being somewhere they don't feel they have to make a choice between "am I a practice person, or am I a parent?". That's why it's the highlight of my year – it's somewhere I just get to be completely whole, completely rounded – because there I am, giving a talk, or leading a meditation, and my children can wander in and say "is it ok if I go in the hot tubs now?" and I say "yes that's fine" and off they go. I think that's why people who have children love it: you have a sense of being with your two loves, your family and your Sangha, your Dharma, and you can have both of them together, you're not having to separate them out. Just the fact that the retreat is there means the two halves have become whole, just the fact you can keep going back to it every year, is very healing, in my experience.

And what that means it's something you carry on into your life afterwards, it's not just that you have this lovely mix when you're on retreat, you can actually take it back into the world when the retreat's over. And if you're reading this and you'd like to come, we'll welcome you with open arms!

*Transcribed and edited from an interview with Candradasa
for FreeBuddhistAudio. The original can be found online at
soundcloud.com/thebuddhistcentre/amaragita-buddhafield-family-friendly.*

Devapriya in the 'Caravan of Love', 2005

THE VILLAGE RETREAT'S
PRINCIPLES AND PRACTICES FOR HOUSEHOLDER LIVING

Little and often. Don't wait for the hour or week you will have some peace to practice. Do it now. One breath is enough. Three breaths is good. 10 minutes an eternity waiting to be woken up into. Places you can practice coming back to yourself: On the loo, drinking tea, waiting for your child/partner/rice to cook/in the shower/in traffic.

Sangha – connect honestly with like-minded people, share your triumphs and fears. Give the gift of your listening.

Do all you can to help parents with babies and toddlers – offer cups of tea, move them to the front at meal times or offer to get their food. It can make the difference between heaven and hell.

Ritual – There will be rituals on different themes through the week. They are fun, participatory happenings to help us connect with the land, each other and ourselves.

Women, Men and mixed lodges (Tipi's). Sometimes it feels right to share things with people of the same gender. Go and hang out in any of the three lodges they are designed to be safe spaces to be sociable and share experience.

Meditation – we will teach meditation for beginners every day. There will be a sit with just bells and a taught meditation for more experienced meditators every day. Look at the programme. There will also be meditation where you can bring your toddlers in the toddler zone.

Puja – a Buddhist practice where we offer incense, chant mantras and sometimes say poetic verses in call and response. We get a sense of ourselves in community aligning with what is important to us and creating a sense of magic. Most evenings this will take place, children welcome and it's fine to leave when you need to.

Contribution – For the retreat to work it takes everyone giving a little. We will have a work period where we will practice bringing mindfulness to work. Some will have their work period at other times of the day. Please let your team leader know if you are unable to come.

GREEN EARTH AWAKENING

Green Earth Awakening, generally known just as the GEA, is the newest addition to Buddhafield's annual calendar. It's a five-day camp exploring a sustainable, socially engaged Dharma, and incorporates community living with meditation, nature connection, creative collaboration, land skills and crafts, Dharma talks, and workshops towards empowerment in social and ecological resilience.

It hosts a platform for groups and speakers such as Dharma Action Network for Climate Engagement (D.A.N.C.E), Eco-dharma, Ecological Land Co-op, Land Workers Alliance, Tyndall Centre, and Mindfulness4Change, plus eco-psychologists, activists, permaculture teachers, climate scientists, musicians, dancers, artists, group facilitators, bodywork practitioners and more.

A proportion of GEA budget is given to support groups, networks and individuals engaged in ecological and social resilience.

For more info visit buddhafield.com or facebook.com/greenearthawakening

Here's some comments from attendees:

"Fantastic — small, intimate, with a rich variety of workshops both creative and informative."

"So much on offer from fantastic, knowledgeable people."

"Felt so safe to bring my daughters here and allow them free range."

"The meditation area (on top of the hill) is the best site I have experienced at any festival / camp. Profound stillness."

Welcome to the GEA 2013

THE BUDDHAFIELD YATRA

Yatrikas walking the South Downs

Yatras are one of the most distinctive Buddhafield events, being a retreat, but a retreat with a difference. Below are two parallel accounts of the 2011 Yatra, one by Lokabandhu, its leader that year, in which he introduces something of its unique etiquette and characteristics; and one by Dave Barr, describing in some detail his experiences as he comes to Buddhafield for the first time.

Lokabandhu writes -

"The highlight of 2011, for me, so far, has been the Buddhafield Yatra. I thought it was totally great; it's unlike everything else we do in Triratna, and I would like to share an account of it with you - if anyone wanted to organize one themselves I'd be more than happy to advise.

In essence, a Yatra is a walking retreat; over 7 days 30 of us walked 60 miles, from Reading train station (an easy place to get to for the start) to Avebury (a vast megalithic complex dominated by the great stone circle: a fine place to finish). It's a walk, but with a distinctive etiquette: we walk in silence, in single file, beginning and ending each hour of walking in a circle, with any words from the leader (or others, who might, for instance, have a poem to share) followed by everyone bowing to one another. The leader then leads off in a spiral, walking around the outside of the circle with everyone following. Behind the leader is a map-reader; at the rear is a backstop who ensures no-one gets left behind. Two vehicles, a van and a run-around car, stay with the day's team of about 4 people; they tat-down the previous night's camp, do the shopping, go ahead with the luggage and set up the next night stop, cook dinner, and welcome the weary walkers as they arrive. The car is available to pick up anyone who can't walk the full distance. The roles all swap around; everyone plays their part. Morning and evening there's time for meditation, Dharma talks, reporting-in, and Puja or other rituals; the silent walking is, of course, mindful and an excellent way to practice Bhante's 'Four Levels of Awareness'.

All that alone would be great, but Yatras are much more too. Five aspects especially struck me this time - the landscape, the elements, the rituals, the community, and the journey back in time. The walk took us along the River Thames and up onto the Ridgeway, a 5000-year-old trackway across the high dry ground of the Wiltshire downs. Water gave way to Earth, Fire warmed us at night, Air buffeted us as Consciousness walked through Space: the Six Elements danced together. For me, this was a delight, a week away from computers simply immersed in the present moment and our surroundings: big skies and big landscapes led effortlessly to 'big mind'. It wasn't all easy: we were fully exposed to the elements, even by Buddhafield's minimal standards. At night, the only shelters were our tents and an awning hung off the side of the van. While walking, the only refuge was to be mindful of (and hang loose to) our experience rather than resist it. And we had weather in abundance - hot sun, strong wind, driving rain, blue skies, cold nights. Happily none lasted too long - we could see for ourselves that all things passed, the Three Laksanas held true...

Almost every night we camped at one or another ancient monument or hillfort, giving a wonderful backdrop to a series of improvised rituals. The first evening we started with the Dedication Ceremony, but thereafter took off into realms of creativity. The first morning by the River Thames, with rain threatening, saw a 'baptism' by Air and Water, based on a Biodanza exercise; that evening another by Fire and Earth - specifically, building and jumping a fire in the woods. The next morning, finding ourselves next to Scutchamer Knob, an ancient collapsed burial mound, we surrounded it, and one by one approached the shrine in the centre of the amphitheatre-like space holding a Vajra, shouting our names to the wind, declaring our intentions for the day's walk - to "walk with confidence, sensitivity, etc.". And off we went... At Uffington, on Dragon's Hill at sunset, in the howling wind, we recited the Ratana Sutta and met, tamed, and befriended our Demons, this time calling their names into the wind. At Wayland's Smithy, an ancient tomb in a beautiful beech tree grove, we began what came to be several ceremonies connecting us with our Ancestors - those unknown people who first walked the Ridgeway and built (with stupendous labour) the many special places we were passing.

We used verses and pujas by Dhiramati, to whom I'm profoundly grateful; he has such a gift with words and poetry. We began with his verses 'To the Ancestors'; that night, by a fire in a field under the starry sky, his beautiful puja to Tara and the Elements. In the wide open space of Barbury Castle Akasaka led us in the Amoghasiddhi mantra and offering our intentions (symbolized by flower petals) to the wind. By this time Reading train station seemed a million miles and several thousand years away!

Approaching Avebury, our destination, for two nights our only campsite and kitchen were the public car park and grass verge by the track: happily we were undisturbed. We'd tried and failed to find a more orthodox campsite for this part of the walk; it was clear how we as Yatrikas had in a sense gone forth from the regular world and (rather like the Buddha and his followers) been forced to take our chances night by night.

Soon after our arrival we embarked upon an all-night vigil inside West Kennett Long Barrow; some 25 of us crowding in with almost 20 staying till dawn. Akasaka and I had drafted a seven-round ritual, recapping and building on the many ceremonies already performed. Each round had several stages, for instance, the first, 'Connecting with the Ancestors' consisting of a welcome talk by Sean (a Druid as well as a Buddhist); entering the Barrow; creating a shrine and finding our places; Dhiramati's 'Verses to the Ancestors' and 'Spirit Song'; the Ratana Sutta and an offering of one sunflower seed each inside the chamber; and finally the Aksobhya mantra and earth-touching mudra. The other rounds were 'Setting our intentions for the night'; 'Evoking our potential' (verses and mantras to Amoghasiddhi and Tara, ending with extinguishing all lights and holding hands in the total darkness); 'Confession and Acknowledgement of Regrets and Limitations'; 'Aspirations and Next Steps'; 'Rebirth and Re-emergence' (in the first light of dawn); a 'Retreat Metta and Transference of Merits' and finally the recitation of Kalidasa's wonderful 'Exhortation to the Dawn' at sunrise at 5.06am. Followed by the long walk back to our camp and sleep! The next day saw us end the Yatra by walking the mile-long Avenue into Avebury and reporting-out among the stones - and meeting Terry Dobney, Arch-Druid of Avebury and Keeper of the Stones, for a formal welcome into and most fascinating tour of the site.

Probably not surprisingly, we were a pretty strong community by this time, even though we'd all spent many hours in silence, simply walking together. Certainly we'd all lived through an adventure together, ably facilitated by the excellent Buddhafield team. For me, it was a great combination of a simple and elemental life, a whacky adventure, and a serious contribution to our great shared enterprise of bringing Buddhism to the West, even, to re-imagining the Buddha. If you're interested, there's photos at http://tinyurl.com/684hpdl. I also copy below a more detailed schedule of the many ceremonies we performed.

previously published in Shabda

Yatra ceremony on top of Dragon Hill

A DHARMA YATRA DIARY
BY DAVE BARR

This is a record of my experiences and impressions of the 2011 Dharma Yatra from Reading along the Thames Path to Goring and then along the ancient Ridgeway to Avebury.

SATURDAY 21ST MAY

I arrived about an hour early at the meeting point, so I had some time to reflect on my thoughts, feelings, and expectations at the time. I had wanted to go on a Yatra for many years and booked immediately I saw this one was happening. I love walking and being in nature, I love the Dharma and meditation practice, and I love ancient places, stone circles, burial chambers and other sacred spaces. So this walk really appealed to me on every level. I tried to approach it with complete openness and not too much in the way of direct expectations. I was slightly apprehensive that everyone would be very strongly involved in the Triratna organisation, which I am only loosely connected with, and that I might feel a bit outside or alienated by too much puja. However, this feeling instantly evaporated at the very beginning of the walk, and there was never even a hint of it during the entire retreat. I relished the element of the unknown for what was to follow, and I deliberately did not look up the route on a map or do any research into the sites. I really wanted to approach everything with fresh eyes and ears, and other senses and experience it in the moment. I did not know anyone on the walk. Everything had an element of the unknown, the landscape, the people, the talks, meditations, puja, rituals, sharing tasks and whatever revelations might occur! I also loved the fact, that at least for this short time I could leave behind the false reality of the modern, capitalist society in which I live uncomfortably, with its work, money, 'entertainment', gadgets, etc. It was a good feeling to turn the mobile phone off and know it was not going to disturb me for this time. In contrast, I was looking forward to reconnecting with nature and the elements, sacred landscapes, ancient monuments, ancestors and my fellow Yatrikas. I was determined to try to fully engage in every moment with as much mindfulness and awareness as I could.

I waited outside Reading station noticing how restlessness and distraction seem to be so prevalent among so many people so much of the time, and gradually other Yatrikas started to appear. There was an instant recognition, and we congregated and began to communicate immediately, if perhaps, slightly tentatively at first. The texts came through about where the van was going to be and eventually we all met up on the other side of the station by the van. We formed our first of many circles and were given our introduction by Lokabandhu, introduced ourselves and our names and began walking silently in a line down a few streets and very soon to the side of the beautiful River Thames. It was already quite a striking sight, nearly 30 people walking mindfully in a line and I noticed everything so clearly; how the sound of the wind changed in different landscapes, blowing around my ears or through grassy meadows or through the tall trees; how the different textures of the ground felt under my feet/sandals; how quickly the sound of the traffic faded, the aromas, the people we passed, the water flowing, the birds, insects, dogs, the sky, boats, my breath, my steps, etc.....etc..... At first, it was easy to become a little insular though, and I soon realised this and made an effort to make eye contact and smile at the person behind me if I opened a gate for them, for example. And so we walked in the sun (fire element), by the river (water element) through trees and over grassy meadows (earth element) and in the constant presence of the mighty wind (air element), which became increasing more mighty and dominant as the days went by.

We set up camp in a beautiful farmer's field by the river, where some people swam. I would have liked to immerse myself in the water element, but I was not alone in submitting to the hindrance of sense-craving for warmth/aversion to cold! We shared our delicious healthy food, had our evening meditation, split into small groups to introduce ourselves in a bit more detail and discuss our reasons for coming, our life situation, our hopes, and aspirations and anxieties. At this point, it was very clear that people on this walk had come from very different backgrounds, spiritually speaking, but all had similar aims and a common focus.

I made a new path to the toilet pit, and it felt good to be doing a different kind of exercise and to be helping towards everyone's experience of the camp, and also to give the camp crew a bit of a rest, because it was immediately obvious how hard they worked to set up camp for us. We had a work circle and volunteered for our 'task meditations'. I chose washing-up for this night, which was another excellent opportunity to connect with people and get to know each other. Everything felt good. During the whole week, everything just felt right for me. There was never a second of boredom or disillusionment, or even real distraction, never any tension between people (that I noticed), and I never experienced any negative emotions. My only obstacle was physical pain with my tendon sheaths around the knees and feet, but I took Ibuprofen, calmly accepted the discomfort and walked!

The night was cold, so much so that it was hard to sleep. I thought it was just that I wasn't used to it, but they got colder, and soon everyone was borrowing blankets for the nights!

I think it was the next morning that we did a ritual based on experiencing air and water. We split up into groups of three and tried to recreate the atmosphere of these two elements on each person in turn, such as by simulating trickling rain on the person's head and making airy sounds and blowing on their skin.

SUNDAY 22ND MAY

Day two, we continued up the Thames into the hills and then stood on the bridge at Goring and said goodbye to the water element as we headed up to the Ridgeway. Everything felt different without the river companion and the trees. Now we were in the open countryside, arable fields and grassland, occasional hedges for shelter, climbing and soon at the top, fully exposed to the wind. I wrote a few haikus about the transition, although it was a few days before I shared them with the group.

Road gives way to path
Motors give way to footsteps
Feet give way to ants

Road gives way to path
Engines give way to Skylarks
Wheels give way to steps

Land gives rise to thought
Thoughts give rise to emotions
All return to land

The wind did become very strong and very chilling until we all seemed to be wearing all the layers we had brought with us. I even had gloves and a warm hat some of the time. But I did not get stressed or annoyed by the wind as I have done in the past. On this walk, working with the elements was one of the main themes, and this meant calmly accepting and appreciating them. I imagined the wind blowing away my unskilful mental states, cravings, aversions and distractions, and helping me to focus. I enjoyed the feeling of adjusting my balance in response to strong gusts, and still I allowed myself to appreciate the shelter of a narrow hedge and a short, partial break from the wind. What a contrast that was!

At Scutchamer's Knob, we camped in the woods beside an ancient, large and partially subsided tumulus (the Knob), which was therefore semi-circular in shape. Lokabandhu talked about the Mahabhutas, Great Ghosts, as Buddhism refers to the elements. These represent the true, fundamental nature of the elements: air expands, water flows, fire transforms and earth resists or supports. He talked about making himself transparent to the wind, which made sense to me and I was conscious of this while walking the next day. It is when I become too opaque to the wind that I try to resist it and feel like it is resisting me. It then becomes a battle I cannot win, and I experience negative emotions towards the beautiful expanding air element – never again!

I wrote in my diary, with homage to Jimi Hendrix,

> 'Kiss the wind
> 'Scuse me while I kiss the sky!'

That evening, we had a large fire and did a transformation ritual of earth and fire, by taking it in turns to jump over the fire towards the Vajrasattva shrine, whilst playing percussion and chanting the transformation mantra of Padmasambhava. This was warming and uplifting and did feel like a seal for how the walk was beginning to transform us and also to make us more aware of the Mahabhutas. It was very clear that we had come a long way and made the physical transition from the city to the river valley and then another to the Ridgeway. It now felt like a very different world we were inhabiting. My mind felt much clearer, more in tune and aware, carrying less extra, unnecessary weight, my heart felt much more open, and we were already really coming together as a community, sharing a lot, emotionally and practically.

We made an offering to the woods by taking something away; we cleared up the litter.

The first time anyone shared anything with the group during a circle was when Ohno shared a thought, something like, 'What you value becomes a part of what you think you are.' I found it very interesting and spent some time thinking about identity, what or who I think I am, what I really value and the link between the two.

MONDAY 23RD MAY

The next morning at Scutchamer's Knob was a highlight, and for me the first really powerful ritual. It was as if the Knob had been built especially for this ritual and thirty people as we now were, was the perfect number for it. We all lined up around the semi-circular ridge and then took it in turns to walk up to Vajrasattva in the middle as people moved around. Then each person, with Vajra in hand, or in my case Vajra in one hand, Dan Moi (my other sacred object) in the other, shouted our names and our aspiration for the day as loud as we could, into the wind. I shouted, 'I am David, and I walk today with openness!' I noticed that 'David' has much more power than Dave. Perhaps it's time to drop the 'Dave'. I thought I had shouted loud until I heard Tam and then I realised none of us had really put our whole being into it like she did! Anyway, it did the job and was really empowering. Openness was what I wanted to walk with, and I think I did. It was quite a demanding day physically, with a very strong wind, some climbs, and even a little rain. Tam pointed out in the evening how she felt so privileged for having so many possessions compared to most people in the world, when we all tried to eradicate even the tiniest amount of discomfort by putting on our raincoats as soon as it started to rain, taking off a layer when it got slightly sweaty, putting on a layer when we felt a touch of coldness, etc. Very true.

We camped at an official campsite under Dragon Hill and the Uffington White Horse, just us and a boys' Grammar School! My hips and especially knees and feet were very sore by now, but I could not miss the opportunity to go up Dragon Hill in the evening for Sean's Druid ceremony of befriending our dragons/demons and a Buddhist ritual to befriend the local spirits of the four directions. The wind at the top was almost overpowering. It made you want to shout spontaneously, so it was perfect for the first ritual, which was a sequel to the morning ritual of aspiration, with Lokabandhu beating a gong. This time we shouted out our names into the wind and the sunset for the transformation of a quality we would like to change. I shouted, 'I am David, and I challenge idleness!' It felt invigorating and uplifting. When we had all finished, we huddled like penguins against the wind and the cold, wrapped up in blankets, in four groups facing out in four directions and threw some grains of rice to the local spirits asking them to protect and guide all visitors to the hill. We warmed up a little, huddling and singing the Padmasambhava mantra.

TUESDAY 24TH MAY

After a cold, sleepless night, I got up in pain for tea and meditation and chopping vegetables; then we regrouped in our original small groups to talk about our experiences so far. There was a release of some very strong emotional issues for some people, associated with their lives before the Yatra, and it felt painful but very beautiful to hear them opening up so honestly, and to feel the compassion which followed.

This day felt very magical. We walked through powerful ancient places, past Dragon Hill and the Uffington White Horse, Uffington Castle and on to Wayland's Smithy for lunch and an ancestor ritual. I managed to find a quiet moment to play my bass Dan Moi inside the burial chamber. Then we had the ritual. Some of us were in the passageway around the entrance, but I was one of the people inside one of the chambers. There were some readings by Lokabandhu, then we all sang a Tara Mantra, then held hands in one connected circle, before coming out. This was a powerful, trance-like meditation and it felt like we were really coming together as a group now, with a single identity and a single goal and shared experience. Emerging from the chamber was a mini rebirth with people touching my head as I walked out – amazing.

At some point on this day, I wrote

> *To walk alone is a pleasure*
> *To walk together is a delight*
> *To walk together as one is transformation*

and that's how it felt.

We camped in another farmer's field, and I felt very appreciative of his stewardship of the land and allowing us to share it with him. Later we wrote cards to both the farmers who had lent us fields for camping, which was a very nice thing to do. I want to be more expressive in future in giving thanks to people and showing appreciation.

Lokabandhu gave us a Dharma talk around the fire later, which was great. He covered the Mahabhutas, the three hallmarks of conditioned existence, the four levels of awareness, the insight which results from this cultivation of awareness and whether or not to act on that insight – concluding, yes with the cultivation of compassion.

This was followed with Tara poetry and readings and a long Tara puja with prostrations, at which point I did feel a bit alienated and very tired, so I overcame my feeling of rudeness and went to bed.

WEDNESDAY 25TH MAY

Had a lovely meditation in the morning as it felt warm at last. After breakfast, there was a work circle, and then a discussion about the pace of the walk, which some felt was too fast. Suryamani led the walk today, which was shorter anyway and definitely slower. There was the daily appeal for two people to help out with driving and setting up camp and I really wanted to help out, but even though my joints were really painful, I was unable to make the sacrifice as Sean rightly described it, and give up a day's walking. Happily, other people did every day. I shared my Haikus and aphorism in the leaving circle today, and Sean told us about the pure spring water we had from the farmer – lovely. Today was a day noticeable to me for the humour that emerged. I think by this point we were probably as connected as a group this size could ever be. Most defences were down; people had really opened up with each other, and there was a lot of laughter. I also noticed that I was just mucking in at the camps now and doing what I saw needed to be done, without waiting to be asked or asking what I should do. I was now searching for things rather than asking for things, taking more responsibility, etc. In conversations, I may not have shared all the New Age belief systems which were very popular in the group, but it did not interfere with my appreciation of, and love for all the individuals within it. While I am not a complete rationalist, the Dharma is supremely rational to me, and I find plenty of magic in the material world and the human mind as they are. I loved the way Lokabandhu would talk about something without trying to explain it or mystify it. Sean did the same later. For example, at Scutchamer's Knob, Lokabandhu said, 'This is Scutchamer's Knob. We don't know what it is, who built it or why, but they did, and it was very important to somebody a long time ago, and we recognise and respect that now.' That's enough for me; I don't need to add Leylines or magical properties to it. It's a wonderful place. It was also a lesson in not over-rationalising, by following the urge to explain everything. I could just try to experience everything as it was, without entering into discursive thought in my mind.

One of the things I spoke about in our small groups on the first day, was my dissatisfaction with work and my work/life balance and today I had a very strong feeling on the walk that I should hand in my notice when I get back, but then some caution crept in, and I haven't done it yet (2 weeks later) although it is still on the cards.

The campsite was near Barbury Castle and had been an official campsite but got burnt down, so it was a little sad for Lokabandhu and others who had stayed there on the last Yatra, with a cooked breakfast, but still, it was a beautiful site.

To get back to humour, even bottom humour was 'released' today. Who can ever forget the spectacularly timed escape of gas just as we all bowed to each other in the arriving circle!

I missed out on the ritual this evening as it was quite a long way away at Barbury Castle and I had already walked to, and around it, and done my own ritual there, and my legs were sore, so I sat at the camp with Kev and a few others. They made a joyful return singing my favourite mantra, 'Om Amoghasiddhi Ah Hum' and I wished I had gone, but never mind. I heard they had thrown a flower into the castle saying the thing they had appreciated most on the walk that day. Most people said the sheep and lambs, a few the horses, but later on, I picked a beautiful, white Clematis flower and said I had appreciated the humour. The lambs were very cute but I found it sad that they would soon be going to the slaughter house, and I had had the impression that the adult sheep, with a slightly mocking tone to their calls, had been saying, 'It's OK for you humans to talk about non-attachment to life, we're living it!' Anyway, we had a lovely gathering around the fire, with people singing and I felt like love was tangible throughout the group, with a sense of real togetherness and cohesiveness. It felt to me as if the world and my whole being were filled with love.

It is relatively easy to write about the community cohesion or the rituals, mantras and meditations, but it is much more difficult to write about the walking itself. By far the most important aspect of this retreat and the one which took the most time, was the walking. It was through walking that the transition from city to riverside to farmland to upland grassland and open, expansive countryside took place. It was through walking that the transition from distracted, restless, busy, cloudy mind to focused, calm, settled, clear and spacious mind occurred. It was largely through walking that the group came together as one. It really began to feel as if we were one long creature, like a giant centipede, with each individual a different segment, snaking our way, single-mindedly along the path, towards a single goal, which was not the destination, but the enlightenment of being fully present. We walked for hours away from any sign of civilisation and crossed very few roads, mostly very quiet, minor roads. It was a true retreat from the rat race in every sense. The spaciousness of the land, the huge skies, and expansive views were reflected by the mind. The four levels of awareness grew by the hour and as I wrote in my haiku, it became very clear how the environment or the land, and our thoughts and emotions are so closely interlinked and all feed off each other, but that ultimately, everything goes back to the ever-changing land. I felt intimately connected to the land and everything around us, almost without any separation, also strongly connected to the past and the future, which we were creating now. The past was present in the now, reflected in this ancient landscape and especially its monuments.

There was one sharp contrast to the spacious calmness when we had to cross a motorway. It was quite shocking and seemed to just leap into our consciousness from some long forgotten dream – a reminder of the other realities we would have to face and apply our new insights to in the near future. It felt exactly like one of those moments during meditation when you lose focus, and the mind drifts off into a chaos of thought. I felt that not only had I had lost my focus for a time, but so had the group as a whole. However, calm, clear spaciousness soon returned, and we were once again snaking through the ancient and sometimes timeless landscape, together as one. There were some occasions when people raced past us on mountain bikes, and it just seemed so hectic and pointless. They were missing so much.

My body awareness was coloured by the pain I experienced in my knees and feet although this is an ongoing problem, so I was expecting it, and I am used to it. It was always much worse in the morning and after rest stops, but I knew after a bit of walking it would not feel so bad. So I took my Ibuprofen to take down the inflammation and relaxed into it, calmly accepting it. Ben said something similar after walking in bare feet. He had to be constantly conscious of not recoiling to every sharp stone, but rather to relax and accept some minor pain, knowing it would not do any lasting or serious damage. It is similar to the reaction to the wind, not fighting it, not reacting to it.

So most of the cultivation of mindfulness occurred during the walk, and this was perfectly complemented by the cultivation of Metta through sharing camp tasks, conversation and giving and receiving practical and emotional support to and from fellow yatrikas.

THURSDAY 26TH MAY

This was the rainy day! The water element had returned, this time from above and sideways, in the ever present, howling wind. It would not have been right if we had got through the whole walk without experiencing a rainy day, so I was happy to welcome it. We were working with the elements after all. We had a rest stop in a lovely Beech grove, but it did not provide any shelter for lunch. We saw a circle of planted daffodils although they were past flowering and lying down on the ground by now. We made our own circle around it and once again Lokabandhu said we did not know what it was, but it was beautiful, and we acknowledged and appreciated it, before moving on for lunch behind the shelter of a tall patch of Hawthorn hedge.

At some point, I remember standing with my back to the wind and rain noticing how the water hit the resistant earth of my body, flowed down my raincoat, and was evaporated by the expansive air taking away some of the transforming fire in my body. In other words, the rain felt very cold even through my raincoat and warm layers!

I was surprised when we walked through a lovely area of limestone with huge Sarsen rocks lying around. They looked like the stones at Avebury, and we found out later that they did indeed come from here. Up to this point, we had been walking through chalk, and I thought the whole area was chalk. Another notable feature in the landscape on this day, was the waves being blown across the beautiful, yellow-green barley fields and I wrote this haiku:

> *Wind blows the barley*
> *Waves ripple across the field*
> *I breathe, the field breathes*

The walk was not so long today, and we soon arrived at the end of the Ridgeway near the Avebury complex, with Silbury Hill, the village of Avebury and West Kennett Long Barrow in sight. In a sense, this was our destination, but it felt a little dissatisfying as some people walked off to the tumuli where we were intending to camp, some to the car park and some stood around. We seemed to have lost our unity for a while, and it was unclear what was happening. Probably the rain and wind made people a little impatient and restless. We had to wait a while for the van to arrive and we met Phil, a traveller who was already parked up in the car park in his truck. He told us the National Trust would evict us if we camped in the tumuli, so we thought we would probably spread out along the verge of the Ridgeway to camp. I was struck by the totally different energy of Phil and other travellers that we met there, and although they were friendly and nice, I noticed the ego coming through and the way they did not really listen, but rather just talked! I became very deeply appreciative of the shared Buddhist/mindfulness values of our group, where people really did listen deeply. In fact, the protective separation that I normally reserve for myself was now being projected onto my extended self, as the group had become, and at first I felt a bit invaded by Phil. I quickly realised the error of this way of interacting and opened up again, enjoying his company and his different energy. I found this a very interesting experience though and a valuable lesson. At first, I just wanted to set up camp, and I did not want to hear about the National Trust. I suppose I naively thought, 'They'll see that we are harmless environmentally sensitive, mindful Buddhists and they'll let us camp there, and if we have to move, then we move' I suppose I had a bit of sense-craving to camp in the tumuli as it seemed really special, but the prevailing mind was to avoid any potential conflict, and so we camped along the verge, quite spread out. I managed to find some shelter from the wind behind a lonely and charismatic Elder tree and camped there next to Kev.

At dusk, most of us began the walk up to West Kennett Long Barrow for an all-night vigil and ritual. This was one of the most amazing and transforming things I have ever experienced, a major highlight of the Yatra and a genuine rebirthing.

Sean gave us a lovely talk when we arrived about the history as we know it and the theories about its role and the continuity between the ancestors and us as the ancestors of the future. Like Lokabandhu, he also said that we know very little, and it is mostly conjecture, again increasing the sense of mystery. For most of the night we had lanterns with night lights burning, but we had a period of darkness whilst singing the Tara mantra, which was intense. The night was structured in several sections: greeting the ancestors, ourselves, letting go, confessions, solitary time outside to offer confessions to the elements, transference of merit, greeting the dawn outside, resolutions and retreat metta, then emerging together into the sunrise singing the Sabbe Satta Sukhi Hontu (*"May all beings be well"*) mantra. There were so many intensely powerful moments for me during the night that I cannot begin to capture them all in writing, but this was definitely another transition into a different world, a different time and a different consciousness. One of the highlights for me was during the Metta Bhavana practice. I think I entered a kind of intermediate bardo, but I was definitely not nodding off or sleeping. I had very strong visions, which did not fade, but changed with each stage of the practice. Some of it involved hands reaching upwards and outwards, combined with corpse-like skin and ghosts (well we were in a burial chamber). The hands were much bigger when I was focusing on people closer to me, and they got progressively smaller as I moved to more distant contacts. I took it to have two meanings: 1. people reaching out for metta, and my role in offering that metta, (more for people closer to me) and also, 2. people's grasping and attachment leading them towards death and away from life and joy. The largest hand belonged to one of my work colleagues who is also a close friend and before I went back to work, I thought 'I must reach out to her' and 'perhaps I should use my hands more in communication through touch.' When I got to work, she asked 'Are you all zenned out then?' to which I replied 'Yes, I really am.' Then she said, 'Let's feel it then' and held my hand with both her hands. This made me very happy and seemed to fulfil the vision.

The confessions section was also interesting. Some people had a problem with the concept of confession and its implications with sin and guilt, but there are things in my life, which I have done unskillfully when I should have known better, that bother me still. Ideally, I would like to make amends, but the opportunity to tell someone else about them did feel like a small burden lifted. This was an exercise in trust, honesty and openness and powerfully liberating. We had been told about the structure of the night earlier, so I had some time to think about what I would like to confess, which was useful. Also, it was done in groups of two, or in my case, three as my chamber brother was asleep at the time. This was definitely easier than to the whole group.

The resolutions section near the end was also very powerful and helped to make sense of the whole night and the entire Yatra. We wound a single piece of string around our wrists, so that we were all linked together and took it in turns to cut the string and tie it around our wrists while announcing our resolutions, i.e., what we want to take back with us into the world, as if we were concentrating the energy of the group into ourselves for our future interactions. I said, 'I will take the caring and sharing of this group into the community where I live and to all people I encounter.'

Apart from the rituals, readings, and mantras, many interesting things were said during the night although much of it I missed due to a lot of shuffling around in noisy waterproofs. Many people spoke about their aspirations for the night and the fruits of the journey, about love, death, personal quests. Alobhin talked about how his father had died about a year ago and how he felt he did not have much in common with him, but realised now that if he had brought him on this Yatra, he would have loved it. This got me thinking about what my own father would make of it, and at first I thought I could not even imagine bringing him, but gradually I began to think that he might also enjoy it and might get a lot out of it, hmmm. Something to think about if it happens next year!

Finally, emerging into the sunrise really did feel like a rebirthing. This was a new day in every sense and a new world and a reminder that every day should be experienced in this way. We walked back in the early morning, and I still did not feel tired, but I slept really well from about 6.30 until 10.00.

FRIDAY 27TH MAY

I shared yesterday's barley haiku with the group in the morning circle. We had a lovely meditation in the wooded tumuli (our planned campsite), followed by an early dinner, and then set off on our yatra, led by Sean into Avebury Ring itself, via the avenue. When we arrived at the avenue, Sean took his boots off. While this may have been just to feel the soft grass under his feet, since he is a practising Druid, many of us followed his example. I was thinking this was his temple and just as I would take my shoes off on entering a temple in India or Japan, I thought it appropriate here also. There were amazing faces on the stones and some bullocks with strong personalities! One seemed most put out by having to move away from us, and he stood watching us all pass, looking left and right repeatedly.

It was a great feeling to enter the massive, ancient presence of Avebury Ring and the giant stones. We stopped around a horizontal stone and took it in turns to give our thanks and describe our impressions from the whole yatra week. This was very moving and lovely.

Eventually, we met Terry Dobney, the 'Keeper of the Stones', and the present day Druid who leads most of the ceremonies there. It felt a bit strange to meet him in the pub car park, next to the road rather than in the circle, but the reason for this soon became clear. He walked us out past the last stones so that he could welcome each of us in turn and invite us into the stone circle. He was quite a character, but again, he had a very different style to a Buddhist guide! He was not embarrassed by letting the ego show, and he was also quite theatrical. In fact, from what he said, it was clear that Druidry is, and probably always was, very theatrical and not afraid of using the odd conjuring trick; one reason why they built, or at least used, calendars and clocks in the form of great theatres. He was very knowledgeable, but I confess to being slightly suspicious and very sceptical about a lot of what he said. What he did for me though, was to 'conjure up' a very vivid and striking picture of how the place would look and would have looked during a big Druid ceremony, and also how the people would have lived, thought and felt in those ancient times. Terry's tour was very long and detailed, and he left 'no stone unturned' you could say, but I did get very cold and was probably still tired from the all-night vigil. The highlight of the tour was at the handfasting stone, where he performed a simplified and shorter version of the handfasting ritual for Conn and Nicky, which was lovely and very moving. Eventually, we walked back to the camp for a fire and a very special late night chat, including some philosophical debate on Terry's form of Druidry, new age beliefs, and puja.

SATURDAY 28TH MAY

The gong or bell did not make it up as far as my tent, so I missed the morning meditation today. I chatted a bit with Kev instead. As we were packing up our tents, Andy walked all the way up to tell us porridge was ready, so we went down to join the rest of the group and write our messages on lovely cards for all the crew. Then the goodbye hugs started in earnest. It was so warm and very moving. They were not just hugs; everybody spontaneously said what they had genuinely appreciated and liked in the other person. Alobhin, who had been in my original smaller group on the first night when I discussed work dissatisfaction, said he appreciated my haikus and asked if I do any teaching or workshops. So that became a suggestion for action, one which I will take up to try and address this issue. It would be very satisfying if I was to come out of the Yatra with such a practical result.

The van took our bags to Avebury for more goodbye hugs, then a lot of us got on the very hot bus to Swindon, where we started to scatter and spread the Buddhafield... I got the train to Reading with Akasaka, Sanghadaka, Priyadaka and Suryamani. I asked Akasaka to remind me of the different events and stages of the all-night vigil, and I wrote them down as a memory aid. We saw the Uffington White Horse from the train, and soon it was full circle, back at Reading station, where I felt like a very different person; much more open, loving, confident and happy; ready to apply whatever I had learned and developed to the challenges waiting for me...

> *I am walking, walking, walking*
> *I am walking, walking, walking,*
> *I am walking, walking, walking*
> *I'll keep walking*
> *And there is no*
> *place I'd rather be.*
> *The whole world*
> *travels with me.*
> *There's no place*
> *the sun has not kissed*
> *And there is no*
> *love greater than this.*

Prajnaparamita at Avebury, following a Buddhafield Yatra

YATRA CEREMONIES 2011

The 2011 Yatra saw a rich mixture of ceremonies, culminating in an all-night puja inside West Kennet Long Barrow. Most were created 'on the spot' to suit the place and the moment, drawing of course on traditional sources from the Buddhist tradition. Here's some of what happened:

Saturday:

AM: meet at Reading Station, begin walking

EVE: Thames meadow. Dedication Ceremony

Sunday:

AM: Meditation. Baptism by Air/Water in threes. Small groups saying hello.

Eve: Scutchamer Knob burial mound: Baptism by Fire/Earth: Jumping fire in woods, being caught by (supported by) community, taking off/landing on earth.

Monday:

AM: Form circle around mound, individually walk into centre of collapsed Scutchamer barrow, holding vajra, shouting name and aspirations for the day: "Today I walk with..."

EVE: Uffington, Dragon Hill at sunset: Ratana Sutta and meeting/ taming/ befriending our Demons: calling their names into the wind.

Tuesday:

AM: Small check-in groups at camp, Verses to the Ancestors at Wayland's Smithy.

EVE: Fire under sky, Dharma talk on Wisdom/ Compassion/ the Elements

Tara and the Elements Puja.

Wednesday:

EVE: Barbury Castle: Offering of flower petals to the wind; Amoghasiddhi mantra.

Thursday:

EVE: Avebury: vigil: walk to West Kennet followed by Seven Rounds all-night puja:

1: Connecting with the Ancestors and Spirits:

Welcome talk by Ratnadeva

Creating shrine and finding our places inside,

Dhiramati 'Verses to the Ancestors' and 'Spirit Song',

Ratana Sutta and offering of one sunflower seed each inside the chamber.

Aksobhya mantra and earth-touching mudra.

2: Connecting with ourselves:

Go-round speaking intentions for the night and fruits of the yatra.

Body-Awareness meditation

3: Evoking our potential:

Reading of Amoghasiddhi as the Green Man

Amoghasiddhi mantra

Tara and the Elements puja

Reading: 'Appearance of Tara.'

Tara Mantra

All lights go out, chanting in darkness

Holding hands in darkness, feeling ourselves as one consciousness

4: Acknowledging Regrets and Limitations:

'Acknowledging our Regrets' from the Celtic Puja

'Confession' from the Sutra of Golden Light

Confession in pairs

Vajrasattva Mantra x7.

5: Voicing our Aspirations/Next Steps:

Verses from Bodhicarya puja

Connecting everyone with string

Go-round saying "When I leave, I will...

Cutting string and tying on wrist.

6: Rebirth (first light of dawn):

'Bone Seed' Verses by Dhiramati

Spoken Padmasambhava Mantra

Re-emerging reborn

7: Retreat Metta and Transference of Merits:

Retreat Metta

Verses of Blessing and Healing.

Transference of Merits

Sabbe Satta mantra

Emerging just before sunrise (5.06am)

Kalidasa's 'Exhortation to the Dawn'.

Return to camp approx 6am.

Friday:

AM: meditation by tumuli.

EVE: Yatra walk into Avebury, formal arrival at stones. Reporting-out.

Meeting the Keeper of the Stones Terry Dobney and tour of the stones.

Saturday:

Transference of Merits

Tat-down and depart.

THE BUDDHAFIELD CAFÉ

The Buddhafield Café is a not-for-profit festival catering provider, offering a varied menu of organic, vegan food, substantially run by a volunteer team. We operate as a Buddhist work-as-spiritual-practice environment at an annual programme of festivals, camping events and large retreats mostly in the South-West of England. We have a strong environmental ethic: we prefer to use bakers and organic veg suppliers local to the event we are attending; we use our own, custom built solar power rig and hot water heating system, and we operate a scrupulous recycling policy. The Café can also provide a sauna, showers, hot tubs, a cinema space, extra geodesic domes and its multi-sized 'Parthenon' tents to other events.

The Café began in the early nineties as a fundraising venture to cover the costs of taking a meditation teaching space to Glastonbury Festival. It's grown into one of the largest festival cafés on the circuit, feeding hundreds of people a day on delicious freshly cooked, organic, vegan food and providing a welcoming haven of warmth and friendliness in a 'no-drink-no-drugs' environment.

Although a core team works for Buddhafield and the Café all year round, some people join just for a season, and many more dip in and out. Not everyone is a Buddhist or even aspires to be, but everyone contributes to its unique ethos.

There's more later in this book about how the Café works: its menus, work roles, kit, policies – everything you might need to start your own!

TEACHING AT FESTIVALS

Buddhafield started life in the early 1990's with a small group of people based around the Croydon Buddhist Centre. Frustrated with the ethos of the Centre as it was then, they came together and decided to raise the necessary money to go to the Glastonbury Festival and teach meditation in the Healing Fields. The name 'Buddhafield' had not appeared, and they were simply known as "Buddhist Meditation Teaching", with a makeshift banner to match! But thus began Buddhafield's proud tradition of meditation teaching at many of Britain's alternative festivals - Glastonbury, The Big Green Gathering, Wildheart, Sunrise, Megatripolis, Earth First!, even the Green Party conference, a tradition which continues to this day.

For some years this was all the project did - though it was quickly obvious that the classes were hugely popular, and the obvious question arose - what 'next step' could we offer the people coming to the classes? Our presence at the Glastonbury Festival was facilitated by Jacob Jones, manager of the Healing Field, and we discovered he was also in the business of putting on camps for a variety of spiritual groups, mostly in two beautiful fields near Shepton Mallet owned by Teddy Stones, an eccentric and much-loved gentleman farmer. Jacob agreed to provide the infrastructure for a 'canvas retreat' and the first Buddhafield retreat was held - though still without the name 'Buddhafield'. Jacob also offered us the opportunity to take a café pitch at Glastonbury, and the 'Green Buddha Café' was born, forerunner of the Buddhafield Café.

Meditation teaching and practice in the middle of a noisy music festival is necessarily very different to practice in a tranquil, insulated urban Buddhist Centre or retreat centre - but Buddhafield discovered it didn't seem to matter: you can still go surprisingly deep into meditation surprisingly quickly. If nothing else, it gave those who came a taste of meditation - and at that time at least, many people at Britain's festivals were seeking for new perspectives on life and spirituality.

Buddhist Meditation classes at the Glastonbury Festival

47

THE PRAJNAPARAMITA SANCTUARY

AN INTRODUCTION BY SAGARAVAJRA

Central to the land at Broadhembury is the Prajnaparamita Sanctuary, a separate but closely related project created and managed by Sagaravajra, also a member of the Triratna Buddhist Order and part of the original team which 'won' the land in the first place. Here're some notes outlining his vision for the site, now a beautiful, unique, secret, and totally unexpected part of the Devon countryside. He says -

BACKGROUND

During my life as a Buddhist, I have had an enduring interest in how intangible, spiritual qualities and values can become embodied in form. This interest by stages led to a practice of sculpture and ultimately to producing the sculpture of Prajnaparamita. At a later stage in this process, as I began to make the plinth and nimbus for the sculpture, I began to notice how these contextual elements dramatically amplified the qualities of the figure. I began to realise, with surprise, how the context that surrounds a sculpture is as important if not more important than the sculpture itself. I began to awaken to the significance of what are traditionally known as sanctuaries, and began an informal study of traditional sanctuaries. I discovered that there were several characteristics of sanctuaries that transcend religious and cultural boundaries.

Sanctuary: a Definition

Fr Latin - sanctus *holy* arium - *ary*
A consecrated place
The most sacred part of any building
A place consecrated to some god esp. ancient Greeks and Romans that may be open (as in a grove) or enclosed and often built around a temple
A place held to be sacrosanct
A sacred and inviolable asylum: a place of refuge and protection
A place of resort for those who seek refuge from turmoil and strife
A place of refuge for birds, game or other animals

A SANCTUARY IN PRINCIPLE

A sanctuary is a sacred or ritual space whereby one's perception is encouraged to undergo a transformation, one in which ordinary objects, actions, and sounds are transformed into significant objects, actions, and sounds.

A sanctuary is defined by some symbolic central organising principle set inside an enclosure. This enclosure is defined by a perimeter wall which defines and contains the sacred space within.

Entering a sanctuary requires the passing through or over a threshold; this marks the point of passing from the ordinary world outside into the realm of heightened significance on the inside of the sanctuary.

AIMS AND OBJECTIVES OF THE SANCTUARY AT BROADHEMBURY

We are trying to create a Prajnaparamita pure land. I see the sanctuary at Broadhembury as containing the following elements:

1. A sacred ritual space. The central organising principle is that of Prajnaparamita, the Mother of the Buddhas, who represents transcendental Wisdom and Beauty.

2. In addition Prajnaparamita has several important symbolic associations which will be included within the sanctuary precinct. These include Nagas, water, and the Mandala of the Five Buddhas.

3. The sanctuary will exist and be defined within an enclosure. It will be defined by a boundary. It is important that people who enter the sanctuary cannot easily see or be seen by people outside the sanctuary.

4. The entrance to the sanctuary will be marked by the passage through a threshold.

5. The sanctuary will be landscaped to enhance its existing natural beauty; over time, it will be planted and landscaped to create an environment that amplifies and embodies the qualities of Prajnaparamita.

6. The sanctuary will be designed to encourage a visionary, imaginative journey that recapitulates the elements of the Prajnaparamita sadhana. These principles will be advanced by the design of paths through the site that will lead to thematic sculptures representing Nagas, the Five Buddhas and ultimately Prajnaparamita herself.

7. Finally, I imagine the creation of a contemplation/walking meditation path modelled on the design of the Chartres Labyrinth. I have experienced this as a very profound setting for walking meditation contemplation. In a sense, this path will be a microcosm of the sanctuary itself: a centre, a circumference and a journey linking the two. This area will provide for a more intensified area for internal reflection.

Prajnaparamita seated in the Sanctuary

WORK AS PRACTICE IN BUDDHAFIELD

For Buddhafield, Buddhism is not just something to be practised at shrines or in temples, its principles are routinely applicable to daily life and should be practiced there. In the Café and on Buddhafield retreats – and at the Festival – Buddhafield encourages the development of awareness at work; mindfulness in actions, speech and thoughts, and the cultivation of kindly and generous impulses. It encourages its teams on all its events – whether Festival café or retreat site crew - to meditate, reflect and discuss the Buddha's teaching and explore how it can be applied to the tasks at hand.

Individuals in Buddhafield and the institution itself are guided by the same set of ethical principles, out of which come Buddhafield's ethical and environmental policies: to look after ourselves, those around us, and our environment; to treat ourselves, each other and our world with the respect that they and we all deserve, in the understanding that none are separate.

Buddhafield strives to keep waste to a minimum by recycling and composting whatever it can. All the food it prepares is fresh, organic and/or fairly traded, bought from local growers and suppliers wherever possible. It prefers to support local economies and small businesses, promoting sustainable methods of food production, and unlike many festival cafes, it usually uses ceramic plates, bowls, and mugs, metal cutlery - or compostable alternatives if necessary. Power for the music and lights in all Buddhafield structures comes from solar panels.

Putting up the Buddhafield Café: teamwork essential!

50

A Buddhafield retreat poster: Living an Abundant Life

BUDDHAFIELD DHARMA:
TEN TALKS AND A PROSE-POEM

What follows are edited transcripts of ten talks given by members of the Buddhafield teaching team and the Triratna Buddhist Order, covering many of the core aspects of Buddhafield's unique approach to Dharma practice.

Akasati, in her introduction 'Ecology, Buddhism and Buddhafield', explores Buddhafield's origins in the 'Festival culture' of 1990's Britain, and some of its subsequent trials and adventures as the new project attempted to make real its vision of an idealistic spiritual community willing and able to spend substantial time both on retreat in nature and teaching meditation in the middle of the wildest festivals.

Akuppa and Lokabandhu, in a pair of essays, 'Nature as Dharma Teacher' and 'Shouting Out Beauty: Listening to the Wisdom of Nature', celebrate the many lessons to be learnt by living and practicing close to nature. More philosophically, in 'The Living Elements', Kamalashila introduces Buddhism's understanding of the six elements and links this with our need to reconnect with the more 'elemental' qualities of the natural world. And Paramananda, one of Buddhafield's most popular meditation teachers but previously a self-confessed 'city boy' by lifestyle and temperament, describes, in 'Being in Nature and in Silence: a rare and precious opportunity', his own first experiences of being on retreat 'Buddhafield-style'. And Ratnadeva, a long-time Buddhafield stalwart, follows this up with a thoughtful exploration, based on his own experiences, of a possible 'marriage' between Buddhism and Druidry as part of Buddhism's process of inculturation in the West - the way religious teachings necessarily adapt and evolve as they are presented to other cultures.

The following four essays look more at Buddhafield as a community and its relationship with the wider society it exists within, and how the one could or should respond to the urgent needs of the other. Khemasuri draws on her long interest in 'systems theory' to offer 'Building an Ethical Underworld: Lessons from the Mafia', a series of reflections suggesting why Buddhist practice and ethics might be especially effective in affecting our world for the better. Akuppa, in 'Strive On! Five ways to stay sane and true and survive global meltdown' distils theory into practice with five simple precepts for action.

In connect.empower.liberate Guhyapati, founder of the EcoDharma community in the Catalan mountains, explores in some detail how the three key practices of connection, empowerment, and liberation can transform and heal both individual, society, and environment; also how also spiritual practice rooted in Buddhism can help the activist sustain and deepen their efforts. And Kamalashila, in 'Community, Nature, and Reality: Buddhist Community in Depth', explores how even the 'lone wolf' Dharma practitioner needs to be rooted in a vivid sense of connection with both community and those who have gone before, our ancestors.

The last essay, at times more of a heartfelt prose-poem, by Dhiramati, is entitled 'Myth, Poetry, and the Goddess: Another way of Imagining' and asks us to develop exactly that, lest we, along with much of our society, suffer a catastrophic "loss of soul".

Hundreds more Dharma talks have been given in Buddhafield over the years, many of which can be found in their original audio form on the Buddhafield page of FreeBuddhistAudio.

ECOLOGY, BUDDHISM, AND BUDDHAFIELD

BY AKASATI

In the last decades of the 20th Century, two movements of human thought and practice emerged as significant influences in Western society. One was the growing environmental movement, encompassing a broad range of concerns from the wellbeing of indigenous peoples, rainforests and wildlife habitats to community lifestyles, organic farming, and issues related to the ever-expanding human use of resources. Meanwhile, the two and a half thousand-year-old Buddhist tradition has become an increasingly familiar and respected presence in the cultural landscape of the West, to the extent that it is no longer unusual for its core meditation practices such as the mindfulness of breathing to be used within major organisations such as the British National Health Service.

The dialogue between urgent contemporary issues and timeless Buddhist wisdom is the central theme of this volume, which itself has its roots in Buddhafield, a collective running a variety of outdoor, eco-Buddhist projects, mostly in the west of England. These include a festival, an itinerant vegan cafe, an annual programme of retreats under canvas and organic growing projects. Most of the talks and teachings on which the following chapters are based were originally given at Buddhafield, either at the festival or on a retreat. Although this is not primarily a book *about* Buddhafield, as the common context which draws the different threads together, some background may be useful.

BUDDHIST PRACTICE ON THE LAND

In the twenty-first century Western world, an increasing number of people are drawing inspiration from the teachings of the Buddha. We have burgeoning volumes of written teachings available in translation, from the Pali texts of early Indian Buddhism to the sutras and commentaries of later schools throughout Asia. However, our comfortable, push-button lifestyles are a long way away from the profound simplicity of the Buddha and his early followers' lives.

From the day he left his family home, the man destined to become known as the Buddha lived outdoors: in forest groves, on the banks of rivers and outside the villages and cities of northern India. At times he penetrated deep into the jungle to confront his own fear, or for respite from human society. Apart from taking shelter in huts during the monsoon, Siddhartha Gautama and his followers slept in the open; at the roots of trees, under the stars, close to the elements and the creatures of the non-human world. In keeping with the culture of the time, early Buddhists perceived the land as alive with meaning, filled with sacred groves inhabited by local deities and the spirits of trees and brooks.

Some Western Buddhists have wished to explore not only the written teachings of the Buddha but also the example of his pared-down lifestyle, rooted in landscape experienced as alive and sacred. Buddhafield is one expression of this exploration.

Buddhafield is what its name suggests: Buddhism in a field. The name is also a play on words from a scriptural source, the *Vimalakirti Nirdesa*. In this sutra, enlightened beings (Buddhas) are seen to arise at certain times, in certain places and under certain conditions in what is conceived of as a vast or infinite universe. The term 'Buddha-field' refers to the field or sphere of influence of a given Buddha, with the expectation that all beings within that field may themselves attain enlightenment in due course through the influence and activities of that Buddha. Put another way, a 'Buddhafield' exists to the extent that living beings within it practice the Dharma. It is, amongst other things, a field of positive thought, high resolve, virtuous application, generosity, and tolerance. It is a field of meditation and wisdom.

Since the mid-1990's Buddhafield has given thousands of interested people the opportunity to experience Dharma practice in the outdoors, in a context of material simplicity. To that extent, it is both literally and metaphorically a true 'Buddha-field'!

UNTAMED DHARMA: FESTIVAL ROOTS

Buddhafield's distinctive style grew out of a network of influences. While the seeds of Buddhafield were first emerging, moves towards non-urban, simpler and more sustainable ways of living were being explored amongst a section of the UK population. Festivals such as Glastonbury were a focus for debate and sharing of ideas. The project that later became Buddhafield began when some members of the (then) Western Buddhist Order[3] and friends went to teach meditation at Glastonbury Festival and later the Big Green Gathering, supported by their 'Green Buddha' café.[4]

As well as being a new context for connecting with people from alternative communities who might be interested in meditation and Dharma teaching, for those pioneering the project these events were also a welcome escape from city life and an opportunity to be part of the relaxed, counter-culture vibes of the festival scene - a very different environment from the comparatively restrained atmosphere of a city Buddhist centre or retreat, which some people found restrictive.

No path is without pitfalls. In Buddhist circles a potential danger has been noted: that the necessary application of restraint in the practice of mindfulness and ethics can be confused with a state of alienation, blocked energy and denial of whatever feelings and drives appear not to fit into the picture of a 'good Buddhist.'[5] Whilst many Buddhist practitioners focussed on cultivating spiritual purity (and sometimes, human nature being what it is, concerns about being *seen* to do so), others were more interested in opportunities to explore energies that were less amenable to conscious control, in an environment which encouraged free expression. Although hard-and-fast distinctions between 'conformity' and 'dissent' tend to lead to unhelpful polarisation, the presence of 'counter-culture' alternatives has nonetheless provided many a liberating context for something fresh and creative to be born. So it was for the pioneers of Buddhafield.

For dissenters and 'bad boys/girls' who felt they did not fit into the 'Buddhist mainstream,' the festival scene was a gift. Glastonbury in the nineties was a relatively uncontrolled environment, certainly by UK standards, with all the opportunities for creativity and underworld dealings one might expect. The festival scene typically blended Eastern influences with New Age ideas, and miscellaneous shamanistic traditions of varying degrees of authenticity with holistic healing methods, creating a potpourri of ritual and spiritual practices (alongside the proverbial sex, drugs and rock and roll). Buddhist meditation, chanting and puja (devotional practice) were readily absorbed into the mix, to the extent that many festival goers did not -- and still don't -

---

3 Now the Triratna Buddhist Order

4 As well as the 'eco' inference, 'Green Buddha' refers to Amoghasiddhi, the green Buddha of the Tantric Five-Buddha Mandala, who symbolises fearlessness and unstoppable energy.

5 Sangharakshita: 'Alienated and Integrated Awareness'

distinguish Buddhism from New Age ideas or the various branches of Hindu belief and practice that made their way West via the hippy trail.

The influence of the festival world went much deeper than opportunities for Buddhists to let their hair down. It was also a focus for activists, campaigners and people following alternative, low-impact lifestyles. These people were engaged in a serious critique of mainstream, consumer values. Buddhafield from its inception has been conscious of the ethical imperative for low-impact living and has provided a context for dialogue between the ecology movement and Buddhist teachings such as non-violence and interdependence. This dialogue continues to be a fundamental working ground for how all Buddhafield projects are run. A radical critique of contemporary Western values and lifestyles remains at the heart of the project.

The founders of Buddhafield had a sense that Buddhism had something substantial to offer eco-activists and the alternative scene. They could pass on their meditative experience and mind-training techniques, and a non-theistic system of ethics, as well as a wealth of first-hand experience of living and working in community. They also saw that they in return had much to learn from the activist community, many of whom exemplified the practice of 'going forth' into a life of material simplicity and who often had a greater awareness of the social and political dimensions of ethics and the various forms of institutionalised or structural violence in our society.

Another influence of the festival scene was a culture of doing-it-yourself, whether that meant chopping wood for a fire to stay warm, fixing one's own van, or rigging up a bender from locally coppiced hazel. This in itself was a protest at an increasingly tightly regulated, specialised society and the potential dependency, even disempowerment, which can result from that kind of system.

CHALLENGES AND JOYS: COMMUNITY AS PRACTICE

Buddhafield is a community, or rather a number of interlocking, overlapping communities. This includes a small 'core' organisation working together year-round, to a variety of seasonal groups and teams that come together to put on the festival, join the café team, engage with land-management events, or run or attend a range of camping retreats. It is an ever-growing and ever-changing community. New enthusiasts get involved each year, and a new generation is also arising from within the existing community as some of the young people who came on the family retreats throughout their childhood are now taking some of the responsibilities of running them.

Central to the project are Buddhists – order members and 'mitras' (friends) from the Triratna Buddhist Community - who have made an explicit commitment to shared Dharma practice. They work alongside many other people who would not consider themselves to be Buddhists but have similar values and outlooks and whose skills and contributions make these projects possible. There are sometimes differences of values, too, which can cause tensions but may also be an opportunity for creative dialogue, not just in theory but in the most hands-on sense, whereby members of a diverse community have to communicate and negotiate with one another. One case in point is that while festivals are more usually places where alcohol and drugs are consumed in quantity, Buddhafield makes every effort to be drug- and alcohol-free. This issue has sometimes led to heated debate, although many people attending the Buddhafield Festival have been surprised and delighted by how much enjoyment they can have without recourse to mind-altering substances, instead having direct experience of 'mindfulness clear and radiant' as described in the positive formulation of the five key Buddhist precepts. It is also a much-valued space for recovering addicts who can continue to enjoy the festival scene without the temptation of readily available intoxicants.

Cooperating with other people is always, sooner or later, a challenge. Views and egos bump up against one another. It's all too easy to talk about the Buddhist virtues of compassion, generosity, truthfulness and so on, and quite another thing to put them into practice. The closer we live and work together, the more revealing our day to day interactions are likely to be about where we actually stand in relation to these precepts and principles. Like deepening one's meditation or ethical sensibilities, building sangha - community-based on Buddhist values - is a demanding practice, requiring a genuine willingness to change. It also brings unexpected joys.[6] Often on Buddhafield events, a deeply satisfying sense of community arises in adversity. On an event dominated by torrential rain, levels of co-operation and mutual helpfulness can reach their highest. As well as helping us to understand the ways in which we need one another, difficult conditions can enable us to appreciate how we can work more effectively together against a 'common enemy' – in this case, the weather.

Looking back over my time with Buddhafield, one retreat stands out as being a particularly insightful experience. It was called the 'Green Retreat' and was on the Buddhafield land at Broadhembury. The theme wove together an exploration of Dharma teachings, along with understanding of the nature of things from ecological sources. We also did some shamanic practices for coming into more direct contact with the elements, leading in my case to a wonderful experience of 'communication' with a beech tree which led into a deep sense of being unconditionally loved by the Earth. But that's another story.

However the 'Green Retreat' progressively became known as the 'Brown Retreat'. The rain was torrential, without let-up throughout the whole 10 days and the site turned to a mud-bath. We campers became increasingly wet and in many cases miserable. Along with others, I found myself internally trying to do deals with the weather: "surely it has to stop soon, it has to stop! I want it to stop now!"

But the rain didn't stop. Paths became impassable swamps. A couple of people left early. On the final day, the shrine tent had completely flooded: the various trenches that had been dug to protect it, overflowing. That morning we did a closing ritual, part of which was filmed and I think can still be found on YouTube. Looking back, it was a gut-level revelation: we couldn't control the world! Resistance was utterly futile! I understood viscerally that there is only one realistic path: to let go of expectations and attempts to control and simply open to what comes. This experience of complete surrender to 'what is' was a moment of great joy in my life. I felt joyful for weeks after that retreat. Of course I didn't stop having expectations and trying to irrationally control things. However, I learned something of the freedom that comes from living with reality, not fighting against it.

Thank you rain. Thank you mud. Thank you Buddhafield.

The practical demands of living outdoors, away from most of the gadgets that make modern life so comfortable, frequently have other unexpected benefits. It is surprising how satisfying it is to be called upon to use our ingenuity rather than having everything laid on as we have come to expect. Rigging up a shower bucket from a tree or chopping wood for a fire can be a wonderfully empowering experience. The vast majority of people who leave their comfortable lifestyles to spend even a short period camping out in the elements seem to be visibly more alive and 'present' within a few days. Unconsciously

---

6 The spiritual benefits of living and working together (at least for periods in our lives) have been much emphasised by Sangharakshita, the founder of the Friends of the Western Buddhist Order; a practical teaching which has been intensively followed within the Buddhafield community.

we realise how dependent we are on machines most of us don't understand for our very survival in the modern West, let alone the complex systems such as global agriculture and trade that are way beyond our control. The human capacity for innovation and specialisation has created unprecedented wealth for at least some of us on the planet, but at a huge cost. In addition to the heavy and unsustainable environmental impact of our current lifestyles, a further individual cost is an underlying anxiety of being ill-equipped to fend for oneself in the world. The theme of 'survival' seems to be part of our current zeitgeist, on various levels.

NATURE AS TEACHER

Living outdoors, even temporarily, it becomes obvious that community extends beyond the human realm. Camping on a piece of land and actively cultivating awareness, we naturally begin to tune in with the creatures who already live there: insects, birds, badgers, foxes, and deer. The presence of the elements in the form of trees, a stream or the earth itself, becomes more vivid and alive. Buddhist teachings on the conditioned and, therefore, interconnected nature of all phenomena reveal themselves in myriad new ways, especially to the great majority of us who have grown up in urban environments to some degree disconnected from the natural world. The experience of arriving in a field to set up an event and having to find a source of clean water and to deal with one's own waste, through earth toilets and composting, can give us new perspectives on some of life's essentials that we normally take for granted. Eating local, organic vegetables, we see how elements emerge from the earth, move through the body and back into the earth, ultimately as the rich compost that 'hu-manure,' in time, becomes. Food and excrement, those two 'ends' of the same process that classically give us occasion for greed and aversion, are fertile ground for reflection on the whole of life as a process of arising and passing away of which our own bodies are a part. From this more immediate experience, it is easier to appreciate directly the importance of balancing what we receive and what we put back in relationship to the physical world.

In shamanic traditions across the planet, the natural world is taken as the great teacher. Qualities of strength, agility and far-sightedness are learned from animals and birds. Through sustained contact with the non-human world, adherents come to a deeper understanding of the meaning and nature of life. Even people coming to live on the land for just a week or a month generally notice how deeply they are affected by the presence of the elements. Camping next to a great oak tree or brook and being awoken by the building crescendo of the dawn chorus, our spirits are nourished and regenerated. Of course, the elements are always present, whether we are in the remotest wilderness or the greyest corners of the inner city. But when we are inside four walls, away from the touch of the breeze or the sound of flowing water, we generally feel less connected to this web of life of which we are intrinsically a part. And we do not need to look far to see what damaging and dangerous consequences this perceived disconnection is having between human society and the rest of the biosphere.

Unlike many religious and philosophical viewpoints, Buddhism sees the whole of life as a continuum and does not separate human beings into a special category. The traditional Buddhist view does not even place humankind at the 'top' of the evolutionary tree, listing 'devas' – beings in subtle bodies – as existing in more refined, happier realms than ourselves (though the deva worlds, owing to the de-motivating effects of sustained bliss, are not necessarily advantageous in the business of attaining liberation).

As the Jataka or 'Birth' stories[7] show, perhaps naively for contemporary tastes, traditional Buddhism sees consciousness as manifesting in a series of rebirths by which an individual (though ever-changing) mind-stream might manifest now as a hare or a monkey, and now as a human being, with its nature and tendencies in the present impacting on future manifestations. Buddhist ethics link us humans in very firmly with other species. The first precept of non-harm is towards all beings, not just other people. It is to be applied as much as possible to the whole of life. Although the threat of the collapse of ecological systems on a huge scale was not an issue in the Buddha's time, and so not addressed directly, it is not difficult to find teachings that are relevant to the predicament in which we find ourselves. One of the key aims of Buddhafield and of this book is to explore the relevance of Buddhist teachings to some of the most urgent issues of our time.

ELEMENTAL EMBODIMENT

Any attempt to bring about real transformation of the individuals who collectively constitute society, however, must be grounded in the self-knowledge that comes from a degree of introspection. Retreats on the land allow people the opportunity to take time out of hectic schedules for meditation and reflection, surrounded by the beauty of nature. Meditating in a tent, seated on the lumps and bumps of the earth beneath, and feeling the cool touch of the breeze, is different from meditating in a room. In a camp situation, we use our bodies more than many of us would normally. Tents have to be erected, water carried and wood chopped. We need to take care walking over uneven ground especially on a dark night, far from the glare of street lights. We are less protected from the elements than we would be in a building, more likely to get wet when it rains, hot when the sun comes up and cold when it goes down. Away from our insulated lives and computer screens, we can begin to experience ourselves as more deeply 'embodied'. Barefoot walking meditation, for example, treading on the very earth and with the expanse of the sky above, allows us to experience directly how connected energetically we are to these great elements. Reflection on the six elements (adding space and consciousness to the classic list of four elements) is intended to deepen our insight into the profound continuity between what we experience inside our bodies and what we experience as 'outside.'

A capacity to extend our awareness to include not just the contents of our head but the direct, non-discursive sensations of the body, is a pre-requisite for entering more settled, meditative states of mind. The importance of attention to the body has been emphasised since the Buddha's day when he urged his followers to cultivate sustained mindfulness of the body and its functions: its posture and movements in space, the experience of temperature, pleasure and pain, and the 'substances' that make it up. In spite of this unmistakable emphasis, many of us have a tendency to disregard and even denigrate our own bodies in our pursuit of spiritual growth. Although we may feel some influence from the Buddha and his teachings in our lives, most of us carry more powerful, less conscious influences from our own culture. According to a Buddhist critique, theistic religions tend towards an 'eternalistic' view whereby the body is regarded as fundamentally separate from the eternal soul, which is seen as our essence and the most important part of our being. From Greek philosophical influences through the dominant Judeo-Christian heritage, there has been a major cultural strand whereby the body, and indeed the whole of nature, came to be seen as something separate, inferior and to be subjugated. Serious study of the Dharma by Western students tends

---

7 A body of canonical and non-canonical stories relating the former lives of the Buddha and his disciples, in some cases as animals.

to lead back to an examination of our own received views. A vigorous critique of such enduring views, and the cultivation of an alternative way of perceiving the world as radically interconnected may turn out to be the most useful contribution Buddhism has to make to the current ecological debate.

MYTHIC REALMS

No introduction to Buddhafield would be complete without the presence of Padmasambhava, Tara, Amoghasiddhi and the archetypal Buddhas and Bodhisattvas, who are the focus of chanting and devotional practice on many events. The practice of ritual, drawing not only on Buddhist but also pagan, Celtic roots, is a vivid experience for many of the people who come to Buddhafield. Whilst an analysis of the meaning and power of ritual is not the intention of this volume, the mythic dimension, like Tibetan incense pervading a tent, is quietly present.

Words, as we all know, have limitations. Ultimately all of these themes are best explored through direct, individual experience. In the end, we cannot fully experience the beauty and magic of meditation and Dharma practice in community and on the land by reading about it. We need to actually do it!

NATURE AS DHARMA TEACHER

BY AKUPPA

Is there any difference between meditating in a field and meditating in a building?

In the Buddha's lifetime, meditation seems almost always to have been done outdoors, except during the rainy season. For those who had 'gone forth' from the household life, there would have been little choice. But it seems that the Buddha and his followers chose to meditate in forests, not through lack of an alternative but because natural surroundings in some way supported or enriched their practice. When the Buddha was looking for a place to meditate, he later tells his monks that he came upon a "delightful stretch of ground" and waxes lyrical about the place where he goes to sit and where he eventually attains awakening.

There is also the account that the Buddha gives of the time in his youth, before he was the Buddha, when he was sitting in a grove under a rose apple tree, very calm, overlooking a scene where some men were ploughing a field. Quite spontaneously, without trying to, he entered into a very expansive, peaceful state of mind. It wasn't until years later, after he'd been on quite a journey of experimenting with ascetic practices, that he thought back to this experience. He had come to see that his ascetic path – being so hard on himself to try to break through to some kind of enlightenment – was a dead end. He was looking for another way forward and, at that point, he thought back to the incident under the rose-apple tree. This seems to have been very significant for the Buddha. It acted as a kind of signpost for him. There were two things that he recalled about the scene: one is that the place he was in was very beautiful; and the other, that he was already in a state of mind that was free from any gross form of craving. He was free enough from any disturbing states of mind to be open and receptive. It seems to have been a combination of his surroundings and his open state of mind that gave rise to this spontaneous experience of bliss.

Years later, it was the recollection of this experience that set the Buddha onto the path of meditation that was eventually to lead him to the Bodhi tree and awakening. So it lies at the very heart of the Buddhist tradition. The origins of Buddhism can be traced, amongst other things, to this experience of beauty in nature.

This relationship with nature was a theme that would continue throughout the Buddha's life. There are accounts of him, for example, taking time away from his disciples and from teaching the Dharma, just to be alone in nature. And it is also something that he passed on to his disciples. Maha Kassapa, who was one of the most prominent of the Buddha's followers, was particularly known for his love of wild, natural places.

> *"These regions are delightful to my heart*
> *Where the Kareri creeper spreads its flower wreaths,*
> *Where sound the trumpet-calls of elephants,*
> *Like towering peaks of dark-blue clouds,*
> *Like splendid edifices are these rocks,*
> *Where the birds' sweet voices fill the air,*
> *These rocky heights delight my heart."*

This poem by Maha Kassapa is a very early example, perhaps even the earliest example, of nature or wilderness poetry. Until then in India, poetry that referred to nature, for example in the Vedic tradition, was overlaid with archetypal symbolism. Buddhist thinking and practice, immersed in the forests of India, seems to have brought something quite new – a naturalistic appreciation of nature for its own sake, not mediated through a theistic belief system.

So what might it be about being in nature that might make a difference to how we meditate? Nature often (though not always!) offers peace and quiet and freedom from distraction. But perhaps there is more to it than just this. If we are open to it, nature also acts as a kind of Dharma teacher. Being in nature is a constant reminder of reality. This can work on a very conscious level, in that we can look at the natural world and reflect upon a fundamental truth such as 'interconnectedness.' But, more importantly, nature teaches us wordlessly through our senses, speaking not just to our reason but also to our intuition. It can have a direct effect on our minds and hearts, and on the quality of our consciousness. In particular, it is through our openness to beauty that we can learn deeply from nature.

To begin with, nature has the capacity to delight us in a very simple way. There are particular arrangements of shape, colour, light and sound that are able to arrest our attention, at least for a moment, such as the sight of a beautiful flower or the sudden glint of a kingfisher as we walk along a riverbank. Our whole attention can become instantly focussed in such moments. Certain experiences have an ability to grab our attention and lift us, as it were, out of any negative states of mind, if only for a moment. We respond especially to certain brighter colours and to simplicity of form. Whatever previous state of mind we might have been in, we are suddenly, if momentarily, transported into a state of delight. We are liberated a little. There are some who may despise this kind of appreciation of beauty as being too easy and too sentimental. But it is, at least, a beginning, what the writer James Hillman talks about as the "beginning of the road to beauty".

Another kind of experience is of beauty as order and harmony. We might, for example, look out over a pastoral landscape or ancient forest and our senses intuit that there is a certain order, harmony and stability, that nature isn't just a completely random collection of stuff. In a forest, for example, there is a clear and stable pattern of organisation with certain plants on the forest floor, others that are somewhat higher, and yet others that form the highest canopy.

This appreciation of outer harmony can evoke an experience of inner peace, perhaps combined with a sense of wonder that such intricate harmony can arise from apparent chaos. Human beings feel a need for inner order and harmony. We have within us all sorts of energies – physical, erotic, mental, emotional – that need both to find expression and also to be brought into harmonious relationship with each other if they are to be meaningful and to lead to happiness. Perhaps, in these experiences of the stability and harmony of nature, we intuit this possibility. We have a sense of our own wild energies being expressed as a harmonious and meaningful whole that is greater than ourselves. We intuit the sublimation of hatred and greed, allowing our own personhood to fully emerge.

Sometimes our apprehension of the beauty of nature is simply ineffable. Occasionally, we can be surprised by a beauty around us that is simply beyond words; that just cannot be expressed. Even a skilled poet might be lost for words. Walt Whitman, for example, writes in the 'Song of Myself' that "the press of my foot to the earth springs a hundred affections – they scorn the best I can do to relate them." A similar sense of being lost for words is suggested by Shantideva: "lakes adorned with lotuses where the calls of the geese steal the heart beyond bounds." These experiences of nature render dumb our whole apparatus for expressing them, our very language – we are taken beyond language and our conventional ways of perceiving and understanding. This is itself a liberation – it helps us to see beyond our conventional view of the world.

There is a school of Chinese and Japanese poetry, called Yugen, dedicated entirely to this subtle profundity. One writer likens it to "an autumn evening under a colourless expanse of silent sky. Somehow, as if for some reason that we should be able to recall, tears well uncontrollably." This quality is often evoked with scenes of mist, things that can't quite be seen, or cries of animals that can be heard but not seen – things that are suggested, but that can't quite be grasped.

One of the greatest gifts that nature can give is a deeper understanding of transience. There is a long tradition within Buddhism, going right back to the Buddha himself, of using natural images to evoke the truth of transience. The classic image of this is the dewdrop. The Buddha often likened human life to a dewdrop on the tip of a blade of grass or a bubble caused by a fat raindrop falling into water. These are all, he said, comparable to human life – "limited, trifling, of much stress and despair." What we need to do, he said, is to "touch this truth like a sage, and live a skilful, holy life."

These images that the Buddha used cascade right down through the Buddhist tradition. The Diamond Sutra concludes with the words:

> *"A lamp, a cataract, a star in space,*
> *an illusion, a dewdrop, a bubble,*
> *a dream, a cloud, a flash of lightning –*
> *view all conditioned things like this"*

And Tsongkhapa, in the fifteenth century in Tibet, evoked these images to turn our minds towards our deepest purposes in life:

> *"All worldly things are brief,*
> *like lightning in the sky.*
> *this life you must know*
> *as the tiny splash of a raindrop,*
> *a thing of beauty that disappears*
> *even as it comes into being.*
> *Therefore set your goal.*
> *Make use of every day and night*
> *to achieve it."*

The image of dew also comes down to Japanese poetry. The tenth-century anthologist Ki Tsurayuki talked about the images that would inspire a typical Japanese poet of his time:

> *"When on a spring morning,*
> *he sees the scattered blossoms;*
> *when, on an autumn evening,*
> *he hears the falling leaves;*
> *when he sees the dew on the grass*
> *and the foam on the water,*
> *expressions of his own brief life."*

Dew and raindrops are a gentle reminder of mortality. But nature isn't always so subtle. In the same passage where the Buddha talks about dew and raindrops, he goes on to evoke the image of a torrential river rushing down the side of a mountain, carrying rocks and trees in its wake. Transience is not always gentle; it is sometimes terrifying.

But even in this aspect of nature, there is the possibility of beauty. Edmund Burke describes it as a kind of satisfying horror, a tranquillity tinged with terror. And Rilke writes:

> *"Beauty is nothing but the beginning of terror,*
> *which we are just able to bear,*
> *and we wonder at it so*
> *because it calmly disdains to destroy us"*

If there is one image that encapsulates this aspect of beauty, it is the tiger. This comes up very early in the Buddhist tradition, when the Buddha meditates in the forest in the night, aware of the danger of tigers but conquering his fear. The Tibetan Yogi Milarepa meditated in a cave where there lived a tigress with her cub. He meditated with the fear, sitting with it and overcoming it. There is a kind of beauty in this transcendence. Sangharakshita, in discussing this episode, describes:

> *"A kind of terror that is so invigorating*
> *as to be strangely pleasing.*
> *The proximity of danger makes you feel stronger,*
> *more courageous and heroic.*
> *Trembling with fear can put heart into your practice,*
> *and positively drive you to practise harder*
> *with the awareness that whatever fearful experiences arise,*
> *they are finally no more than that –*
> *just appearances, not fixed realities."*

And there is an image in Zen Buddhism of the Zen Master being like a tiger's cave, where there are footprints going in, but none coming out. There is something terrifying to the ego about approaching Buddhist practice, or going to a Zen master, because the ego goes in but doesn't come out. If we can stay with the terror, we will find a certain freedom on the other side of it.

From a Buddhist point of view, we're not separate from our surroundings, or from nature. What we are as human beings is an amalgam of energy, matter, consciousness, and information. These flow in from the rest of reality, and they flow out to the rest of reality. There is no hard edge to us. Buddhism teaches that as human beings, we are a bit like whirlpools. A whirlpool in a stream definitely exists, but not in a way that is separate from the rest of the stream around it. We too exist, but not in a way that is fixed and separate.

There are some experiences of beauty by which we intuit our kinship, or our connectedness, with the world around us. There is a sort of signature in the forms of nature that speaks to our deepest intuition and tells us who we are and where we've come from. The complex form of a human being has emerged from nature, and the forms that we see around us have also emerged from nature. In the West, there is a long tradition of recognising this. Euclid, the mathematician, realised that there is a particular proportion that can be found again and again in the forms of nature – the pattern of twigs along a branch or of leaves along a twig, the spiral of a seashell unfurling, the scales on a pineapple or the florets on the head of a sunflower, the gyre of a falcon, or even in the arrangement of tiny unicellular organisms. This proportion, called 'the golden ratio' (approximately 1:1.618) derives from the way in which complex patterns in nature arise from more simple conditions. It is a signature of natural processes, of self-organisation. As human beings, we are sensitive to this 'signature', like recognising one's own mother's handwriting. There's something in those forms that we recognise intuitively. Depth of complexity 'out there' speaks to depth of complexity 'in here.' Deep speaks to deep. Again this is beyond words. We don't need to understand Euclid or Darwin to experience this – it comes directly and intuitively through our own senses. In our appreciation of beauty in nature, we are remembering our deepest origins.

This might even take the form of a kind of communication with nature through a sense of the numinous. The Latin word *numen* refers to the spirit that inhabits a sacred grove. It can also mean 'the nodding of the head of a divine being,' indicating some kind of positive affirmation from nature. It hints at a view of the cosmos as something basically alive rather than dead. Perhaps it is what Wordsworth refers to as "a motion and a spirit that impels all thinking things, all objects of all thought, and rolls through all things." In the appreciation of beauty, there is something two-way about certain experiences. There is the sense of contacting something in nature – and of something in nature nodding back. Most traditional cultures regard nature as essentially alive; many indigenous cultures have words for the sense of an animated cosmos to which Wordsworth was eluding.

Some people, maybe just once in their lifetime, have a spontaneous experience in nature of a vast expansive connectedness. Jung calls these 'oceanic experiences'; Maslow calls them 'peak experiences.' It's a sudden experience of oneness with nature whereby the senses are completely overwhelmed with nature and, for a time, the very sense of self as something separate disappears. Something of the numinous might also arise in encounters with animals in nature. Some American poets have used the Greek word 'noumenon' in this context, to refer to an animal that somehow embodies the spirit of a place. In the encounter with such an animal, it can feel as though the place as a whole is looking back. There can be a strong feeling of privilege in these experiences and of being a part of nature.

What underlies all of these different experiences of beauty is that each of them represents a sort of liberation, whether a temporary liberation from mundane states of mind or a more profound liberation from our whole sense of self. That is what beauty is. Beauty is freedom, and the intimation of freedom. Kant said that beauty is essentially boundlessness. This is also what our Buddhist practice is, freedom from limited ways of thinking about who we are.

The Buddha talks about a succession of meditative states called the 'vimoksas.' In the first two of these, we are getting beyond a state of gross craving. He called the third vimoksa 'the release called the beautiful.' In meditation, this is a simple experience of beauty. The Buddha talks about it as a state where all that can be said is, "Ah, beauty!" This leads onto the fourth vimoksa, a state beyond all sense of self and other. So in this succession of the vimoksas, the path of beauty traverses the whole territory between gross states of craving on the one hand, and transcendence of self on the other. This signifies that what we think of as beauty is the very stuff of the spiritual life. There are all sorts of ways of thinking about what spiritual life is, but the whole of spiritual practice can be thought of as opening up to beauty.

There is one problem with this. The moment that we attempt to grasp beauty is the moment that we lose it, because we've put ourselves back into a state of craving. We can't think of Buddhist practice as 'getting' experiences of beauty. Something more subtle has to happen. What we can do is create the conditions whereby beauty might arise. In nature, that implies an actual physical, sensuous contact with the natural surroundings, and a presence and receptivity to it. We need an attitude of openness to what nature has to teach us of impermanence, insubstantiality, and suffering. Combined with a study of Dharma teachings, being with nature can open us to beauty and truth on a profound level. And it begins with a still body and a still mind, immersed in nature, with all of the sense alive. The philosopher Arnold Berleant writes:

"The boundlessness of the natural world does not just surround us; it assimilates us. Not only are we unable to sense absolute limits in nature; we cannot distance the natural world from ourselves... [When we perceive] environments from within, as it were, looking not at it but being in it, nature... is transformed into a realm in which we live as participants, not observers... The aesthetic mark of all such times is... total engagement, a sensory immersion in the natural world."

If we meditate in this spirit, without walls of any kind, then perhaps we can say that not only are we meditating in nature, but that nature is meditating in us.

Easterbrook: site of the Total Immersion meditation retreat

SHOUTING OUT BEAUTY:
LISTENING TO THE WISDOM OF NATURE

BY LOKABANDHU

The old pine tree speaks divine wisdom;
The secret bird manifests eternal truth.

INTRODUCTION

This chapter started life as a talk for the 2009 Buddhafield Festival. As I struggled to collect my thoughts, I realised that I was trying to reflect on fifteen years of open-air Dharma practice, mostly with the Buddhafield Sangha, and condense all those memories, experiences and reflections into a single coherent talk. This process of reflection felt far from finished, partly because much of that time I had been part of a collective and experimental experience. Three central questions arose in my mind. Firstly, how might 'open-air' Dharma practice play a part in a modern Western Buddhist's spiritual life? I knew I was powerfully drawn to practicing in this way, but I couldn't articulate why. Second, how can traditional Buddhist teachings be applied to the urgent environmental questions of the modern world? I desperately wanted it to be relevant, but much traditional Buddhist discourse seemed indifferent to the natural world, even dismissive of it. And third, arising out of this, what might traditional Buddhism have to learn from a modern environmental and scientific outlook?

By the time I became interested in such topics, I'd been a Buddhist for some fifteen years. Much of that time had been spent at the London Buddhist Centre, where I worked as Centre Manager and lived in a community upstairs. Life there was busy, rewarding and very 'inner-city', with an almost constant noise of sirens, helicopters, road drills and traffic all around. Perhaps not surprisingly, there came a time when I found myself filled with a yearning to be alone, to be outdoors, to be 'in' nature, fully immersed in it. On train journeys, I found myself glued to the window, spotting places I could camp up and hide away. In the end, I followed this intuition, embarking on what became six years of homelessness. Joining Buddhafield, I lived out of a rucksack and spent a lot of time outdoors, albeit as busy as ever, helping organise many of Buddhafield's retreats. Along the way, a constant companion was one of my earliest Buddhist influences, the *Zenrin*, which I'd found soon after I became a Buddhist in a tatty 1970's paperback, 'The Gospel According to Zen.' I'll quote liberally from it as we go along. It's a collection of over 5000 Buddhist verses from Japan, each one intended to be taken up and used for meditation practice.

What follows is in two parts, corresponding to the Paths of Vision and Transformation, which together make up the Buddha's classic teaching of the Noble Eightfold Path.

THE PATH OF VISION

The Path of Vision is that which starts us off on our spiritual journey. It is also that which sustains us as we go, and also that which finally comes to be fully and permanently embodied in us at the end of our spiritual journey. The word 'vision' implies an act of seeing - seeing deeply into certain truths. For me, it became clearer and clearer that all the truths of which the Buddha spoke were immediately visible in nature. I simply had to go outside and look. What this also meant, for me, was a realisation that no religion, and no person in any religion, could claim any monopoly on truth or teaching All truths about the nature of existence are immediately accessible to everyone. As the Zenrin sings,

> *Nothing whatever is hidden;*
> *From of old, all is clear as daylight.*

This view is in contradiction to those of most priesthoods of most religions, including Buddhism, some of whose schools have emphasised lineages, 'ear-whispered' teachings handed down in secret ceremony, initiations, empowerments and so on. None of that is essential. Vision into the nature of reality comes simply from seeing deeply enough into things "the way they really are." To achieve that, you just have to open your eyes and look.

I like to play a game with myself asking, "What would the Buddha have said?" Of course, I cannot know for sure, but I think he'd have said that priesthoods, including Buddhist priesthoods, were not necessary. Teachers, yes; priests, no. As the Zenrin says:

> *Taking up one blade of grass,*
> *Use it as a sixteen-foot golden Buddha.*

Who needs priests when you have a sixteen-foot golden Buddha? And who needs a sixteen-foot golden Buddha when you have a blade of grass?

So, if we did really open our eyes, what would we see? What *is* the nature of reality? The Buddha's fundamental insight was into what is known in Sanskrit as *pratitya samutpada*. It was this insight that 'enlightened' him and gave birth to the entire Buddhist tradition. Unfortunately, *pratitya samutpada* is rather a mouthful and hard to translate. Variously rendered as 'Conditioned Co-Production', 'Dependent Co-Arising', 'Mutual Causality', or even 'Interbeing', it states that all phenomena whatsoever - physical, psychological, spiritual - arise in dependence upon conditions, and exist only so long as the appropriate conditions exist to support them. When conditions change, things change, which in turn cause other things to change, and so on. This is simply the way things really are, according to Buddhism. To develop deep insight into it, as opposed to mere intellectual comprehension, is to become 'liberated'.

As befits a general law, *pratitya samutpada* is necessarily somewhat abstract, and, therefore, easiest seen in some specific applications. This is where nature can be such a wonderful teacher. Here are three examples: interconnectedness; actions and their consequences; and ethics.

INTERCONNECTEDNESS

Working for Buddhafield, I saw how everything depends on everything else. Nothing stands alone. Running up to a dozen retreats a year was an extraordinary logistical operation, and the Buddhafield Festival ten times more so. At first (though in truth there was no 'first'), there was a field and a farmer, and animals which had to be moved off well in advance, thereby avoiding fresh cowpats! There were thistles and nettles to be scythed, often growing especially strongly on last year's rubbish or fire pits. There was publicity and thus the need for computers, printers, and the postal service. There were food and fuel, a network of suppliers and personal relationships with organic farmers and timber yards in the local area. There was the meditation shrine, with more exotic items brought in from far away.

There were people, many people! And a rich web of connections between them, passing on the accumulated wisdom of the camps that had gone before. There was our waste, with no dustbin-men to take it away out of sight. That was a shock! Above all else, there was the weather, ranging from torrential rain to blue skies, from deep frost to blistering heat. Our 'retreat' in an isolated field was tangibly connected to the rest of the world in a million ways, and much more visibly so than any retreat in a building. Maybe it was the immediate experience of our reliance on one another and on the fundamental elements of life, like the warmth of the sun after a freezing night's camping. "Stop and realise," say the Buddhist teachers. Sometimes we could.

> *Mountains and rivers, the whole earth -*
> *All manifest forth the essence of being.*
> *Wind subsiding, the flowers still fall;*
> *Bird crying, the mountain silence deepens.*
> *The voice of the mountain torrent is from one great tongue;*
> *The lines of the hills, are they not the Pure Body of Buddha?*

ACTIONS AND THEIR CONSEQUENCES

Two great 'beauties' of a Buddhafield retreat are its beginning and ending. It begins with a large empty green field, and ends with the same thing, albeit looking a bit trampled! In between, wonderful things may happen, extraordinary magic may be created, but on the land, we aim to leave no trace. It has always reminded me strongly of the image of the blue sky that begins and ends Buddhist visualisation practices. From an ultimate point of view, the 'blue sky of pure being' is always there, and nothing we do can ever sully it. As the Heart Sutra puts it,

> *All things are by nature void,*
> *They are not born or destroyed,*
> *Nor are they stained or pure.*

From a more pragmatic perspective, fields and other living things are fragile and easily spoiled. On a rainy day a single car, carelessly driven across the field, can leave a rut that lasts for years. A blanket left out in the rain remains soggy for days. Looking and seeing in this way, we're led to see more clearly the way things "really are." There's nothing mystical about this. We simply see, deep in our being, that things really are interconnected, impermanent and fragile, that there really is a natural law of cause and effect, and that actions really do have consequences. Seeing in this way deepens into knowing, into wisdom. A perceptive and receptive contact with nature will reveal to us the basic truths of existence, the way things really are. Nothing whatever is hidden. This is the Path of Vision, and it leads to insight.

ETHICS

Following directly from this understanding of interconnectedness, and that actions have consequences, is a natural desire to live more harmoniously with the world, which includes living more harmoniously with ourselves. We come to know in our very being that if we harm our world, we harm ourselves, and vice versa. The Buddhist teacher and activist, Joanna Macy, refers to this as the 'Greening of the Self', saying,

> *"..we are beginning to realise that the world is our body. It would not occur to me to plead with you, 'Oh, please don't saw off your leg. That would be an act of violence'. It wouldn't occur to me because your leg is part of your body. Well, so are the trees in the Amazon rain basin. They are your external lungs... we are beginning to realise that the world is our body".*

Buddhist ethics are born from the recognition of this interdependence. If we do *this*, *that* happens. If we want *these* things in our lives, we need *those* conditions to sustain them. If our minds are coloured by *this* mental state, our day tends to unfold like *that*. As we become more aware, we become more skilled in the art of living and things begin, almost magically, to go more smoothly, to unfold with greater and greater ease. Old patterns begin to drop away, and old traps and pitfalls are avoided, almost by instinct. The path ahead becomes ever clearer.

THE PATH OF TRANSFORMATION

A deeper immersion in nature can help us to integrate our insights so that they become an integral and permanent part of our being. In principle, we can simply open our eyes to the nature of reality at any time. In actuality, most of us need more specific practices to follow. The following sections outline four areas where contact with nature might help us in our practice, namely anxiety, gratitude, insight and (perhaps more problematically) beauty. This is not a traditional 'Buddhist' list, nor a systematic path to be followed, but simply the areas where my own spiritual life has deepened through time spent practising outdoors.

ANXIETY

One of my first experiences with Buddhafield was an anxiety that seemed to creep up on me and to wrap me in a suffocating embrace. We were about to host our first-ever retreat. The 'punters' were due to arrive, and there were rainclouds on the horizon! What if it rained? How would we cope? What would people say? I feared that everything would be ruined if it rained. Of course, this being England, it did rain, but in due course, it stopped. I got wet, and then I got dry. People got miserable, and then they cheered up. As a consequence, several small but significant insights grew in me. Everything changes, it really does. Things really are impermanent. And, more prosaically, it's only water! Water trickling down the back of your neck is not necessarily pleasant, but it's just a sensation, and sensations are bearable. Why worry? So I stopped worrying.

Later that season, in October, we had a long weekend retreat where it rained from beginning to end, thanks to an endless procession of clouds blown in from the Atlantic. We not only survived but we, in fact, had an extraordinary time. We composed songs I still sing to this day. So much of our energy is devoted to a never-ending quest for comfort, while at the same time, many of us suffer from on-going, low-level, corrosive anxiety. Rather than forever running away from the reality of 'what is' in pursuit of comfort, far better to stop and 'be with' our actual experience. That way lies true freedom and happiness.

Meeting, they laugh and laugh -
The forest grove, the many fallen leaves!

On an eight-day solitary retreat at Tipi Valley in Wales, my tent was located high on a hillside and, from my vantage point, I could see the smoke from the tipis curling up between the trees below me. It was tempting to play 'I-spy' on the people as they moved about, far below. Having come from a very busy period at work, I found what I really wanted to do was simply sit for hour after hour and gaze at the view, the hills stretching into the far distance, the clouds and mist (it rained a lot here too), and the to-ing and fro-ing of the busy bumblebees.

As the days went by, I could sit for longer and longer in perfect happiness, just being. It was deeply satisfying. Bit by bit, almost imperceptibly, my consciousness widened into a broader perspective which ultimately included a consciousness of mortality, of life and death itself, even my own mortality. And with a greater acceptance of my own mortality, another level of anxiety dropped away. In a way, there's nothing to be done except take that bald knowledge of the reality of life and death, and absorb it deeply into one's being. As the Zenrin sings,

> *Sitting quietly, doing nothing,*
> *Spring comes, and the grass grows by itself.*

More challengingly, it also tells us,

> *To save life it must be destroyed.*
> *When utterly destroyed,*
> *one dwells for the first time in peace.*

GRATITUDE

The Buddha said that his teaching had one taste throughout its length and breadth, the 'taste' of freedom. At the same time, Buddhism teaches us to recognise our interdependence with all life, our interconnectedness. From this comes gratitude. The Buddhist word for gratitude is *katannuta*, meaning 'knowledge of benefits received.' Through spending time outdoors, in closer contact with the earth, I've found intense gratitude welling up in me for what I've received from 'Gaia,' Mother Earth herself, as well as from human society and civilisation.

> *If you don't believe,*
> *just look at September, look at October!*
> *The yellow leaves falling, falling,*
> *to fill both mountain and river.*

One especially strong experience came to me when walking the hills on Iona: I found a sheep. The poor creature was heavily pregnant and had tripped and rolled upside-down into a little hollow from which she could not get up. She was lying there with her four legs in the air, a very strange sight. More shockingly, all around her face was blood and bits of wool, and part of her face seemed to be missing. Gradually I realised that a crow had taken advantage of her helplessness to peck out her eye. As I realised this, a voice came into my head; I don't know where from, saying "there is no compassion in nature." I then felt grateful for my human consciousness, that I was able to conceive of the notion of compassion, and sometimes even act upon it. Happily, I was able to find the farmer who took the sheep into his barn to nurse. It was a strange day.

Another pivotal experience came on retreat in the mountains of Spain, where twenty of us were on a long ordination retreat. Out walking early one morning, enjoying the fabulous clarity and freshness of the air, the sunlight on the rocks, and the sound of the birds, I realised with something of a jolt how utterly dependent we were on the supermarkets below and the diesel-powered Land Rovers that brought our food up to us. Without them, life up in the mountains would be almost impossible. What I experienced as beautiful abruptly also appeared harsh and barren. I felt deeply grateful for the benefits conferred by modern science and civilisation.

Within Buddhafield, pretty much every camp is created from scratch and meticulously dismantled at the end. An extraordinary number of skills are needed, plus many people working behind the scenes, to set up and run the retreats and the Festival. At first, I just turned up and enjoyed it all with very little thought of how it all got there. But as I became more conscious just how much hard work went into them, I found more and more gratitude welling up for everyone involved. I could almost feel their presence in every cup of tea, with all the blood, sweat, and tears they'd shed.

INSIGHT

'Insight' is one of those 'big' words, deeply alluring and yet, it seems, always tantalisingly far away. It's often spoken of as something other people, great practitioners of the past, perhaps, attained to, but not us. Buddhist discourse in this area can be rather confusing. One moment it depicts insight as relatively easily attainable, at other times 'way over the horizon'. This ambiguity can extend to the way we relate to our 'elder' practitioners and teachers, sometimes exalting them almost as living Buddhas whilst at the same time, becoming critical of them if they dare to hint that they themselves might have attained any degree of insight. Can we calibrate this elusive insight? Is it really so hard to attain, so far away? As already noted, insight can be equated in essence to a deep seeing into the nature of reality. In principle, that's possible in every moment, anywhere. True insight, however, implies actual transformation of the way we live our lives and manage our relationships. After an experience of insight, things can never be quite the same again.

This transformation has to extend right down into the nitty-gritty details of life. That's where the truths of existence are played out. Actions have consequences. Everything we do has an impact, however unpredictable. One quality of the Buddha is that of *akirika*, that he is 'the Trackless One'. As the Zenrin says,

> *Entering the forest he moves not the grass;*
> *Entering the water, he makes not a ripple.*

In the Buddha's day, life was much simpler and more localised. He and his followers could see where the things they used came from, and what happened to them afterwards. We live in a globalised world, where our actions still have consequences but often out of sight, even around the other side of the world. Classic Buddhist scriptures teach about awareness in terms of direct perception, but the consequences of our actions in the modern world are not necessarily visible to direct perception, although they are just as real. We cannot possibly perceive many of these consequences, however observant we are. We have to make the effort to learn about them, adding education to our practice of awareness, an 'informed awareness.' Dispassionate scientific observation, enquiry and research are crucial if we want to act skilfully.

Actually, this notion of 'out of sight consequences' is nothing new. There's a lovely story in the Buddhist scriptures of some monks going to meditate in the jungle, choosing a grove where some tree spirits lived. The monks couldn't see the spirits, and were unaware of how distressing their presence was going to be to them. The spirits became more and more actively hostile to the monks, who eventually couldn't stand the ghostly apparitions any longer and fled back to the Buddha. He upbraided them for their lack of sensitivity and taught them the Karaniya Metta Sutta, the teaching on loving-kindness. The monks returned and made friends with the spirits, and harmony was restored. This story illustrates that sometimes you just may not be able to perceive what's going on, and can only make progress by learning the truth of the matter from an outside source.

For us today, this 'informed awareness' needs to enter every area of our lives. It may at times seem as though simple decisions are made impossibly complex, but it's just a necessary working-through in detail of how actions have consequences in a globalised world. Within Buddhafield, one way this awareness has manifested is in a loving attention to the retreat food, which as far as possible will be locally-sourced, organic and healthy. It's more expensive in short-term financial terms, but far less costly for the planet.

BEAUTY

To say that nature is beautiful is a cliché, but we do say it, and we feel it to be true. At the same time, 'the beauty of nature' is a surprisingly modern notion. Reading the Pali Canon, one of the oldest strata of Buddhist scriptures, one has the impression that in the Buddha's time it never occurred to them to see nature as beautiful. In fact, many of the Buddha's metaphors praise paths and cities over trackless wastes and jungle, and extol the benefits of uprooting creepers. What beauty really is, or what it means, is hard to say. For myself, it's about finding nourishment, happiness and contentment in simply being out of doors, in the woods and fields of England. On returning from a Buddhafield retreat to an urban setting, by contrast, so much of what our society offers seems flat, artificial and hollow. Supermarkets and shopping malls appear as mirages populated by ghosts. It's hard to imagine how people can turn to them for nourishment after a hard week's work, yet people do in their thousands.

I love the beauty of nature, and yet I've come to be somewhat wary of the notion of beauty. My doubts crystallised one year on a summer retreat in Suffolk. Out walking one day, I became transfixed by the beauty of a field verge. The grass was a luminous yellow, the earth a gorgeous chocolate brown, the sky behind a cerulean blue. Yet as I stared at the grass in wonder, I realised that something was not right about it. It was yellow, luminous and sort of beautiful, but totally dead. I realised in fact that it had been sprayed with a systemic weedkiller which had killed it from the roots up. I knew this because the sprayer had been past the retreat centre a few days before and a little of the spray had wafted over the garden, maiming some of our newly-planted trees. In that flash of recognition, the perception of beauty disappeared. It became ugly, even horrifying. Reflecting upon it afterwards, I realised that understanding had to come before beauty, a deeper seeing into what is really going on, augmenting and informing one's sensory perceptions.

In this way we can become 'positively disenchanted' with superficial 'beauty'. Modern culture seems to see newer, bigger and faster as better, more successful, and more beautiful. These responses become deeply ingrained in us, too. However, our feeling-responses can and will change as we increasingly recognise the true cost of our lifestyles. Buddhism asks us to practice stillness, simplicity and contentment. Our task is to embody them so deeply that this perspective becomes an instinctive part of us, so that we would quite literally see the world differently.

CONCLUSION

Practicing in nature, mostly with the Buddhafield Sangha, has led me to a much more intimate appreciation of the Buddha's teachings and to a greater confidence that the possibilities of insight and awakening are available to us right here, right now. Nature is a teacher, a giver both of vision and transformation. We need her and she needs us, both, perhaps, as never before. Buddhism is coming to the West, in a decades-long adventure of which I feel privileged to be part. I hope the encounter will change both parties, that it will help us in the West to realise through Buddhism the ignorance and violence with which we assault the natural world, but also help traditional Buddhism to speak with a new voice, in answer to the new needs of our time. When the Buddha lived, civilisation could be seen as a series of fragile oases in the ever-encircling jungle. Now the 'jungle', if it exists at all, is a fragile oasis in the worldwide wasteland of 'civilisation'. Our society is vigorous, inquisitive and innovative, but deeply unsustainable.

This society and we ourselves have to change. But how to bring that about? Telling people what to do doesn't seem to get anywhere! Meanwhile our own authentic perceptions are endlessly assaulted by the advertising and lobbying industries. Yet cultural shifts can and do occur, though usually slowly. Buddhism uncompromisingly asserts that our mental states are our own responsibility and that we can change them at any time. We can choose, step by step, to unsubscribe from the most destructive aspects of our culture. No one says it'll be easy, but it is at least partially possible, if supportive conditions, such as contact with like-minded individuals, are in place in our lives. What we can do is develop ever deeper awareness, and encourage others to do likewise, in the confidence that awareness leads to different perceptions, different feeling-responses and ultimately to better choices, freely made. In this way, we may bring forth people's natural goodness and empathy. Very few people, if any, really want to act with violence, although many so often do in ignorance and unawareness. A new situation requires new voices, languages and metaphors, ceremonies, rituals, and practices. They'll probably all have to be worked out painstakingly through trial and error. Buddhafield's approach is part of that experimentation, and we're getting there.

See you in a field!

Tents on the 'International Retreat', Taraloka

THE LIVING ELEMENTS

BY KAMALASHILA

OUR NEED TO RECONNECT

To ancient peoples from across Europe to the far shores of India, the basic constituents of life and matter were considered to be earth, water, fire and air. The early Buddhists added space and consciousness, making six 'elements'. These describe, in pre-scientific terms, core human experience, the physical reality of how we live and experience the world. More recently, modern science developed its own ideas of the significance of this as it began exploring the essential properties of physical matter. This project eventually gave rise to the Periodic Table which today lists 117 elements, including a number of synthetic ones.

However, the traditional view of the nature of the physical world differs radically from that of science, as does its purpose in dividing human experience into 'elements' in the first place. For Buddhism, the elements provide a useful analysis of what people actually experience from moment to moment, rather than what scientists have placed on record. The six elements cover what we experience subjectively, as well as what we perceive 'out there'. Elementally, being alive is an experience of subjective perceptions of an objective world, the elements making up both of these aspects. It comprises all the variations of solidity, wetness, heat, movement, space and awareness of which our lives consist.

For traditional societies, elemental energies animate special life forms, such as earth and water spirits, that are imperceptible to ordinary consciousness but become apparent at times when conventional perceptual boundaries soften. Early and contemporary Buddhism share an animist outlook on the world. The universe is not an infinity of dead matter, or a cosmic illusion. Even the densest rocks and vastest spaces are considered to be real and vividly alive. From this point of view, the world contains many unseen energetic forms with needs, desires and activities which not only affect us, and which are also affected by our wants and deeds. Since there is this mutual relationship, the non-human beings in one's environment may be considered as part of our community and be acknowledged as such.

Perhaps some strands of this kind of thinking may be helpful to us in the West. We cannot force ourselves to believe in 'supernatural' beings or to think in ways similar to those of early Buddhist and other traditional communities. For now, it is perhaps enough to keep an open mind. But somehow, we need to find a fresh way of looking upon the natural world of which we are a part. The viewpoint that we inherit from our Western cultural history has largely disconnected us from nature and brought us face to face with some very serious problems. It is as if someone had drugged us so that we overslept and just woken up late, struggling with a hangover and trying to block out the realisation that last night's intoxication has had extremely grave consequences. Similarly, we are coming to terms with the realisation that, in our ignorance and self-indulgence, the way we have generally treated mammals, fish, reptiles, insects, plants, land, air and waters has damaged them terribly. We now realise that we are all in a web of intimate relationships, and that our every action eventually affects everyone else. We have forgotten our part in this and our deeds are now blowing back into our faces, like sand thrown against the wind. For a while we have tried to ignore what we had done and to carry on as before. But it is no longer possible, and we are beginning to look for ways we can change.

All we need do is reconnect, understand nature in a less impersonal way, and learn how to behave better. However regaining what is lost looks like taking far more effort than we realised. Over the centuries our finer feelings of relationship with the nonhuman world have become blunted. Yet we can no longer ignore our need to find a new, healthier approach to the natural world.

We can get help from so-called primitive forms of society that have largely been lost in the onrush of technological progress. These people appreciate nature not just as something for humans to use, but in far broader, multi-dimensional ways. This is how we might try to assess for example the elemental life forms that were mentioned. These, whether seen as mythical, 'supernatural' or solidly real, are often awe-inspiringly powerful. Nagas for example are great water spirits who guard the secret of wisdom in the depths. A point for us is how their striking forms and legendary deeds express something about the living quality of liquid nature. This quality is a quite separate dimension from the physics of H_2O, amazing though that is, and is even more important. Moreover this living quality is something everyone is in touch with constantly, whether they can recognise it or not – and is of great spiritual importance to us, since it has a potential to open up our narrow view of the world.

Consider the falling rain, a tsunami or the depth of one of the great oceans. Think not only in terms of various facts you know, but the quality you feel in each. Feel especially how the nature and power of water is immeasurably greater than our own. The elemental nature of water, as we have said, refers not just to the physical properties of liquids, profound as those are, but also to a quality of the mind which perceives or reflects it. The water element is something one feels personally and which is also felt universally, by all beings. Among the overwhelming emotions it is capable of arousing are deep awe, admiration, terror and peace. Elemental water thus includes instinctive, aesthetic, emotional and subtle perceptual experiences. These are considered to be aspects of the water element too; since no observer is ever really separate from what is under observation, and vice versa.

The other great elements are similarly multi-dimensional. Our feelings and perceptions about the great earth, and the sun with its heat and light, go deep as life itself. Solidity and light are so basic to our existence that we take them for granted, just as we tend to assume that our own life will continue indefinitely, despite (in our heads) knowing otherwise.

Because it was so characteristic of his teaching method, the Buddha called himself an Analyser (*vibhajjavaadi*). His interest in the division of experience into elements, already traditional in his time, was its usefulness as a method. Seeing what really happens in experience will enable anyone to liberate themselves from ever-present, deeply held assumptions – views that are false and undermining. For example we tend to become attached to our physical body because it is unconsciously held to be 'me' or 'mine' (resulting in reflections such as, "Oh, I've got such an ugly nose"). This kind of thinking betrays a basic delusion, the emotional power of which increases the more we unwisely reflect upon it, something we normally do many times in a day. Its power causes us to cling to an exaggerated idea of 'me' in ways that create all kinds of suffering for both ourselves and those around us. People and those around them become happier when they learn to let themselves go a bit, to accept and ride along with the continually transforming (i.e. real) world that the elemental analysis is pointing at.

If we could connect much more fully with the basic elements of life, we would more easily cut through the accumulated cobweb of our complex delusion. Getting down to the elements was probably a lot less necessary in ancient India, where people lived in much closer contact with the land, but clearly even then the Buddha felt people needed to simplify their vision of the world. Nowadays our disconnection from the earth is extreme and it is happening worldwide, as 'developing' nations increasingly take their cultural cues from the privileged West.

When we consider the psychological alienation and grim ethical consequences that have arisen from this disconnection from nature, a purely spiritual quest like overcoming fixed views could seem like a luxury. Of course it is not, for in the long run insight into our real nature is going to help everyone. Yet right now, while our peculiar disease threatens to take our entire society over an ecological cliff-edge, it remains a matter of urgency that all of us begin to reconnect with the natural world.

Meditation is a good way for us to tackle both of these issues, i.e. the global ethical imperative as well as our inner existential ignorance. Buddhist practices in general get us experiencing the elements more clearly in our body and the world outside, putting us in a position where we may realise their real nature. The great classic meditation for heightening awareness in the body is *anapanasati*, mindfulness of breathing. However more directly linked to this particular purpose is the meditation which follows: the visualisation of the stupa of six elements.

MEDITATION ON THE STUPA OF SIX ELEMENTS

From Nepal to Japan, various forms of the Buddhist stupa are well known in the East. They were originally monuments for holding remains of Buddhas or other saints, and nowadays are often honoured – by circumambulation, usually – as though they themselves actually are Buddhas. The stupa also represents the six elements because, in the spirit of 'ashes to ashes,' they are what we are produced from at birth, and what we relinquish at death. Hence the classic stupa consists of six symbols, one for each of the elements. They are stacked vertically starting at ground level with the symbol for earth, the other elements arranged above in order of subtlety. Occasionally only four, or even just two elements are represented. The Buddha is said to have designed the first stupa in the simplest possible form: asked what kind of burial mound would be appropriate after his death, he silently folded a yellow robe into a cube shape, placed it on the ground, and laid upon that his upturned begging bowl.

So the yellow cube symbolises earth. Square shapes express some of the qualities of earth: solidity, strength, support and so on. We are not required to imagine this as a clear stable picture as though on a screen. (It is interesting incidentally to explore the manner in which we actually do imagine. Do we think in pictures or do other in-turned senses play a part?) Here, for the purpose of the elements practice, we need only get a sense of the symbol's earth quality – some feeling or sensation, some kind of holding impression which enables us to dwell easily on the characteristics of earth. We use our direct sense experience as well: noticing for example the solid floor supporting us or the hardness of our teeth and nails.

Then above the cube we imagine the water element. In the stupa meditation water is represented by a white dome or a globe like the full moon. Though the water element expresses the quality of flowing, fire and air also flow. The distinctive character of liquid matter is its cohesiveness. So the white sphere could be seen as like a bubble or a drop of water that in nature holds together as though by magic. To support your engagement with the water element notice the wetness of your eyes and tongue; swallow and trigger your awareness of the liquid nature that pervades the whole body.

Getting more deeply involved with the elements can be oddly satisfying. Perhaps there is some relief in being able to acknowledge a level of experience that was present before we were even born, for we were intimate with the elements, and in a very lively way, well before we were self-aware. The fact that we are embodied beings is a profound mystery, and to reflect like this stirs a sense of insight ready to unfold.

The energy of earth is stable and unmoving; the holding energy of water moves only downwards. Now with the fire element, we contemplate energy which flies upwards. Fire is symbolised by a bright red cone, rather like a flame. As we allow this new form, especially its colour, to have its influence in our mind, the brilliant qualities of temperature and light become more present to us. We notice that the eyes are actually receiving light, and feel our body's warmth.

Above that, the symbolic element of wind (or air) is a light green dish shape, delicate like porcelain. At least that is how I imagine it; we are free to play as idiosyncratically as we like with these forms. They can be lively, even comical. I see this like a sensitive satellite dish, picking up sensations and vibrating with them; or as a light green Frisbee, juddering as it skims through space. The air element is not about air alone; air here is an idea which symbolises movement. Hence the alternative term 'wind' (Sanskrit *vayu*). The essential characteristic of this element is movement. So we tune into the pulsing of the blood, the tidal flow of breathing and the progressive relaxation of muscles as the body stills in meditation posture. In Tantric Buddhism, the movements within the body's subtle energy channels are known as winds (lung). And indeed if we watch very closely and gently, the play of thoughts and emotions is sometimes observable in particular parts of the body, riding as though upon rushing winds.

Everything that exists, inside and outside, not only has movement but is often moving in several different ways simultaneously. Even if something could be completely solid and stable, which is impossible, it would still be moving, for the planet itself is moving in several different ways. So the element air, in a spirit even livelier than the up-rushing energy of fire, spreads out in all directions at once.

No movement, temperature, coherency, or stable matter can exist without some space being there to contain it. The element of space is symbolised by a single location point, a 'drop' that is gently flaming, showing its vibrant living quality. Elemental space is definitely not an empty vacuum! The single point symbolises the fact that space is everywhere all at once: it is infinitely out there and is also infinitely 'in here,' in the endless micro-spaces within the body. Notice how distinctly (and also how emotionally) we are sometimes aware of the particular location of various parts of our body. Everything has to take place somewhere. So this 'flaming jewel drop', as it is sometimes called, stands for the fact that this space here is one of an infinite number of possible location points.

Finally, the element of consciousness or awareness is the 'space' within which space itself happens. That is not to imply the solipsism that 'it's all in the mind', but to offer the simple reminder that (whatever the ultimate truth may be), earth, water, fire, movement and space are all experienced by our mind. We could call this the element of experience. Philosophical questions as to whether the elements take place outside experience and exactly how – though interesting to think about at other times – are not relevant here. We are creating a rare and precious opportunity to dwell on the experience of experiencing itself. Is this sensation 'me', or is it mine – or otherwise what is its nature?

This most basic of all the elements is symbolised by an open sky which is clear, blue and boundless. In fact the practice begins here. Start with the blue sky and let it contain, one by one, the symbols for earth, water, fire, wind and space.

The stupa of the elements, surrounded by its clear blue sky, symbolises our entire experience and response to a world filled with many sensations of resistance, coherence, temperature and movement in space.

As we meditate on each element, we experience its special qualities directly in the body as much as we can. We appreciate its particular life-energy, its role in our existence. Once the connection is there, we reflect that despite our habitual attitudes, this characteristic of our body experience is not something one could possibly own in any literal way, but whose nature is completely free. We let go as fully as we can into that quality of freedom. For this letting go to be meaningful, it will be necessary to acknowledge – to feel – the particular ways we grasp on to experiences and sensations as 'me' or 'mine.' These may not be obvious at first. In the end, the practice requires a commitment to the deepest reflection and a genuine desire to enquire into what really happens in our thoughts and feelings about ourselves and the world. This will come in time if we want it to – depth and skill comes from applying these reflections in a sustained way.

Concluding the practice is done in a special way to reflect that profound process of 'letting go.' Just as they are conjured up within the blue sky of awareness, the elemental symbols all dissolve back into it. In turn from the top, each symbolic form melts and dissolves into the element beneath. The space element melts down and is absorbed into the wind element, then wind melts into fire, fire into water and water into earth. The earth element melts into the sky. The sky itself dissolves like mist... and gradually we return once more to the direct experience of the six elements as again and again they emerge, solidify and dissolve in the course our daily lives.

If pursued, this meditation will develop our real, living connections to the elements and with nature generally, supporting us to live more ethically and in harmony with the earth. All Buddhist meditation methods have this kind of effect, since the tradition is one of awareness stemming from mindfulness of the physical body and its elements. The same feeling of harmony arises as we engage with other Buddhist methods such as ethics, wisdom, right livelihood, study and community.

A PROCESS OF TRANSFORMATION

It is not surprising that the stupa is held in such high honour in the east, representing as it does both the wonders of the natural world and the amazing nature of the Buddha – that is, the 'Buddha Nature' which can be awakened in all of us. Beware thinking of this awakening in purely mental terms, however, for Buddhahood is also a profound physical transformation. The stupa represents this in particular, referring to the body of an enlightened human being: it is a reliquary mound supposedly housing the physical remains of a Buddhist saint in whom the elements have been completely harmonised.

The idea of an 'enlightened body' may seem odd on the face of it, but we get a sense of it ourselves when we meditate. As concentration deepens, the mind opens and becomes clearer, and with that the body too undergoes numerous changes. Physically, we become progressively more relaxed and energetically balanced. Overall there develops a subtle body sense which, with experience, becomes an active component in our approach to meditation. These are the raw beginnings of our bodily process of transformation into, ultimately, that of a Buddha.

Actually experiencing our body and mind being transformed through the practices stimulates our confidence in becoming more awake and alive. Feeling even slightly closer to the Buddha's realisation makes it clearer that this is what we want. The Buddha called this deepening impulse a 'going for refuge' – to practices, methods and ideas that bring us closer to doing what we need to do to realise Buddhahood.

There is a particular progression in this transformation into an 'enlightening' human being, a process which takes a particular shape, even though its form varies greatly from person to person. Once we really start practising the Dharma, we first start noticing all the ways in which we are not the same as the Buddhas. We realise more exactly what it is we need to do – all kinds of qualities still need bringing alive in our experience. This clarification is essential: we accept that becoming aware must entail facing up to our faults and weaknesses.

An elemental perspective is useful in understanding these particulars, for (as with everything) our dukkha – the turmoil and discomfort in our lives – is elemental. When we are upset, the disharmony of the elements manifests in our body tissues. So when feeling uncomfortable in a conversation, say, we can look at the actual quality of that discomfort. It is like the sensations and assumptions we have explored in the elements meditation; and seeing that it is so may afford us some small insight enabling us to avoid getting unnecessarily caught up in it. We may feel for example that we are 'losing our ground', or may feel 'all over the place' – scattered by the wind. We might feel hot anger or passion, or become cold with fear or anger. We may feel all dried up, or flooded – overwhelmed by emotion. Or we may feel that we have 'no space'. All these expressions are rooted in our common cultural experience of the elements.

The process of realisation is not limited, thankfully, to facing our shortcomings. It is also about rejoicing in ourselves. We live in a world of beauty. Yet we rarely feel that we have the space to let go and let some of the beauty in. Appreciating the marvel of the natural elements both in and outside us helps us do that. The golden beauty of the earth really is there, supporting us. We are refreshed by the nourishing waters and inspired by the brilliance of fire. The elements are what can make our lives amazing and wonderful. We cannot make much progress until we can fully appreciate their blessings.

We can meditate on the elements, or we can just lie on the grass, look at a fire or sit by a stream appreciating what water is and does. Nature is a place we can find peace – it has a healing effect, and the return to health happens almost immediately and automatically. It is why we go to the beach, to woodlands or high mountains. It is not entirely automatic though: we do at least need to look, listen and feel. Something here is a key to the process of realisation being described. When we open to the healing of the elements, we find in ourselves a greater capacity to be truthful and real. We feel our heart more easily, whether happy or in discomfort. We can see our faults and even our joys in a bigger context. This brings us to the high point of the transformation process (which generally unfolds again and again in many forms and on many levels): somehow, in some way, we open to receive the wisdom teachings of the elements.

AWAKENING TO WISDOM

Awakening to wisdom can be brought about by a series of reflections based on the insights of the Buddha. These may be undertaken deliberately, or may simply arise spontaneously in ways that cannot be captured by the relatively crude descriptions which follow. Because the transformation is brought about not just by reasoned thinking but through some kind of opening up, i.e. something that is at least partially emotional, we need to ask for the teachings. The request may be not uttered externally, or even verbalised at all. But the receptivity involved is essential to the process.

Firstly, as already touched upon, we can reflect that the elements are 'not mine'. We spend so much of our lives grasping after things, but we do not in fact need to do it, because whatever we want, the elements will always come and go freely according to their natures. No-one can ever own the earth, the water, or any of the elements.

When it comes to our own body we think we do have some ownership. But when we look deeply at own body and the bodies of others, we have to acknowledge that we have come into the world having had no say in that fact. We arrived here in a particular package which looks like this, feels like this, and is composed of many substances - some of which we would be reluctant even to touch! We have very little

80

control over this body and (again, totally disregarding our wishes) it will sooner or later come to an end. We cannot say 'it is mine' with any real meaning. The elements are 'not me' and they are 'not mine.' And this is fine once we can accept it. With that acceptance we can let go of all that grasping after possessions and advantage and thereby find in life much more that is useful, interesting and productive.

Much that is harmful in our world has arisen out of grabbing attitudes, which are cut right through by this kind of reflection. This is a practice, therefore, which will bring benefit not only to ourselves but to the entire planet.

The second reflection is that all of the elements are experience. For example, we may presume that our car is outside where we parked it. The point for reflection is that at this moment we have a mental image of it. It is a memory, an experience in the mind. This is not an examination of what this entails philosophically, but the simple instruction to reflect on the fact that everything that we know exists, essentially, within someone's experience of it. No one can get outside experience and find a more 'objective' viewpoint.

The third reflection is that none of the elements exists in themselves. We cannot find the earth element itself. There are endless examples of its quality of resistance, but no one thing is 'earth'. The element water is simply wetness or cohesion, and so on. What makes an element is its elemental quality, which can be found in things that may at first sight seem of a totally different nature. A rock does not seem to be liquid but it does have a certain cohesion and even flows in some ways (if we look over time, or at its molecular structure). The quality of 'holding up' is characteristic of the earth element, but air and water also support things.

The fourth reflection is that the elements are inconceivable; no one can really capture them in concepts and words, despite the best efforts of writers and speakers. Yet just because they cannot be described or even clearly conceived of does not mean they do not exist. The elements exist in a way which we cannot adequately describe, simply because something like 'hardness' is not, in itself, an idea. The elements are not concepts – and nor is anything. Nothing is ever really conceptual, apart from the concepts themselves which we use as references for the real things.

The fifth of these reflections, following on from the truth that things do not exist as concepts, is that there positively is a way that they do exist. Too much analysis of how we see things falsely, that things are not like this or like that may get us into the subtle wrong view that nothing really exists all, that it is all a vacuous illusion. So it is vital also to reflect that there positively is a reality that is the way things actually are. This is what the Buddhas realised, and the goal of our practice is to fully open to that positive dimension of things. That is the ultimate connection to nature and the natural world.

So in the process of realisation which unfolds from the 'going for refuge' to awakening, we allow the elements (which, we must remember, is simply the world around us) to make us mindful of our imbalances and shortcomings, awaken a capacity for great joy in our good fortune; and to teach us the true nature of things. This sequence is often celebrated in rituals such as the Buddhist puja.

But there is one more stage yet. This stage arises from the fact that we will have gained something highly significant from this reflection. So now we have something that we can give – a surplus, one could say – and to narrowly keep that surplus to ourselves would, in time, limit its trajectory. What we can do is dedicate the goodness of our growing realisation for the benefit of all living beings. It can be done wordlessly, incorporated as part of our attitude and affecting everything we do. Having that sense of the big picture as our context helps make all our actions free of a limited sense of 'me'.

And that attitude might also be expressed, just to sum everything up, in the form of an aspiration:

Just as Earth and Water,
Wind, Space and Awareness,
All contribute in countless ways
To the good of beings throughout endless space
So may my efforts support like the Earth
All beings for as long as time lasts.
May the strength of my practice hold them like Water,
Energise like Fire, and move them like Wind towards Dharma,
Until every single one has discovered
True and genuine peace.

The Buddhafield Stupa with prayer flags

BEING IN NATURE AND IN SILENCE:
A RARE AND PRECIOUS OPPORTUNITY

BY PARAMANANDA

The extraordinary patience of things!
This beautiful place defaced with a crop of suburban houses-
How beautiful when we first beheld it,
Unbroken field of poppy and lupin walled with clean cliffs;
No intrusion but two or three horses pasturing,
Or a few milch cows rubbing their flanks on the outcrop rockheads-
Now the spoiler has come: does it care?
Not faintly. It has all time. It knows the people are a tide
That swells and in time will ebb, and all
Their works dissolve. Meanwhile the image of the pristine beauty
Lives in the very grain of the granite,
Safe as the endless ocean that climbs our cliff. -As for us:
We must uncenter our minds from ourselves;
We must unhumanize our views a little, and become confident
As the rock and ocean that we were made from.
(Carmel Point, by Robinson Jeffers)

The historical Buddha lived over two and a half thousand years ago, in Northern India. As one would expect, many legends and myths have attached themselves to his life over the centuries. However, a careful reading of the Pali scriptures, the oldest accounts we have, gives us a vivid impression of the life that he led. From the time of his Enlightenment at the age of 35, until his death some 40 years later, he lived the life of a wanderer. Only during the three months of the rainy season would he settle in any one place, the rains making travel difficult. The rest of the time, probably with a small band of followers, he would wander from one village to the next, dressed in a simple ragged robe, with a minimum of possessions: a begging bowl, a blanket, a razor and little else. Just before noon he would take his begging bowl around the huts of the village and wait silently to be given food. When he had enough for his daily needs he would retire under the shade of a tree and eat the only meal of the day. We can imagine in the afternoon and evening, people coming to hear him give instruction on the Dharma and meditation. All types of people would come - nobility and the poor, men and women - for advice and guidance. If we were to encounter such a figure today, perhaps we would take him for a tramp. But in ancient India, and still to some extent today, wandering holy men were revered and valued. It was understood that they had something precious to give to the rest of society and that their way of life, far from being one of poverty, was rich and profitable spiritually, rather than in the materialistic sense that so dominates our ideas about life these days.

During Margaret Thatcher's tenure as Prime Minister, laws were introduced forbidding Travellers to gather freely together. There is a long tradition of settled society persecuting those who do not choose to live such a life. It is as if travelling people threaten the security of settled existence. One wonders what it was that so frightened Margaret Thatcher that she felt she had to introduce legislation. Related Planning laws mean that Buddhafield are also unable to put up structures for retreats or other events for more than 28 days a year on any piece of land, even its own. It is sobering to reflect that such laws could have stopped the Buddha from resting for a few months in one place during the rainy season!

Despite these restrictions, however, Buddhafield has managed year after year to run a successful and innovative programme of retreats. Those on which I have taught meditation have been some of the most important and enjoyable retreats I have been privileged to lead in thirty years. They are simple affairs, held in a field. Participants live in tents or vans. We meditate under canvas and eat in the open air. The particular ones that I have taken part in have been intensive meditation retreats, held over a period of a month. They are conducted largely in silence, with just a brief period at the beginning and end for people to talk to one another. Throughout the retreat the teachers are available to give help with meditation and any difficulties people might encounter. There is a dedicated support team that take care of the retreatants, cooking, maintaining the showers and hot tubs, and generally making sure that all runs smoothly so that the participants can dedicate themselves to deepening their practice.

Why are these retreats such a rich and delightful experience for not only myself but, I believe, all that take part? First, and rather obviously, the retreat takes place outside. When first asked to lead one of these retreats, I felt some sense of trepidation, having hardly camped since I was a child and now being in my 50's and partially sighted. I thought it might be something of an ordeal to live under canvas for an extended period. However, as soon as I arrived my fears were assuaged by the care of the very experienced and dedicated support team who understand this work as part of their practice as Buddhists. I was also struck by the beauty of the environment, a large field bordered on one side by a stream and on the other by a wood of ancient oak trees covering a hillside. On the site were two large meditation tents, one dome-shaped, supported by an intricate network of branches, the other a larger arched tent with ample space for all of us to gather in comfort. Both of the tents were richly decorated with hangings, rugs covering the floor, and Buddhist shrines to act as a focal point. Over those few weeks we would spend a lot of time meditating, performing rituals, and listening to talks and stories inside one or other of these structures.

Given the vagaries of the English weather, we often found ourselves meditating as the rain drummed its intricate rhythms on the taut canvas. Sometimes it was so loud one could not make oneself heard, at other times as gentle as a lover's fingertips. When the sun shone, the tent would be full of a diffuse golden light, the sound of birds singing, and the canvas gently breathing in the breeze. I often found myself feeling that we were living and practising in a manner that would have seemed quite familiar to the followers of the Buddha thousands of years ago. It is a very different feeling than meditating in a building, whether in a city or at a retreat centre in the countryside. This is due, in part, to the sense that the natural world is all around us and indeed under us. Instead of sitting on a smooth flat floor, we are sitting on the earth. When we sit down in the early morning, we can feel the coolness of the night still in the earth beneath us. The uneven surface means we have to take a little more care to arrange our seat, checking that the slope of the ground does not mean that our posture will be thrown out of alignment. On a cold morning, we might need an extra blanket. Yet we find ourselves welcomed to our seat by the morning chorus of the birds that live in and around the field.

For me, such conditions provoke a different approach to meditation practice. In the city, one usually tries to find a relatively quiet place to meditate so that the surrounding sounds are kept to a minimum. In the countryside, the sounds seem to support rather than disturb one's attempt to cultivate calm and kindness. Now when I sit to meditate, wherever I happen to be, I follow a practice that has developed from the experience of meditating at Buddhafield. I imagine the landscape I was sitting within. I remember it.

In the case of Buddhafield, I call to mind the old trees and the meadow flowers that cover the field, and I invite the sound of the flowing water just a few feet away. I listen to the bird song. I think of the land right under me, supporting me. The first verse of an E. E. Cummings poem often comes to mind when I sit in the morning:

may my heart always be open to little
birds who are the secrets of living
whatever they sing is better than to know
and if men should not hear them men are old

The use of the actual situation as an aid to 'grounding' in meditation, has become a central element in my own practice and in my teaching. People often have an idea that meditation has something to do with escaping from the world, a kind of going into a pure abstract space of awareness that is above the everyday world. This is not how I understand what we are trying to do when we meditate. I am reminded of a line from Wallace Stevens, 'The way through the world is more difficult to find than the way beyond it.' The point of meditating is to come into a fuller relationship with the world, not to move beyond it.

One of the most resonant stories in the mythology of the Buddha's life is the incident of the 'calling of the Earth to witness'. In this story, Siddhartha (the Buddha-to-be) is on the verge of gaining enlightenment when he is challenged by Mara. 'Mara' represents a kind of Buddhist version of the devil as tempter, and he challenges Siddhartha as to his right to be sitting on the 'Diamond Throne'. In reality, he is just sitting under a large Bodhi tree, but this place is transformed into the central point of the universe (the Diamond Throne) by his enlightened presence. In reply to Mara's challenge, the Buddha stretches out his right arm and taps the earth with his fingertips. The Earth responds to this gesture of earth-touching by manifesting itself as a goddess, who testifies that he has every right to be seated where he is. This story, which is far richer than this short telling captures, is central to the mythos of the Buddha's life, a fact reflected in the countless images of the Buddha which show this earth-touching gesture. One could say that this illustrates that the Buddhist tradition, in Stevens' words, is one that seeks a way through the world rather than a way beyond it. That is to say, it is a human tradition which does not postpone the fruits of its practice to another world, but accepts its location in this world just as it is, and on a moment-to-moment basis.

When we first start out, we might have all sorts of ideas about what our meditation practice might offer us. We may think that it offers some sort of solution to the difficulties of being in the world. We may have a fantasy that it is going to let us rise above all the problems of our lives. But this is not really what meditation is about. It is not some kind of magic bullet, nor something that is going to put us on a 'higher plane' from which we can look down on all those other neurotic human beings who are struggling in their 'unenlightened' ignorance. That said, when we first begin to practise, this can seem to be an aspiration that might well be realised. Fresh to meditation, we often experience unfamiliar mental states of calm and peace. However, for most of us, this does not last very long. In a while we begin to understand that we can't just leave our old selves behind. Rather, we have to come into relationship with ourselves in a deeper way. Meditation begins to reveal itself as a means of experiencing ourselves in all our different aspects. When we sit in meditation, we come into a more intimate sense of ourselves. We begin to see the constant, neurotic activities of our mind, the avoidance, distractions, suppression and denial. This can be very uncomfortable, and is possible only to the degree that we learn to sit with awareness and kindness.

One of the factors that helps us to be with ourselves in all our heights and depths, is a sense that the world is 'on our side'. When we feel the earth under us and remember the world all around us, we can begin to cultivate a sense that the world supports us to be ourselves. The Robinson Jeffers poem, cited above, offers a clue to this process and the potential movement from a life dominated by an ego-centric way of being in the world, to one in which we feel part of that world. When we go on retreats like those offered by Buddhafield, we put ourselves in situations where we have the chance to see how the mind really operates. Moreover, we put ourselves in situations where we feel actively supported by nature's conditions to undertake this sometimes difficult journey. The fact that we are doing it with others, is also of great importance. We not only then have the opportunity to work with our own minds, but also to support (and be supported by) others as they do the same. Our practice is a collective effort, and if we are able to open up to this sense of solidarity, we have already begun to move from a self-centred understanding of our practice to one based in compassion.

Just as when the Buddha sat under the tree of Enlightenment, whenever we sit to meditate, we too can become the still-point of the universe. We can encourage the feeling that we too are supported by the Earth. In this sense, the idea of grounding is not just feeling centred in our bodies, but also being intimate with this world of which we are part and on which we are completely dependent. To sit in this way *is* the practice. There is not something more that we need to seek. Rather, the practice of meditation is to sit fully present in and aware of the world, and directly sensing the world is a great aid to establishing this kind of attitude. In her poem 'Wild Geese', Mary Oliver writes, 'whoever you are, no matter how lonely, the world offers itself to your imagination'. Although not talking specifically about meditation, she nonetheless expresses something fundamental about practice, the sense that we sit in order to be in the world and, when we sit in that way, the world offers itself to us.

For me, it is this intimacy with the world that makes Buddhafield retreats so special. They also come with a sense of having 'gone forth', albeit in a temporary way. The notion of 'going forth' from ordinary everyday life in order to embark on a spiritual journey or quest, is even older than Buddhism. It seems this was already an established tradition when the Buddha-to-be took leave of his privileged life and became a homeless wanderer. From a Buddhist perspective, this radical choice is understood as a way of freeing oneself from the constraints of a 'worldly' householder life. As modern practitioners, the notion has become rather more symbolic or metaphorical. Few of us may be prepared to 'go forth' on a literal and permanent basis, but even doing so for just a few weeks can offer a fresh perspective on life. Most importantly, life becomes very simple as its day-to-day concerns are stripped away. Most of us normally have a multitude of things to do, and even when we have some 'spare' time, there are more and more ways to readily distract ourselves. We may find that we go from year to year without really considering our lives, unless interrupted by illness, depression or some sort of unexpected or tragic turn of events. Or we might find our lives slowly drying up.

We might do all sorts of things but, without time for reflection, these become little more than a series of events that happen to us. There is a distinction we can make between 'events' that happen to us and what we might call 'real experience'. For 'events' to become 'experience' in the sense of having real depth, there needs to be time when the things that occupy our minds are allowed to settle, time when the ceaseless activity of life at least slows a little. When we go on retreat and live in a field for a few weeks, that is a radical interruption of our normal pattern of life. We find ourselves without the television and the computer, without the possibility of going to the shops or the pub. To find ourselves in such situations can be disconcerting to begin with, but in only a few days we begin to feel the benefits of living in a simple way, close to nature. As we meditate, do simple work, walk, eat and participate in collective practices such as chanting and devotion, there is a slowing down in the rhythm of the day. This begins to hold us in a heightened awareness of our own selves and the world of our immediate surroundings. The flowers become luminous. The sounds of the stream and the singing of the birds replace the constant chatter of our own minds, and we begin to experience moments of real serenity.

Of course we also experience moments of confusion, periods when we wonder why we are living in a field using compost toilets in the rain, when we have a very nice bathroom at home. Such retreats are certainly not all plain sailing. 'Going forth' and living close to nature can also be very challenging. Our insecurities might confront us with a new intensity, without the distractions of our normal roles and props of life. But, nevertheless, the practice of meditation and the wonder of the world, will eventually work its magic. Increasingly, there are moments when we can let go on a deeper level than we may have done for many years. And as we let go into the moment to moment experience of 'being', we can have the sense of really belonging in the world. There arises the sense that life does not have to be a constant attempt to assert our ego on the world, a constant struggle to protect our fragile sense of ourselves in the face of a world that can seem hostile and harsh.

One of the more surprising aspects of these retreats is the deep sense of community that develops within the silence. We begin to understand that so much of our normal communication is, in fact, a way of keeping people and things 'in their place' in relation to our sense of ourselves, a way of trying to maintain control. This constant desire to control the world is a source of strain and tension. When we are free from the demands of speaking, we find that we begin to notice others in a new way. We realise how much we can sense about someone by the way they walk or hold themselves. We begin to notice the same for ourselves, how we express ourselves in everything that we do. We might begin to realise that much of our regular communication is about hiding our real selves. We begin to feel that sitting with others in silent meditation can be a profound act of allowing ourselves to be seen.

Teaching on these retreats, much of what I am trying to encourage is for people to just relax. Then I notice that over the weeks, people's faces undergo a radical change. The mask that many of us wear for the world drops away. After a while we sit together stripped of the social faces that we so often put on. One is increasingly struck by the experience of sitting with others, soft-faced, feeling that we are all together, implicitly encouraging one another to be fully ourselves, free from all the pressures that we feel in other social situations. The act of sitting with others in meditation, becomes an opportunity to be with them in an atmosphere of unconditional kindness. It is a chance to support others to experience themselves in all their depth and uniqueness and also to feel the unconditional support of others at the same time. This moving away from being concerned just with our own mental states towards a sense of solidarity with others, is one of the most important aspects of being on retreat. For this to happen, we need to begin to relate to one another less through our particular personalities, likes and dislikes, and increasingly through a feeling of shared humanness and a sense that we are all part of the same world. It seems that being in silence for a while is a great help on this movement from egoism to altruism and fellowship.

Being together in nature and in silence offers a new way of experiencing ourselves that is relatively free from the stresses and strains of our normal lives. It is a privilege to teach on these retreats, to share with others the experience of being more fully oneself and, for a few weeks of the year, to live a simple life in the open air. To 'go forth' from a daily life in which so many of our interactions with others are largely utilitarian and short-lived, fitted in within the demands of busy routines, and to be with others in deep-felt kindness and awareness is of such great importance, and an opportunity all too rare.

COMMUNITY, NATURE AND REALITY:
BUDDHIST COMMUNITY IN DEPTH

BY KAMALASHILA

Creating effective and satisfying community is perhaps the most urgent and difficult challenge we face in our individualistic, disconnected world. But maybe something can be learned from Western Buddhists who have been experimenting with various approaches to communal living since the 1960's.

My own interest in community life comes out of experiences in solitude, which is not really as peculiar as it sounds! Some years ago I spent eighteen months on retreat in some woods on a hill in south-west Wales. It was the most inspiring time of my life and years later I am still assimilating its effects. I passed the time happily alone in my dome tent, burning wood and drawing water from the hillside, and discovered that being close to nature provided wings for my fledgling understanding of things. Afterwards it seemed that, rather than spending the rest of my life in continued busy-ness and travel, I should stay in one place and continue exploring the Dharma in natural surroundings – but this time with others.

My dream was of an ecologically aware Buddhist community. Yet when I started my solitary retreat, I was not at all interested in ecology. My reason for going to the countryside was to escape the distraction of other human beings. I expected insights and realisations to arise in meditation, not out of my surroundings. I knew I would learn about lighting fires, tying knots, chopping wood and conserving water, but I never expected natural things themselves to give insights into the Dharma. Yet in the event, every single insight came from these things. You could say they were instigated by the elements and local spirits, for whose teachings thirty years of traditional Buddhist training had prepared me.

Living alone and simply, I became sharply aware of events around me: seasons changing, the opening of flowers, birds, grasshoppers, frosts and dews. Becoming connected with so much living, interacting variety was like entering a timeless sacred community, as in the Navaho chant:

> *All day long may I walk,*
> *Through the returning seasons, may I walk*
> *Beautifully joyful birds, on the trail marked with pollen*
> *With grasshoppers...(and) dew about my feet, may I walk*
> *With beauty before me... behind me... above me... all around me*
> *In old age, wandering on a trail of beauty, lively, may I walk*
> *It is finished in beauty.*

Solitary life was not always marked by beauty and joy. I managed several dozen times to get myself trapped in some very unsettling situations, like getting completely lost one night in a fog until the small hours, or slipping knee-deep into my toilet! However, because there was unrestricted time to deal with such events, and no one else around to confuse me with their scorn, disgust or anxiety, each situation could be experienced much more thoroughly, and the outcomes were always transforming and positive. Through accepting my situation again and again, there came a growing rapport with the surrounding natural world in which the Dharma (i.e. the true nature of existence and the conditions necessary for seeing it) was far more evident than usual. Moreover, such experiences gradually undermined my natural human pride and rigidity, leading to a series of experiences in which my idea of myself collapsed, along with the world I assumed I was living in. This illuminating period especially transformed the way I felt about others. I had loved people before with the usual variations, but now my love came from somewhere deeper. And despite the isolation from the human world of the solitary retreat, I felt an immediate connection with all life that I had never experienced before.

As Buddhist practitioners understand, the conditions for such a transformation were many and varied. No doubt a major influence was the daily commitment to hours of meditation and reflection. But an equal part was surely played by the surrounding landscape, which constantly reminded me in the most uncompromising ways of the purpose of my retreat. Along with my inconstant moods, nature appeared variously beautiful, ugly, gentle or harsh, but there was never any escape from the reality of it. Whatever the weather or my state of health, if I needed to urinate or get water and firewood I was forced go outside. I was in my mid-fifties, never in the best of health, and my retreat started in December. Over the freezing winter months of 2001 (during which there was a record number of days' rainfall), whenever I felt very cold or ill, I longed for the convenience of piped water and mains electricity. I became impatient with practical matters, cursing the need to tie a knot or split logs with frozen fingers. However, as I got used to my situation, my tetchiness and anxiety dissolved. I began feeling at home in it all; I began to love it. I saw increasingly that my resistance to any painful experience – to the irritated person experiencing pain, and the direct experience of pain itself – was actually quite unfixed. These were things that could teach me everything about the Dharma, if I could only let the smokescreen of my outrage disperse and become curious instead about what was really happening. Little insights like this enabled me eventually to become a real local, a native who easily inhabits his environmental niche. And from that point, I came into a creative and Dharma-inspired relationship with every local plant and animal.

In the years since leaving my retreat, I sense that my delusions have been re-establishing themselves, which inevitably happens with any incomplete insight experience. However, their dissolution was surely real at the time, and I am inspired by the possibility that others could make the same kind of shift under similar conditions. Even more important would be to do so within a community of practitioners who can help each other absorb such experiences into ordinary life. This is what has aroused my interest in a nature-based, Dharma community. Insight is not so hard to achieve; the real work is in its integration and continuance over the following months and years. It is the possibility of doing that in company that appeals deeply to me. My vision is of establishing something large and land-based with a diverse population, a community that would eventually evolve its own ways of Dharma teaching. It would be lively, even controversial in some respects, yet helpful to society and attractive to visitors who would come and attend retreats, meditate and explore the Dharma from the point of view of nature and deep ecology.

NATURE AND COMMUNITY

Nature must have informed the Buddha's own feeling for the Dharma. He chose to live in nature even though, after his Awakening, no one would have surely thought any less of him had he returned to a more conventional indoor life as his context for teaching. His decision to remain in the wild seems to indicate that it supported his realisation better. The Buddha became as considerate towards the needs of non-human beings and plants as his own kind, teaching his disciples how to cultivate love even for snakes and other fear-inspiring creatures. And his central teaching of *vipashyana* is a revelation of the vastness and profundity of Nature as it is, beyond all concepts of space, time, location and relationship – yet is applicable right here in the so-called 'real world', in ethics, love and helpful activity. Any modern nature-based approach to Dharma would come from this essential revelation. It would need considerable articulation. It would not be not enough to live in nature with mindfulness and curiosity; we would also need to gain some realisation of *vipashyana*, talk about the experience, study others' writings on it, reflect on it, and write and argue about it.

Though spiritual practice is always something individual, in an ecologically aware culture, personal relationships are a very important aspect of Dharma practice. Nature is an infinite field of relationship, and awakening to reality must involve insight into the implications of what this means. Reality is personal. Even though, from a Buddhist perspective, beings are seen not to be permanent entities, each has a personal history that is unique and unalterable. The connections made with others are inescapable, and are reinforced in every meeting, thought and decision. These connections live vividly in all minds, whether awake or asleep. They are a core aspect of this personal reality. Because ecological awareness is about relationship, the ideal eco-dharma community would include families and partners as well as single individuals. Although it could also be an excellent situation for a monastic community, or the kind of single-sex community that has prevailed within the Triratna tradition, the emblematic ecological community is a mixed-sex environment reflecting the whole of life.

Because the Triratna Buddhist Order is non-monastic, it has been single-sex situations that have tended to provide a setting for intensive Dharma practice. They offer its younger, unattached members especially, a working ground that is clearer and less distracted by the powerful forces of sexual affairs and relationships. However, in the last two decades, it seems that many seasoned practitioners have left these environments to live alone or with a partner, and not simply because they were blown off-track by the 'worldly winds'. Single-sex communities are usually geared to the needs of newer and younger people, an emphasis that gradually becomes of less interest and relevance to more experienced practitioners. Even though the absence of the opposite sex often fosters deeper, more relaxed friendships, not everyone experiences such environments as friendly. For myself, I have benefited greatly from the many years spent living in single-sex communities, and would do most of it again, yet I also know that the experience for a significant number has been disappointing overall.

So perhaps the time is ripe for the exploration of new, mixed-sex, Dharma practice situations such as ecologically-based communities, even though they will inevitably involve big challenges. Family and sexual ties involve strong attachment, and it will take considerable collective experience to manage these well. Since we have yet to acquire this experience, there will surely be difficult lessons to learn. No doubt it will help if the mixture contains many trusted elders living close by. We can also draw upon the experience of others within the tradition, such as Dhardo Rimpoche, Sangharakshita's friend and teacher in 1950's, whose community in Kalimpong included a large school for Tibetan refugee children. The Triratna Movement has in fact learned a lot about community dynamics during its formative years, often inspired by the teachings of Sangharakshita, especially concerning the relationship between the ideal of spiritual community and the tendency to fall into group patterns.

Ideally, every member of a spiritual community consciously works on themselves. They reflect, meditate, practise the precepts, and thereby come to understand essential truths about themselves. Unfortunately, in a real life situation, people can lose interest in such truths, cease to cultivate meditation practices and ethical principles, and become insensitive to the thoughts and feelings motivating their actions. When that happens, it strengthens the tendency to engage in negative group behaviours such as bullying, deference, favouritism and competition. These tend to arise within a group when over-dependence on others undermines the capacity to take personal initiative in communication. We may begin relating unconsciously to a perceived pecking order. We might become over-compliant, unwittingly afraid of offending some authority, or have an unnoticed tendency to manipulate those who put us in that position of perceived authority. Everyone is subject to group patterns like these, but one of the purposes of spiritual community is to allow its members the freedom to reject such dynamics and to relate to each other as true individuals.

In practice, this is a challenge. Within families and sexual partnerships, especially, it is not easy to be so free from group pressures. The attachment we feel towards a lover, parent or child can enclose us in a kind of bubble. A couple at the beginning of their relationship may look to one another for emotional support in such an exclusive way that they disengage from community life. Or parents, feeling intensely protective of their children, may keep them away from other community members. And when others react, people may start feeling isolated and unable to share. Such group-based feelings are natural enough, yet they can undermine genuine community life. However, in the context of an apparently disconnected wider society, where increasing numbers of people live and die alone, it seems worth making the effort to form communities of all kinds. As Sangha members get older, living in community and sharing with like-minded friends offers the possibility of a richer quality of life, not to mention the mutual inspiration to practice. The alternative is hardly attractive; people living isolated from the Sangha in old age could easily lose their vision of the Dharma.

THE DHARMA AND ECOLOGY

Mahayana Buddhism and Deep Ecology unite around the point that all biological organisms have needs. All beings whatsoever need others to support their existence. The ideal Mahayana practitioner – the Bodhisattva –appreciates this. He or she knows the need of everyone in the web of life, and especially what is needed most of all, Enlightenment. Very few of us are able to see that Enlightenment is a need. The majority of humans, not to mention other organisms, have to occupy themselves with needs that are far more basic, and they certainly need attending to! Indeed, our accumulated neglect of the needs found in nature is a terrible disaster. It is most unfortunate that we have so naïvely and so appallingly exploited the earth and its peoples. Yet there is no point descending into despondency. A Buddhist ecological community can easily educate itself about these needs, practise Dharma, help wherever possible, and avoid doing further damage. It can generate as much of its own power as possible, eat mainly local, organic food and be more politically active. In short, it can set a much-needed example of how everyone will need to start living in a sustainable future.

The need for such an example is very great. The privileged portion of the human race living in the 'developed' nations, entertained and ensconced in its comfortable homes, has come to feel that nature hardly touches it, and even that it is more powerful than nature or, as a race, beyond it. Yet one only has to consider the effect of natural events like volcanic eruptions, orbital shifts and global weather patterns to see the foolish arrogance of this. Nature can never be something outside our lives; it is simply everything, from Buddhas to barcodes, Birkenstocks and bee-eaters. And, as Frank Egler (1977) famously expressed it: "Ecosystems are not only more complex than we think, they are more complex than we can think."

We must cooperate if we are to find solutions to the ecological challenges facing us, and which we have, at least in part, created. The Buddhist approach is to consider causes, especially those embedded in our own minds, fixed deeply in our attitudes, relationships and views. Arguably, for example, our perfectionism, our apparently unlimited desire for convenience, safety and orderliness, has been an important condition for human abuse of the natural world. And in our inward justifications for that misuse, we are influenced by the embedded idea that nature is evil. European culture, after two thousand years and more, is still adjusting to the authoritarian suppression of pagan values which contain a far more positive understanding of nature. Throughout the Christian era, nature (including human nature) has been seen as something to be mastered, risen above and transcended if we wish to make spiritual progress. We have been told that the world was made for the benefit of humankind, and that nature is for our use and profit. Accepting this idea has done little good, it seems. Even the more enlightened ideology of custodianship of, rather than dominion over, nature presumes the pre-eminent place of humanity within the natural order.

Rather than viewing the environment as our enemy, a slave or somewhere we do not belong, it would be more constructive now to recognise it as our precious community, as our home. For as ecological science has shown, all beings and all things are in relationship. By ignoring this we have gradually fallen, as it were, into a tragic mess of family betrayal. The world we have been busily creating has been intended basically just for ourselves. All other beings have been regarded as expendable, second class, mere commodities. And the relatively few of us in the world benefiting from this stratification (i.e. those in the privileged richer nations) seem increasingly disconnected and distant from the natural world of which we are a fundamental part. We are also getting more and more disconnected from one another, preferring to live in increasingly smaller social units, often just a couple or entirely alone. We are even becoming increasingly disconnected from ourselves, as our busy lives afford less and less time for reflection. We tend to identify ourselves with our shifting surface awareness with its endless complexes of likes and dislikes, perceptions and prejudices. As a result, the deeper inner world of feeling, empathy, ethical sensibility, clear thinking and heartfelt communication is becoming less and less available to many people.

It could be argued that a certain atomisation in society and a disengagement from the dynamics of the group are desirable from a Buddhist point of view. A popular view of Buddhism is as a path for the lone individual, more or less separate and disconnected from others. It is true and important that the training helps individual people struggle with and transcend their particular conditioning, including social conditioning. Yet, at the same time, its methods make reference to learning from, giving to, and collaborating and sharing with others. Buddhism speaks to the individual yet is not an individualistic, narcissistic teaching. It is lived at least as much for others as oneself. This implies community. Relationships with others are vital if the practices are to work. The Buddha himself went forth on his quest for awakening because of other people. Having seen that sickness, ageing and death are universally inescapable, and then being inspired by an encounter with a spiritual practitioner, he was prompted to radically change his way of life for the sake of all beings.

We need something of that radical motivation, too. It may be the case that what moved us originally to start meditating and seek insight was our own suffering, not that of others. However, as we practice, the impact of our personal suffering and preoccupation with our own concerns may lessen, and sooner or later we might open up to the reality not only that others exist, but that their sufferings and perceptions are at least as valid as our own. This is an opening to the beginnings of compassion which, from a Buddhist perspective, is completely inseparable from insight. Hence, there is the value of extending our idea of our community to include all that lives.

In Mahayana Buddhist countries spiritual practice is always dedicated 'for the sake of *all* beings'. And for indigenous peoples generally, it is considered civilised to be sensitive to the existence of non-humans. It reduces our pride and arrogance and makes us better people. Witnessing the special concerns, troubles and joys of other creatures brings us down to earth, reminding us of our responsibilities and our proper place in this world. From a biological perspective we may be at the top of the evolutionary tree, but many animals also demonstrate significant levels of intelligence. Others are far stronger, more sensitive, more industrious and much more persistent than most humans. Traditional tales like Aesop's Fables entertain us with stories about the special qualities of nonhuman beings, as in the race between the hare and the tortoise which is surely instructive in the present context. There is much that we can learn by observing how other species live, but first we must acknowledge them as our 'brothers and sisters' within the natural order. One of the worst effects of our ignoring the lives of other beings, human as well as non-human, is how that maintains our own considerable ignorance. Conversely, to cultivate more awareness and appreciation of the individual lives of others, however apparently simple they may be, would surely transform our understanding of life generally.

REVERING OUR ANCESTORS

There is a play of reciprocity between ourselves and those in our immediate communities. It also takes place across time, as the experiences of our ancestors offer lessons to us in the present. All human communities have evolved ways to hold their ancestors in memory. Shrines are often created for the purpose, as when an offering table is set up for the Buddha in a meditation room, a kitchen shelf is specially dedicated to the local spirits, a mossy log under a tree functions as a nature shrine, or some hero's monument is erected at the centre of town. All these give communities a focus for their highest values. Dedicating a special location to those we respect provides a medium for connecting to and celebrating them as part of our community, whilst also enhancing everyone's appreciation of community culture itself. This can be seen in war memorials and graves, and in the roadside sites of tragic accidents and other community shrines at which people make offerings as a way of expressing appreciation of this connection.

Such shrines are beautiful despite sometimes being dirty and untidy, because they are expressing something beyond this world. 'Beyond-ness' is what makes a true shine. Their simple beauty can be enhanced with lovely arrangements of flowers, skilful woodwork, silk hangings or golden images, and the devotion thus expressed can be deeply inspiring. Yet attention to the aesthetic aspect can be overdone, with a loss of the sense of connection with the other world. A true shrine is never merely a decorative feature or an art object. It has to be a portal to another dimension, giving actual access to the worlds of the Buddhas, the 'spirits', or our ancestors, or indeed all three. In the past, the celebration of ancestors has played a prominent part in community awareness, whereas a component of modern alienation seems to be our loss of a sense of ancestry. It is perhaps increasingly common for modern people to feel virtually nothing about their own ancestors, something that would be considered a great impoverishment in any indigenous culture.

In some Buddhist meditations one imagines not only the Buddha in front of us, but also, to the surrounding horizons, all beings starting with one's own mother and father. It seems important to connect our feeling for the Buddha with our sense of having grown up into a world of supportive beings. This may be particularly evident in the 'cultivation of loving-kindness' meditation practice (*Metta Bhavana)* which is often connected with gratitude, and in which we might reflect upon the many influences we had received in our lives, especially those (like the Buddha's) that had brought us to practising the Dharma. We might come to realise how strong an influence (positive and negative) our own family has been and, from there, all our forebears going back into history. The connections and memories evoked by reflecting upon our ancestors can be intense or even painful, though through awareness and ritual (such as the creation of 'ancestor shrines') we can transform any associated feelings and their sometimes devastating effects. Such ritual practice can help us to acknowledge these ancestral influences upon us and bring them not only into our current sense of community, but also into our spiritual practice.

Though influences from the past can be fascinatingly powerful, we often know very little about our own ancestors. Members of more traditional tribal communities such as those in West African villages or the indigenous Buddhist cultures of Burma or Tibet, would have inhabited their land for millennia and shared the same ancestors, memories of whom would be evocative for everyone in the village. Such connections with the ancestors are generally weaker for most of us in the West. Billions of us have dispersed in migrations throughout the world and we usually have scant knowledge of previous generations, and often scant interest too. There is even a strange tendency to feel that life began with our own generation. The impressions we have of the past, even the recent past, can seem quaintly irrelevant, like fading sepia-toned photographs.

This really quite severe loss of an appreciation of the past's living influence on us in the present, can exacerbate our sense of disconnection. How lonely many of us are these days. Yet, in truth, the ancestors remain as influences and memorial facts even amidst the complexity of modern life, and can offer a rich wellspring of inspiration. Likewise, spiritual practitioners always have the great teachers of the past available for recall. And even if we know nothing whatever of our great-great-grandparents, our collective culture still possesses a rich array of shared myth and history. Reading myth, or listening to it, opens a channel to the influence of our ancestors. In the opinion of Malidoma Some, a West African shamanic teacher, we in the West need to acknowledge as ancestors major cultural figures like Shakespeare and Socrates as well as other poets, writers, philosophers, teachers, artists and social activists.

I did not grasp the importance of any of this until, on a month-long retreat I was leading, I noticed how profoundly our retreatants were moved by one of the shrines we were building. It began with hardly more than a mossy tree trunk, but soon people began to add appreciations of deceased family members written on wood. Then all kinds of offerings started appearing – flowers, stones, branches, grasses, drawings and carvings – and, after a day or so, someone dug a small well and filled it with water. A model boat and some paper fish then appeared, after which inscribed stones and even money were seen lying at the bottom of the well. The well seemed to symbolise the possibility of drawing refreshment up from the depth of the past. Everyone, including me, found ourselves drawn to sit by what had become a shrine to our ancestors, with its evocative, slightly eerie atmosphere.

After witnessing the feelings involved, I saw how much we need to feel proud of our human inheritance, and that our own life is worthwhile. Honouring the ancestors reminds us that people in the past, like our parents, had strong faith in us and the lives we would live after them. The ancestors, in a way, act as mentors, encouraging us to activate what is good and creative within us. Remembering them, we wish for their blessing. A significant memory of this retreat for me was a tangible sense that collectively, including both British and German retreatants, we had 'healed' something of the pain of two major wars, through opening to what our grandparents and great-grandparents had gone through.

As well as that of the ancestors, we need the blessing of the living, too. How tragically wasteful it seems, from this perspective, that we have become so uneasy in our dealings with the elderly. For indigenous peoples, the knowledge of the elders may be vital for survival. No-one else may remember how to deal with a set of conditions that last appeared, say, fifty years ago. The elders are a precious resource. So it is sad to see, in our own society, how the elderly can be dismissed so readily by the less experienced. It is even sadder to see how fearful men and women become at the onset of ageing, afraid they will be seen increasingly as unattractive or irrelevant. The characterising of seniors as useless, distasteful, slow and expensive is another of our culture's great family betrayals. Yet all of us are on our way to becoming elders, just as our elders are on their way to becoming ancestors. Any elder's life experience is invaluable. Elders are, by and large, good company, and their wisdom and experience has a potential to profoundly change lives. If this is valued, their memory will stay alive after death as they join the 'world' of the ancestors.

We can speak of family, cultural and spiritual ancestry. Connecting to the latter is considered vital in spiritual traditions worldwide, but is not an easy idea for us in the West. In ethnic forms of Buddhism, some kind of recollection of the school's lineage, perhaps a visualisation of a 'refuge tree' displaying on its branches its particular teachers of the past, is considered fundamental. Its necessity is unclear to us, but amongst people who live in a nature-connected world it is understood implicitly that, in order to be a community, all must share their lives with the ancestors, the elders and mentors. This brings the blessing of happiness. Indeed, the *primary* function of community could be said to be its ability to channel the blessing of the ancestors, since that connection is what keeps its spirit and culture alive. In Buddhist terminology, this is *adhisthana*, the blessing or 'grace-waves' of the tradition and the culture of Dharma stemming from the life of the historical (ancestral) Buddha, Shakyamuni.

We clearly need some time to develop a realistic appreciation of our ancestors, elders and mentors. Spiritual groups in the West that are drawing upon Eastern traditions and lineages are discovering they need to adapt the customs they inherit to the very different attitudes here. Take, for example, the inherited expectation that a spiritual teacher should be perfect, and the outrage expressed when people discover they are not. Yet teachers will inevitably be imperfect and therefore disappointing, in one way or another. The African shaman and teacher Malidoma Some has some amusing stories about his relationship with his own spiritual mentor, Uncle Guisso, and how irritating he found him. "I remember more vividly the times when I yearned to kill him than...when I wanted him...for my own sake. Almost every time I was with him, something he did or said, something he did not do or failed to say, irritated me profoundly and stole...curses out of my mouth. I must confess that though he is still alive, I can't stand seeing him because our conversation is almost always a slippery journey into the sticky mud of disappointment. Yet I love my mentor beyond what I can say."

This mixed emotion rings very true for me. It reminds me of Buddhist mentoring, where the teacher sometimes seems engaged constantly in challenging students, often causing them embarrassment, irritation and humiliation. Yet evoking these reactions is not the teacher's intention; they are the natural consequence of the ignorance of the student making contact with the wisdom of the teacher. Feeling that disparity can be difficult and challenging. In Tibetan Buddhist traditions, the lama is considered the root of all blessings. In the ordination ceremony the preceptor's crucial act is to pour drops of consecrated water on the crown that flow down and fill the initiate with the water of *adhisthana*. Yet this extraordinary ceremony only draws attention to something that, from the perspective of the ancestors, could happen all the time. For we are already in the presence of the Buddhas, the lineage of teachers, our ancestors. We are, moreover, literally surrounded by all beings on this earth. Their blessings flow from above, below and all directions. If we are mindful of our relationship to all beings, we will surely feel our life and practice witnessed by them all.

DHARMADRUIDS:
BUDDHIST INCULTURATION IN THE WEST?

BY RATNADEVA

According to the legends, the great eighth-century Buddhist yogi Padmasambhava knew a thing or two about getting local spirits on his side and on the side of promoting Buddhism in Tibet. The story goes that in 760 AD, Trisong Detsen, the first emperor of Tibet, invited Padmasambhava to help build the monastery of Samye in his realm, previous attempts having failed. Walls that had been built one day were found completely dismantled next morning. Hostile local demons were blamed for the nocturnal destruction. Padmasambhava had a reputation for working with demons and agreed to the Emperor's request for help. When summoned, however, he did not go straight to the King's court. Instead he spent some months travelling around the wilder parts of Tibet, meditating in the wilderness and befriending the local demons, deities and spirits of place. Finally, he arrived at the King's court to continue the project of building the monastery. The workers set to work again and when they arrived at the building site, they were astonished to find that not only were the foundations and walls still in place, but the walls they had started building were twice as high.

INCULTURATION

This story is part of the larger account of how Indian Buddhism was introduced to Tibet. Tibet had its own established indigenous spiritual tradition, the Bon Religion. This is a shamanic animistic tradition that emphasises respect for non-human life, visible and invisible. Padmasambhava's befriending of local demons may be read as a metaphor for Indian Buddhism's respect for and adaptation to local cultural needs, by accommodating to the Bon tradition. This process of accommodation is sometimes called inculturation. It involves the adoption by an incoming religion of the symbolic language of an indigenous tradition. The advantage of inculturation is that the language used by the incoming religion to express its teachings is more familiar to and therefore already resonates more deeply with the indigenous population. The incoming religion has therefore greater chance of taking hold in its new setting.

The fusion of Indian Buddhism and the Bon tradition offers a historical example of successful inculturation. It gave rise to what we now recognise as Tibetan Buddhism, a Buddhism that can be said to be rooted in the mountainous landscape of the Tibetan plateau. The effectiveness of the fusion of Buddhism and the Bon tradition is evidenced by the fact that Tibetan Buddhism is alive and well today, 1250 years after arriving in Tibet, practiced around the world and still being practiced in Tibet at least at some level, in the face of decades of Chinese occupation and oppression.

Perhaps the marriage of Indian Buddhism and the Bon tradition offers a lesson for modern Buddhism, with regard to its endeavour to establish itself in the West. Buddhism has been introduced to the West only relatively recently i.e. over the past 100-150 years. It comes from the East with many Eastern cultural trappings. In order to make headway in the West, Buddhism is is taking the well-trodden path of enculturation, of cultural adaptation. Part of the challenge for Western Buddhists is to distinguish between what is the essential core of the Buddha's teaching and what is cultural embellishment, a helpful but limited accommodation to a specific historic and cultural context. This can helpfully be replaced by a re-accommodation to Western culture by adopting its unique symbolic language.

FINDING A MATCH

I'm suggesting in this article that a marriage along the lines of that between Indian Buddhism and the Bon religion could provide a beneficial grounding of Buddhism in the West, a marriage between the core teachings of the Buddha and some suitable partner that comes out of the Western cultural tradition. Just as Padmasambhava won the collaboration of the local spirits to build Samye Monastery, perhaps Buddhism in the West needs to enlist the help of the spirits of these lands, these Western islands.

Who then are the eligible partners for Buddhism to consider as a marriage prospect? The dominant religious tradition in the West over the past fifteen hundred years has been, of course, Christianity.

Could Christianity form a partnership with Buddhism? Orthodox Christianity insists on the existence of a supreme being, a creator God, the First Cause, the ultimate ground of reality, who judges, rewards and punishes. In contrast, Buddhism is a non-theistic religion. Belief in a personal creator god is seen as unhelpful from the point of view of attaining enlightenment. Buddhism offers a practical programme for ending human suffering and does not speculate on first causes. The world is governed by an impersonal law of conditionality, rather than by a personal god. Another central tenet of Buddhism is that there is no enduring and substantial self, in the form of a soul. In these ways, at the very least, the doctrines of Christianity and Buddhism are incompatible. In the words of the Dalai Lama, trying to fuse Christianity and Buddhism would be like 'trying to put a yak's head on a sheep's body'[8].

So we have to look elsewhere for a Western marriage partner for Buddhism. What I am exploring in this article is the suitability of the Western pagan tradition of Druidry to fill the role. This requires enquiry into the nature of Druidry and how it might qualify as a tradition that is indigenous to these lands.

WHAT IS DRUIDRY?

We know from classical (Greco-Roman) writers that the Druids were the priestly and intellectual class of the cultures they encountered in Gaul and Britain. They were philosophers, judges, educators, historians, philosophers, theologians, seers, astronomers, even peace-keepers[9]. The Greco-Roman literature (e.g. that written by Julius Caesar) describes how it took twenty years of training to become a Druid and how they were highly respected in society. For example, warring factions would not engage, if a Druid came between them[10].

While ancient Druidry has receded into the mists of time, there have been a number of revivals in the intervening centuries. These revivals have been inspired by the classical accounts of the ancient Druids and from the legends and folk tales preserved in Gaelic and Welsh languages. The most recent revival of Druidry in the late 1960's has gradually developed into a living spiritual tradition. This is evidenced by increasing membership in Druid Orders and the recognition of Druidry as a religion by the Charity Commission for England and Wales in 2010. Modern Druidry draws inspiration from

---

8 Dalai Lama, 1996. The Good Heart: A Buddhist Perspective on the Teachings of Jesus, Wisdom Publications, Boston.

9 Hutton, Ronald., 2007. The Druids, Hambledon Continuum, London.

10 ibid

the accounts of ancient Druidry and from the recurrent historical revivals, but not exclusively.

What does it mean to be a contemporary Druid? On the basis of my personal experience, I've come up with one possible description: "Druidry is a spiritual path that reveres nature and values intimate encounter with nature as a basis for wisdom, universal love and harmony." Unpacking this description will help draw out some of the key elements and characteristics of Druidry, its worldview and practices, at least as I see them.

I describe Druidry as a spiritual path, rather than as a religion, simply to emphasise some key differences between it and the main world religions. The first difference is that Druidry does not have a central originating person or literature. Similarly, it has no agreed and prescribed set of beliefs, no canon, no dogma. Rather than seeking instruction from an accepted body of doctrine, the emphasis is on creative engagement with the Druid tradition, in a spirit of exploration and adventure, informed by personal experience. Paraphrasing Philip Carr-Comm, the 'Chosen Chief' of the Order of Bards, Ovates and Druids (OBOD) - instead of being in the restaurant reading from a fixed menu, you are in the kitchen deciding what ingredients are going into the dishes.

Other characteristics of Druidry follow from the fact that there is no dogma. It is not authoritarian. No one has a monopoly of spiritual truth. This implies an openness to a wide range of beliefs, with some provisos around core values of respect. This makes Druidry highly inclusive. I've met Druids who are Christians, Buddhists, Pagans, Goddess worshippers, Shamans, Wiccans, and Shinto practitioners.

This openness expresses itself as another characteristic of Druidry - its eclecticism. Druidry can find inspiration in any tradition that is consonant with its core values i.e. which honours and respects 'our true humanity,' the earth, and the ancestors. Evidence of this eclecticism can be found in the use of ideas and rituals from the First Nations traditions of North America. For example, on OBOD-inspired camps there is a daily practice of the 'Dance of Life', reported as originating in the Cherokee tradition. This consists of multiple rounds of a sequence of movements and a chant, between them said to encapsulate the Cherokee way of life.

REVERENCE FOR NATURE

I've described Druidry as 'a spiritual path that reveres nature'. This means that Druidry sees humanity as just one element within an ecosystem that includes all life on the planet, albeit a very influential element. The 'web of life' is a popular image that describes this immense and complex system - it illustrates the interconnectedness and therefore interdependence of all life.

An awareness of interconnection can be seen as the basis of Druid ethics. The fact of interconnection means that all our actions have consequences on those beings with whom we are connected. Every thought word and deed has some effect. Therefore, as moral agents it behoves us to take personal responsibility for every act and the effects of our actions. The implication is that each and every one of us can make, and has a responsibility to make, a real difference to the state of this world. This can be scary, but empowering.

Druidry tends towards a 'deep ecology' perspective. Ecology may be described as the science of interconnection. It is that branch of biology that describes the relationships between members of an eco-system and between them and their physical environment. Deep Ecology develops the moral and philosophical implications of interconnection i.e. that nature has intrinsic worth, not just worth on the basis of its usefulness or necessity to humans. Some people prefer the description 'reverential ecology' to distance themselves from some proponents of deep ecology who emphasise the sacredness of the non-human to the detriment of the sacredness of the human.

THE ANTIDOTE TO ALIENATION

The adoption by Druidry of a deep or reverential ecology view of nature is partly in response to the utilitarian attitude to the natural world that modern technological society demonstrates. This attitude relegates nature to a source of resources supplying our greed and a sink for our excessive wastes. The price is damage to the planet, the health of which is key to our survival. The utilitarian attitude is supported by the dominant worldview, scientific rationalism, which reduces nature to mere matter. Nature is desacralised and depersonalised, leading to a lack of emotional involvement with it, which in turn gives rise to a lack of respect and even fear. The result is estrangement and alienation from nature.

Druidry puts forward intimate encounter with nature as an antidote to our alienation from nature. Intimate encounter with nature is the practical basis of the Druid project. It means spending time in nature, experiencing the elements with all the senses - the heat, the cold, the rain and wind, the music of birdsong and of the dawn chorus, the feeling of dewy grass under bare feet.

The Druid organisation that I've been a part of since 2003 (OBOD) has been holding camps to mark some of the principal pagan festivals called the Fire Festivals. These mark and celebrate the passage of the seasons, e.g. Imbolc Camp at the beginning of February, that celebrates the first stirrings of life in the year, the quickening of nature after the dormancy of winter, manifesting in the snowdrops, catkins and crocuses. Camping in nature affords the opportunity to spend time close to nature and the elements, whatever they have to offer.

Camps are an opportunity to connect with fellow Druids and to engage in communal ritual. There are solitary druids who practice on their own, but for me, sharing my experience of ritual is central to my experience of Druidry. Camps offer an experience of community that involves sharing more than just ritual. We share space, food, music, laughter, feelings, appreciation, support, knowledge. This experience of community reminds me how rich and deep the experience of being human can be.

Spending time in nature is a necessary, but not a sufficient condition for developing a deep heartfelt, spiritual connection with it. Unfortunately the agricultural industry is one of the biggest polluters of water in this country, despite the fact that farmers are physically in contact with nature more than most. Intimate encounter with nature requires spiritual depth - a depth of meaning and purpose. Druidry tries to achieve this depth of encounter through use of two principal means: myth and ritual.

MYTH AND DRUIDRY

Druidry espouses a mythical take on the natural world. I use the word myth in its positive sense of an imaginative exploration of life's deeper mysteries, as opposed to its derogatory use to describe something as pure fabrication, without any purchase on reality. Myth explores the world through the language of the imagination - through poetry, metaphor, image and symbol.

This contrasts with scientific discourse which is literalistic i.e. terms are defined precisely and univocally, and claim to fully encompass the reality that is represented. Mythic discourse is ambivalent, evading tight definition. Scientific discourse is useful for communicating the how of things, the facts of existence. Mythical discourse communicates the why of life, the meaning of existence.

Myth-making appears to be a universal human impulse. Cultures and civilisations have used myth from time immemorial to encode their wisdom. Myths are universal because they are a more powerful means of communication of values compared with literalistic discourse. This is partly because they engage us more fully as human beings, on more levels of experience i.e. they engage our emotions, intuition and imagination to a greater degree and they engage us on both the conscious and unconscious levels. The root of the power of myth is the fact that myths tap into archetypes - deep and perennial structural components of the personality that can act as forces within us. To engage with these forces is to engage with our deeper selves and the latent energies that may be locked up in these selves.

In summary, Druidry uses myth to explore the meaning of life, to encapsulate the values that follow from the sense of meaning, to express meaning and value as a basis of wisdom and as a means to tap into latent sources of psychic energy.

ANIMISM

One particular myth that Druidry espouses, in common with other nature-based spiritual traditions, is that of animism. Animism is a mythical way of thinking and behaving that attributes personhood to the non-human. This includes animals, trees, plants and even to objects that are regarded as inanimate such as rocks and streams. In this view of the world, spirit pervades nature - nymphs, dryads, demons abound. Animism may therefore also be described as a mode of consciousness that experiences the natural environment as a living presence, aware of and responsive to our presence[11].

Animism holds that humans are not separate from, or rulers of, the natural world, but that we belong in the natural world, are an integral part of it. Animism therefore seeks to behave towards the natural world with the respect due to partners, rather than the lordly attitude of masters or the superior attitude of stewards. This sense of partnership is the very antithesis of the alienation from nature that is based on separation and estrangement.

THE ROLE OF RITUAL

I've described how Druidry seeks to achieve intimate encounter with nature through espousing a mythical take on the world. For this attitude to be effective it needs to express itself in behaviour and specific concrete practices. One such practice, and perhaps the dominant communal practice in Druidry, is the use of ritual. Druidry uses ritual to explore its myths, to draw out their meanings and underlying values. Ritual us also used to express, and thereby promote, devotion to core values, such as wisdom, love and harmony. It is used to acknowledge and joyfully celebrate our relationship with the natural world and thereby reinforce our sense of belonging within the web of life.

The power of ritual comes from its ability to embody spiritual realities. It uses a range of media to engage and hold our senses - words, song, dance, physical gestures, artistic creations, costume, ritual implements. So often our attention, and therefore our will and energies, are dispersed and therefore less effective. Almost every aspect of a well designed and performed ritual can help focus conscious attention in the moment and the intention of the ritual. Ritual garb such as robes, or indeed ritual nudity, can be used to denote and heighten the sense of sacred space and time. The intensity that ritual generates a context in which to explore myth in which our reason, imagination and emotions are engaged. It thereby integrates our faculties, connects us to the

---

11 Sangharakshita, 2003. Living with Awareness: A guide to the Satipatthana Sutta, Windhorse Publications, Birmingham.

various aspects of our being, conscious and unconscious, and potentially unifies our energies.

DRUIDIC VALUES

I have described how Druidry uses myth to encapsulate and communicate its core values

and how it uses ritual to embody and express them. So what are these values? I describe its core values as 'wisdom, universal love and harmony'. Druidry sees these as the natural outcome of intimate contact with the natural world. 'The book of nature' is our best teacher and source of wisdom.

Most spiritual traditions are defined by a set of beliefs. In the absence of an accepted body of doctrine, Druidry is defined more by:

A culture of basic common values of wisdom, universal love and harmony

Ritual (a means to express and develop shared values, collective myth and to connect with our deeper selves, each other, nature, the spirit world)

Community (of mutual support and inspiration)

COMMON GROUND

The description of Druidry that I have offered above can provide a character reference on which to explore the possibility of a marriage between it and Buddhism. Druidry's lack of an established doctrine and the attributes that follow from this (i.e. experiential, non-dogmatic, inclusive, eclectic) make it an open door to influences from other spiritual traditions. I've described that in the absence of an accepted doctrine, Druidry is defined more by common core values (e.g. wisdom, love, harmony), by ritual and community. These defining elements are very non-prescriptive and therefore potentially open to and inclusive of other traditions. From a Druidic perspective, as long as the core Druidic values and goals are respected by another tradition, it is highly plausible that it would be compatible.

INTERCONNECTION

A primary common ground between Druidry and Buddhism is their shared sense of the interconnectedness of reality. I've described how Druidry sees humanity as just one part of an immense ecosystem or web of life that is interconnected and interdependent. This view is also inherent in Buddhism. A Buddhist scripture, the Avatamsaka sutra, uses the image of Indra's Net to symbolise interconnection. Every element in Indra's net is a jewel, that reflects the beauty of every other jewel in the net. The sense of interconnection follows from the most fundamental of Buddhist teachings, conditionality, sometimes termed dependent co-arising or conditioned co-production. Understanding conditionality involves a deepening of our sense of interdependence to a point where we experience a profound sense of non-separateness from each other and the world we live in. It allows us to broaden the notion of self beyond the boundaries of our skin, to include our fellow human beings and the natural world.

USE OF MYTH

A second fundamental characteristic shared by Druidry and Buddhism is that they both espouse a mythical relationship to reality and in particular, the animistic view of the world. In the canonical Pali scriptures, an animistic perspective is taken as read. The world that the Buddha lived in is portrayed as one filled with spirits, demons and gods and goddesses. Encounters between the Buddha and these beings are frequently recounted. For example, the Buddha may be described as teaching Devas, or angelic spirit beings, dwelling in the 'god realm'.

Like Druidry, Buddhism's animistic worldview promotes reverence for the natural world. The Buddha spent most of his life immersed in nature - in the forests and groves of Northern India. As with Druidry, Buddhism has a particular reverence for trees. Trees are the backdrop to many of the key events in the Buddha's life (e.g. his first experience of bliss as a child under a rose apple tree, his enlightenment under the Bodhi tree, his death under the sal trees.

USE OF RITUAL

On a practical level Buddhism, like Druidry, also uses ritual as a key spiritual practice. In particular, it is used as a means to express and develop devotion to that which transcends us e.g. the Buddha, the Dharma, our own potential as human beings. As with Druidry, Buddhism sees ritual as a means to engage the whole person (involving, in the Buddhist formula: body, speech and mind) including the emotions, in the cause of spiritual progress. An intellectual understanding of the Buddha's teaching is not a sufficient condition for personal transformation. We need to harness the energy of our emotional lives behind the intellectual understanding, by finding emotional equivalents to this understanding, to bridge the gap between knowledge and action[12].

In common with Druidry, Buddhism also uses specific rituals, rites of passage, to mark the significant transitions on our path e.g. Ordination as a rite of passage - an initiation into and public validation of a higher level of commitment. My four-month Ordination retreat in Spain was the culmination of five years of training in the Triratna Buddhist Community. The Druid in me was well satisfied during this course - we lived in huts in the midst of an abundant, biodiverse and constantly changing ecology. We made full ritual use of the mountainous karst landscape, acknowledging and invoking spirits of place.

MY LIFE IN BUDDHAFIELD

Having described some of the common ground between Buddhism and Druidry. I want to briefly illustrate this common ground and the compatibility between the two traditions that this common ground supports, through my own experience.

I started attending meditation classes and studying Buddhism in 1999 at the then FWBO Centre in Sheffield. At the time I was working as an environmental scientist at Sheffield University. As a scientist, my relationship with the environment was heavily weighted towards the rational and objective. After three years of meditation, I realised I had a need to develop a greater emotional connection with the natural environment, to balance my largely cerebral relationship with a more poetic, heartfelt, soulful approach. In particular I remember feeling a need to give ritual expression to my sense of connection with the environment. I had moved to Nottingham to work with the British Geological Survey (BGS) and had begun attending the Nottingham Buddhist Centre. This context for Buddhist practice was mostly urban and did not satisfy my need for ritual connection with nature.

After a brief scan of contemporary pagan traditions, I began exploring Druidry, attracted by its Celtic and environmental emphases. My initial exploration was through a correspondence course and then through attending camps under the auspices of OBOD. From the moment I arrived at my first camp celebrating the pagan festival of Lughnasadh in August 2003, I had a strong sense that I'd arrived home. Soon after this experience I got wind of an initiative to start organising Buddhist camping retreats, an

---

12 Sangharakshita, 1995. Ritual and Devotion in Buddhism - an introduction, Windhorse Publications, Birmingham.

initiative that became Buddhafield North. This gave me an opportunity to combine my developing Buddhist practice and Druidic explorations. I extended my involvement to helping with the Buddhafield Festival in Somerset.

Then in 2009 I got an invitation to work full-time with Buddhafield. The prospect of living like the Buddha and his disciples - a more simple life in community, close to the elements right through the seasons, while promoting the Dharma, was irresistible. I left my job as a contaminant hydrogeologist with the Survey and headed south with a bell tent on a trolley and heavy backpack.

A key motivation for my move to Buddhafield was to find a day to day context for interweaving the two threads of my spiritual practice. My new job was to help organise Buddhist camping retreats and the Buddhafield Festival. Organising camping retreats in beautiful natural locations mostly in the Southwest of England has provided me with opportunities for living in a community of shared vision and practice, working in a team on common projects and all of this while immersed in nature. My previous engagement with Buddhist teaching and practice usually took place in buildings in city centres. At Buddhafield this happens outdoors, or in tent structures, depending on the weather. We sleep close to the earth, meditate in the morning to the polyphony of the dawn chorus, eat and work and rest outdoors. This habitual immersion in nature has nurtured a felt sense of a living universe, full of presences, that are aware and responsive to my presence. It has also supported a simple, embodied and profound experience of the central Buddhist teachings of impermanence and interconnection. I am so much more aware of the passing seasons, the first budding of Spring, the abundance of summer verdure, the shifting leaf colours in Autumn and the stripping bare in Winter.

My life in Buddhafield feeds my need for ritual and imaginative engagement with the natural world. Outdoor Buddhist rituals (pujas) are a regular feature of life on camping retreats. Performing pujas under the sky, surrounded by the elements is a different experience compared within a building - more sensually engaging and resonant. As well as camping retreats I have been involved in organising walking retreats called Yatras as part of the Buddhafield programme. These are Buddhist pilgrimages through the countryside visiting sacred sites and performing outdoor pujas en route. For several years we have walked along the Ridgeway, an ancient walkway in the South of England featuring several significant Neolithic sites like Waylands Smithy long barrow, and Avebury stone circle.

During our last Yatra in 2012 we explored the theme of marriage between pagan traditions of these lands and Buddhism. We enacted a ritual on Dragon Hill next to the Ridgeway, to introduce Padmasambhava to the spirits, Gods and Goddesses of the sacred sites of Oxfordshire and Wiltshire through which we were walking. We recited the names of a Celtic pantheon to the sound of a Tibetan horn before a statue of Padmasambhava. We repeated this ritual at the conclusion of our pilgrimage within the stones at Stonehenge.

Having started this article recounting the story of Padmasambhava's befriending the spirits of Tibet, this description of a ritual enactment of the encounter with spirits of these lands seems an appropriate place to finish. Since my arrival at Buddhafield, the line between my Buddhist and Druidic practice is getting ever thinner and artificial. One way of seeing the mythical and ritual context for spiritual practice that Buddhafield affords is as a practical example of the marriage of Druidry and Buddhism. Time will tell whether this take is just a personal idiosyncrasy or representative of a new phase of Buddhism grounding itself in the West.

Padmasambhava at Dragon Hill, Buddhafield Yatra 2012

BUILDING AN ETHICAL UNDERWORLD: *LESSONS FROM THE MAFIA*

BY KHEMASURI

The process of change is mysterious. Why did the Berlin Wall come down so suddenly in 1989? What factors finally brought the end of apartheid in South Africa after decades of struggle? In 2008, why did the banking system suddenly collapse after decades of apparently working well? What made the difference? This chapter will explore how change happens and how to effect change in the world, both as individuals and through our communities. The question of how to make the transition to a more sustainable, more ethical society is increasingly urgent, and one which demands clarity and creativity. Positive change is ever more necessary for our survival, and the spiritual community has the potential to support this.

As human beings we often resist change, we want to remains safe with what we know, what is familiar. At other times we crave change because of difficulty. We want whatever it is to stop, and we want it to stop *now*. Both of these attitudes to change are based on individual preferences, what we like and what we dislike. Contributing to positive change in the wider world cannot be based on just these emotional responses. If we are serious about such change, it is necessary to have a broader perspective and an understanding of the processes involved. Different sources of understanding and inspiration are available to us. The timelessly relevant teachings of the Buddha are now available to us in the West, bringing much-needed insights into how to live well in relation to one another, and as part of the interconnected web of life. Deep-seated transformation towards a more skilful way of being, personally and collectively, is the purpose of Buddhist practice.

This chapter will look at the essence of the Buddha's teachings on change, but also draw on 'systems thinking', the science of complexity, which has developed over the last 60 years or so. Both the Dharma (the teaching of the Buddha) and 'systems thinking' talk about the conditions that determine the outcome of a process, how change comes about and how we can support and promote it.

PRATITYA-SAMUTPADA: THE FOUNDATION OF BUDDHISM

The fundamental experience of the Buddha upon his Enlightenment was what he later referred to as *pratitya samutpada*, which has been defined as 'conditioned co-production', 'conditioned arising' or 'dependent arising'. When we talk about 'conditions', it is a way of looking at the world that perhaps we are not used to. For example, we say that an oak tree grows from an acorn. But what actually happens is that a set of conditions come together to allow this. The conditions (greatly simplified) would be the soil that the acorn is buried in, rain, the light and warmth of the sun and so on. It could also be dependent on a squirrel burying the acorn for winter food and then forgetting where it was! These are all conditions which enable to acorn to grow. Then we could look deeper, the soil itself is dependent on conditions, not only bacteria, worms and other beings, but also the evolution of the planet and perhaps even meteors that are from outside the solar system.

This spiritual insight of *pratitya samutpada* had nothing to do with any kind of abstract ideas or assumptions about how the world worked. It was a direct, unmediated experience of the world. In the Buddha's time, this was simply known as 'the way things are'. The Buddha could 'see' how things came into being and also how they came to an end. As Sangharakshita (the founder of the Triratna Buddhist Order) says, '...*we must clearly understand that this insight is a purely spiritual attainment, and has nothing to do with any kind of conceptual construction.*' (Survey of Buddhism, p.109)

The Buddha later went on to teach various formulations of this insight as conceptual constructions comprehensible to the intellect, such as the Nidana Chain (most famously depicted in the Tibetan Wheel of Life) and the Four Noble Truths. These formulations were embedded in the existing understandings of Indian culture over two thousand years ago. The Four Noble Truths, for example, were based on a well-known method of diagnosing and treating ill-health by looking at the problem (suffering), the cause of the problem (the cause of suffering), the possibility of a cure (the cessation of suffering), and the prescribed course of treatment (the 'Eightfold Path').

It can be argued that the doctrine of *pratitya samutpada* is not just one Buddhist doctrine amongst others, but is *the* Buddhist doctrine that defines Buddhism as 'Buddhism'. It cuts across all Buddhist schools. The present Dalai Lama calls it 'The Buddha's slogan'. It is not dependent on humanity; it is more like a natural law operative on all levels of existence, from physical matter to culture and consciousness. A famous expression of *pratitya samutpada* is: '*When this is, that becomes; from the arising of this, that arises. This not being, that becomes not; from the ceasing of this, that ceases.*' (Majjhima-Nikaya, 11.32)

Although this sentence looks simple, it is difficult to comprehend in all its richness and implications. Ananda, who was the Buddha's attendant for much of his life, said to the Buddha, '*It is wonderful, Lord, it is marvellous how profound this pratitya samutpada is, how deep it appears. And yet it appears to me as clear as clear.*' The Buddha responds, '*Do not say this, Ananda, do not say this! This pratitya samutpada is profound and appears profound. It is through not understanding, not penetrating this truth that this generation has become like a tangled ball of string...*' (Samyutta-Nikaya, 11 92)

So Ananda's understanding can be seen as merely conceptual. He does not see it in the full sense of enlightenment, does not penetrate the reality of it. It is important to remember that understanding *pratitya samutpada* conceptually is not the same as knowing it through direct experience. As Sangharakshita comments, '...*pratitya samutpada is essentially the general principle of conditionedness rather than any specific sequence of conditions.....*' (Survey of Buddhism, p.127)

The Buddha's teaching of *pratitya samutpada* also points to the possibility of something quite new arising. Qualities that have not existed before can come into being under certain conditions. In modern scientific terms these are known as 'emergent properties', and cannot necessarily be predicted from what has happened previously. When the conditions are appropriate they simply appear. For something to exist in the present, it is not necessary for it to have existed in the past.

Perhaps this becomes clearer when we look at faith. In Buddhism, faith (*sraddha*) has a particular meaning. It does not mean 'blind faith'. There is no need to accept any teaching just because the Buddha taught it. Rather, the Buddha suggested that his disciples should test his words as they would 'gold in a fire', i.e. test his teachings with the 'fire' of their own experience. The experience of *sraddha*, this 'tested' faith in the Buddha's teaching, can be the beginning of the re-orientation of one's whole life. This change of direction will be new and was not present beforehand. In fact, it can come as a surprise!

Sangharakshita says,

> *'Perhaps the best definition of faith is that it is the response of what is ultimate in us to what is ultimate in the universe.'*
> (What is the Dharma?, p.110)

Most of the time, when we experience suffering, we also experience craving. We crave something to take away or cover up the unpleasant experience. Sometimes it is craving for a situation to continue; sometimes it is craving for it to come to an end. But when the conditions are appropriate, an experience of faith rather than craving can arise from the experience of suffering, faith in the doctrine, faith in the Buddha and in his teaching. This is something completely new, an 'emergent property', and is the true beginning of the spiritual life. It can be seen as a paradigm shift, a change of perspective that offers new horizons and new possibilities within us.

TRADITIONAL TEACHINGS AND MODERN UNDERSTANDINGS

The conditions prevailing in our globalised, twenty-first-century society are very different to those in the Buddha's day. It was a different time and a very different culture. It can therefore be difficult for us to relate to the traditional doctrinal explanations of *pratitya samutpada*, so we may need to find ways of understanding it in more contemporary terms. Buddhism, in its 2,500-year history, has spread very widely. It has done so in a spirit of adaptation and assimilation. Sangharakshita, when talking about the rapid expansion of Buddhism through different races and cultures says, *'the Dharma, while remaining essentially changeless, was capable of assuming a thousand forms, because it is in principle simply the means to enlightenment.'* (The Survey of Buddhism, p81)

The Buddha, in discussion with his aunt, Mahapajapati, defined his teaching in positive terms as *'...whatever is conducive to dispassion, not to passion, detachment, not to attachment, leads to a decrease in worldly gains, frugality, contentment, energy, delight in the good, and solitude. This is the Norm; this is the discipline; this is the Master's message.'* (Vinaya 11.10, Anguttara-Nikaya 8.53) The Buddha was asking us to decide what is helpful to us as practising Buddhists in the light of our own experience. The Buddha was helping us to identify for ourselves the conditions that lead to enlightenment through the results of our actions instead of rigid rules.

In this spirit, we can also gain understanding from contemporary sources. Perhaps one of the most useful models to have emerged in recent decades is that of 'complexity theory'. The systems thinking that comes from this can deepen our understanding of how we set up conditions for change and the implications for how we need to act. It is a world-view with a much greater overlap with traditional Buddhist teachings than with previous mainstream scientific models. General systems theory is a conceptual construction of *our* time, and *our* culture, which has grown out of scientific understanding. I believe it can help bring us closer to understanding conditionality, the essence of the Buddha's teaching.

TWO WAYS OF LOOKING AT THE WORLD

The Buddha taught that our thoughts, speech and actions are underpinned by our views about the world. He encouraged exploration of these underlying views. With this in mind, I want to look at the difference between causality and conditionality, two ways of looking at the world. These views are based on distinct assumptions about how the world works, and they have very different implications in terms of the way we view the world and how we act within it.

Causality was expounded by Descartes, Newton and others, and is often known as 'Cartesian thinking'. This approach moved from a holistic understanding of the world to a mechanistic one, in which there is direct cause and effect: A causes B. If you chop down a tree and process it, you get paper at the other end. Cartesian thinking sees the world as being machine-like: there is a direct relationship between input and outcome. This model led to a view that we could control the world 'from the outside', that humans were in charge and separate from the rest of the world. As superior beings, we could dominate the world through our intellect. The world was there for Man to have dominion over. It is important to understand causality as it is the dominant worldview of the modern West, a worldview to which we subscribe without necessarily being aware of it.

In contrast, systems thinking looks at the interplay of conditions which make up the world we live in. So in a straightforward sense, you can chop down a tree and process it to make newspaper. But chopping down the tree also destroys the habitats of living beings. Turning it into paper uses chemicals that have an effect on the environment. The process uses water, which decreases the flow in the river which, in turn, affects its plant life. The process also creates waste products which have to be disposed of, and so on. This complexity of conditions can be seen not only in the material world but also in the 'processes' of culture, of society and in our consciousness. Recognising such complex conditionality means that we can no longer see ourselves as isolated or separate from the world around us.

Systems theory has a very particular way of looking at the world, based on the concepts of non-linear dynamics. Very simply, systems theory says that there are many causes and many effects in any given situation. This complex interplay of conditions can look chaotic and confused but, in fact, have clear patterns of interaction. It talks about systems that are characterised by continual flow and change. These systems can be described as 'living' systems and they are dynamic yet in balance. All systems are wholes in themselves, and also they all fit into larger systems. For instance, I am composed of atoms, which combine to form molecules, which combine to form cells, which combine to form my organs. The organs of my body make up 'me'. I am part of a system known as my family, and my family is part of a society. All systems are systems within themselves, which are connected to other systems, and they cannot be understood fully in isolation.

Systems also have self-generated goals. My body has a self-generated goal to maintain a constant body temperature of approximately 98.6□F despite the temperature of the environment. All systems have feedback mechanisms which act to increase or decrease a deviation from the goal at the centre of that system. When I get too hot my body sends a signal to my brain via my spinal cord to say the body is overheating. The brain then sends a signal back down the spinal cord and tells the body to cool itself by perspiration. In cold weather, the body senses the lower temperature and our brain tells our bodies to shiver to warm ourselves up. These are both known as self-stabilising feedback systems, which decrease the goal deviation in my thermoregulation system, keeping the system stable. There is also self-changing feedback. If my body overheats due to infection and cannot cool down I may end up with a fever. The thermoregulation system breaks down and produces change, namely illness. There are times when self-changing feedback causes a system to collapse, as when a fever cannot be overcome and the person dies. Self-changing feedback is at all levels change-producing, and exists at a point of instability within a system. On a personal level, it is how we learn. At the level of the species, it can be seen to trigger evolution.

Systems can have what are known as 'emergent properties' which are dependent on the conditions and the relationships between them. For instance, the wetness of water cannot be predicted by the qualities of oxygen and hydrogen. When oxygen and hydrogen come together, the water they produce is something completely different. These emergent properties can be reliable and at the same time unpredictable. Systems are not reducible to their constituent parts. Although things do not happen in isolation and without pattern, we cannot always predict what will happen. Systems that work well can grow and adapt, evolve and learn.

EVALUATING OUR ACTIONS

The Buddha taught for 55 years and all the time he was trying to help people understand and put in place the conditions that lead to enlightenment, to liberation. He taught that our actions, our bodily actions, speech and mental actions (thoughts), all have repercussions. *Pratitya samutpada* means that we never act in isolation, and that we contribute to the state of the world continuously if not consciously.

How we see the world has repercussions for how we act. Cartesian thinking and systems thinking lead us to two very different outcomes regarding how we act and our effect on our environment and other people. We see our place in the world differently, behave differently and evaluate the effects of our actions differently. Causality and conditionality are distinct paradigms, two different sets of views and assumptions about how the world works.

CAUSALITY; CAUSE AND EFFECT

Cartesian thinking continues to be the dominant cultural understanding in our world today. It assumes that we do something because we desire a particular outcome, and we expect that outcome to happen. It encourages us to be goal-orientated. We think that if we know enough, we can dominate our environment and that 'mankind' is in charge. Here the understanding is that the end justifies the means. It does not matter what we do, so long as we achieve the desired outcome We tend to be always looking towards the future, at which time we expect to have what we want. Often we regard ourselves as acting in opposition to others who may take what we want from us. We act competitively, and this can also be an isolating way of looking at things. We see ourselves as acting on our own and only in our own interests, an individualistic perspective in which we can become polarised, mentally separating ourselves from other people and the world around us.

Because we see ourselves as being on our own, it is easy to believe that we are in competition with others. And if we see that other people have things that we want we can become envious, which can lead to judgmental blame of others and their actions. If we do not get what we want, we experience disappointment and disempowerment. We may see ourselves as not good enough, and develop low self-esteem. Understanding this set of views and assumptions about the world is important. They are the foundation of westernised thinking in the world at the moment, and it is a worldview to which we subscribe without being aware of it. This is how we mostly think: that if we apply enough effort we can have things our own way.

SYSTEMS THINKING: INTERPLAY OF CONDITIONS

The systems approach says something very different, and talks about processes which involve 'synergy'. The notion of synergy asserts that the effect of the whole system is greater than the combined effects of the individual parts. The way things are (and the way things change) is collective and co-operative. We never act in isolation. Regarding ourselves as isolated individuals is neither realistic nor practical. From a Buddhist perspective, we are all responsible for how the world is. The world in which we live is one that we envisage in our minds. As the Buddha is reported to have said,

> *Our life is shaped by our mind: we become what we think. Suffering follows an*
> *evil thought as the wheels of the cart follow the oxen that draw it.*
> *Our life is shaped by our mind: we become what we think. Joy follows a pure*
> *thought like a shadow that never leaves.*
> (Dhammapada 1, 1-2; trans. Eknath Easwaran)

Our actions arise from how we see the world. Through our actions, we bring things into being. We act in the knowledge that we cannot but have an effect, in everything that we do. We know that all our actions have consequences, but we do not always know what the particular outcomes of those actions will be. Not only is the world more complex that we think, it is more complex than we can ever know. And it is also unpredictable.

Systems thinking does not separate 'means' and 'ends'. How we do something is as important as what we do. Our actions, which include thoughts, speech, written words and bodily actions, all have an effect. AND because of the change-producing feedback mechanisms within a system, very small actions may actually create huge effects. A chance remark, for example, could have a huge effect on the course of a person's life. As a friend has noted, "Small acts of kindness save lives", and she is right. This is what can happen.

SETTING UP THE CONDITIONS FOR SOCIAL CHANGE

In systems theory, social change is seen as the emergence of novelty within a system, brought about by certain conditions. For change to happen, the system involved has to be functioning well and be connected to other systems. This means that there is effective communication in which information can be exchanged freely. Furthermore, because change is an emergent phenomenon, it takes place at a point of instability. This shift starts with an event-triggering process, which could be anything from a chance remark to a cataclysmic event. The event needs to be perceived as meaningful: something we can neither ignore nor adjust to with existing resources. For example, we may hear something that is astonishing and unbelievable, that we cannot accept within our normal understanding, and the individual, or the community, can elect not to ignore it. In effect, it can 'choose' to be disturbed by this event, and if so, information then circulates about this disturbance and its meaning and value. Insofar as the individual and the community cannot absorb the event or the disturbance at this critical point, instability arises in the system.

Instability can lead to all sorts of different outcomes, including chaos, confusion, uncertainty and doubt. When we cannot accept or come to terms with something, it can be uncomfortable. Perhaps it doesn't make sense. It is likely to arouse strong emotions and feelings of fear, helplessness and self-doubt. We'll probably experience this instability as painful. But out of this instability and discomfort there comes a change in the system, either a breakdown or a breakthrough. If there is a breakthrough, it leads to new levels of creativity, novelty and change. Whatever the event-triggering process and the discomfort brought about by it, the problem is not solved at its own level. A new order emerges that cannot be predicted by previous conditions. This new order comprises the 'emergent properties' referred to earlier. Accordingly, looking at the world through the lens of systems theory suggests that, if we want to effect change, it is important to think 'outside the box', to challenge prevailing assumptions.

COMMUNITIES AND CHANGE

Communities are collections of individuals with some sort of relationship to each other, people coming together on the basis of something shared in common such as family ties, friendship, work projects, personal interests and activities, locality, and so on. We are all part of a number of these different sorts of communities.

In systems terms, communities that work well are defined as self-generating in thought and meaning. This means that they are held together through a common system of meaning, information, and open communication. They hold shared knowledge, rules of conduct, and agreement about what constitutes acceptable or unacceptable behaviour. They exhibit a collective identity and generate a sense of belonging for their members between whom there are recognisable bonds. The community is held together by values, principles or goals that are held in common by their members.

WHAT CAN THE MAFIA TEACH US?

These communal conditions can be found in many institutions, organisations and communities, from the criminal underworld to the Sangha, the community of practicing Buddhists. Such conditions are found to be conducive to change, and even 'The Mafia' can teach us something about how change may be brought about in communities generally! In 'The Hidden Connections', Fritjof Capra claims that the criminal underworld (referred to here as 'The Mafia' for convenience) is often more successful in promoting itself than multinational corporations. He argues that they are uniquely successful organisations and he identifies some reasons for this. The Mafia does not originate in the traditional institutions of civil society. They are 'outside the box' and are not bound by convention or traditional values and behaviour. They are, from the outset, an unconventional and non-conforming system within a larger system. Because the Mafia community is not bound by society's dominant values, it can challenge those values and provide triggers for change. The Mafia has flourished in what might be called 'transitional economies' (such as those of the USA, Russia and Eastern European countries, Mexico, and Albania), at times of economic instability, and where law and order cannot be relied upon. Their goal of making money in hard times has been incredibly successful.

The Mafia works as a coalition of grass-roots communities that are bound by a common context and understanding, which support the meaning and stability of the organisation. In 2007, the 'Mafia Ten Commandments' were discovered, a list of rules which emerged from documents seized after the arrest of Salvatore Lo Piccolo, a top 'Godfather' in Sicily. These rules constituted the secret 'Cosa Nostra' (Mafia) code of conduct, whereby the so-called 'men of honour' must avoid bars, other gangsters' wives and girlfriends and be on time! The Mafia use global communication effectively to support their activities, so they have free-flowing systems of communication and information, and also an ability to use symbols and cultural codes effectively. They employ a direct, frank and emotionally charged discourse. There is a strong sense of belonging and an acknowledgement of the discomfort of change. They do not pretend that things are easy. If 'The Godfather' movie is anything to go by, 'the family' is an important symbol. Cultural codes, such as the vendetta, are strong and influential. The 'system' that is The Mafia has clear and recognisable bonds. It values tacit and explicit learning of the culture and skills of the community. When people are brought in, they are taught the skills and values that they need to become part of The Mafia. This knowledge is shared freely within the group.

At the height of The Mafia's power in the USA, as well as its own lucrative criminal activities, it controlled trade unions and sectors of show business, corrupted public officials, and infiltrated legitimate businesses. Wherever there was money to be made, there was The Mafia.

BUILDING AN 'ETHICAL UNDERWORLD'

That we can learn from the success of the criminal underworld in the way that they organise themselves, is not to suggest that we adopt their values! But the Buddhist community, the Sangha, could develop a kind of 'ethical underworld'. We, too, need to promote our own values and principles, particularly our ethics. Modern Westernised society seems unsure of the value of ethical behaviour, and 'liberal capitalism' can be seen to actively promote greed, envy and selfishness. The Buddhist community has much to offer in the promotion of ethical change in the wider world. Sangharakshita offers this particularly inspiring image of the spiritual community as being *'like an earthworm, undermining the existing order and shifting the governing values of the world.'* (Evolution or Extinction: A Buddhist View of Current World Problems, 1971) Acting ethically is no longer simply an option, but a necessity for our global survival. We need to become an 'ethical underworld' exemplifying and promoting a morally sustainable way of living on this planet.

INDIVIDUAL CHANGE

Change on an individual level is the backbone of real transformation of the world. We need to self-develop. How we act in the world is underpinned by our ethical sensitivity and the clarity of mind that comes from meditation practice. Developing awareness is crucial. Without awareness we can't see what is happening around us. We are blind to both our situation and what motivates our choices. Mindfulness meditation practice helps us develop this awareness.

The practice of the Metta Bhavana meditation, the development of loving-kindness, is also very important. It can be thought of as a revolutionary practice. It changes one's relationship with oneself, with other individuals and with society. It also changes how we act. To act from loving-kindness is to change dramatically the whole basis of our interaction with the world. Individual ethical behaviour based on loving-kindness is important because all our actions will have consequences in the world, even though we may not be able to predict exactly what they will be. We do not know what effect our actions will have, but we can be sure that they will have an effect. We therefore need to act as skillfully and as consciously as we are able, and to act in the knowledge that we are not isolated or separate from the world around us. The consequences of our actions are borne by others and by the planet as a whole, as well as by ourselves.

By meditating and acting ethically, we also work against craving. This represents a central shift both in effective Dharma practice and in the transformation of our negative impact on the world on a material level. We can develop lifestyles that encourage low consumption, economic sharing and 'right livelihood' (ethical work). We learn to be more contented with what we have. When we act from what is most important to us, we live so much more freely in the world. That said, ethical acts are self-validating, worth doing in themselves. They do not need to have an immediate and evident outcome.

CHANGE THROUGH COMMUNITY

As we endeavour to bring about communal change, we can firstly consider withdrawing support from groups and organisations that do not support our spiritual values and principles, or which are not in harmony with the Buddhist teachings on ethical behaviour. Where we are unavoidably involved with these kinds of organisations, we can still do something. Sometimes it is just a matter of communicating what we feel is important, because that way of thinking may not have occurred to other people in the situation. We can exemplify a different attitude, without just being awkward, rude or unpleasant. If we do challenge somebody's ways of going about things, we should always try to do it from a position of taking responsibility for ourselves. We might say,

"This is the way I look at it", rather than, "You're doing that wrong." We can explain what we would do in the situation, but leave them to their own responses. So it is not about telling anybody what to do or preaching. It is a matter of being completely responsible for ourselves and what we think is important.

Despite the enormity of the challenges we face, I am personally confident that I can do something meaningful now, with my available resources. We can make immediate decisions about how we live, decisions that feed into our relationships with other people. My friends, family and colleagues know what decisions I make. I decided to write this article because this is important to me. I attempt to do what I can in a wider sphere, although I am only one voice among many and I am not a 'big player'. Every moment, we are making decisions. Our choices may be limited but we do what we can, and we can endeavour to do it with as much determination and clarity as we can manage.

ACTING WITHIN A BUDDHIST COMMUNITY

Another option we have it to be an active part of a Sangha, a Buddhist spiritual community, a network of friendships that can support and affirm our ethical sensitivities. Communities do not necessarily work through personal contact, especially in this age of global communications. We can belong to strong communities with people we rarely see. We can communicate the shared values of the Sangha within a wider social world and culture which has, for the most part, quite different values to us.

We also need to hold in awareness that change is not comfortable. We know this is so on an individual level, but it also exists when there is change in our society, too. Confusion, doubt and insecurity are part of the process of change. To belong to a community that understands this is fantastic. To have people around us who understand what we are doing, and will support and encourage us through difficult times, is something truly precious. To experience this gives us an understanding of why the Sangha is traditionally one of the three most precious things in the world, the Three Jewels, at the heart of Buddhist practice.

When we experience strong emotions, for example being upset by some of the things we see happening in the world, it is because we have a very real, heartfelt connection to what is happening. We are not ill; it is not because there is something wrong with us. Rather, it is an authentic communication between us and the outside world, based on our feelings and emotions. Because it is so easy to deny our deeper, less comfortable, responses, we may need support to be able to express our feelings freely and fully. Our society as a whole is adept at repressing this kind of discomfort. We live in disturbing and difficult times, unstable times, but it is this quality of instability which is the forerunner of change. As Rudolf Bahro, the German philosopher, said, *'When the forms of an old culture are dying, the new culture is created by a few people who are not afraid to be insecure.'*

It is also good to share our experience, knowledge, abilities and skills, not least within our spiritual community. This free flow of information and energy makes for a community that is thriving, connected and effective. We can teach people what we know, and we can also learn from other who know more than us. In this regard, the use of symbol and myth can promote an internal culture that will strengthen the Sangha. The Buddhist tradition is rich in symbols, some of which are already entering and influencing Western culture. So, as well as our own internal culture, we have the opportunity to promote and communicate an alternative vision of the world for those outside the Sangha. Furthermore, a system that is functioning well, welcomes diversity. United by common values, diversity strengthens the Sangha and brings opportunities for it to evolve. Diversity in all its guises can be change-enhancing and should be welcomed.

The Sangha can use its networks to communicate its values, principles and ideas as a spiritual community. It can use its Centres and retreats to teach meditation and ethics to others. It can encourage others to develop themselves in positive ways. This is all important work. It is also open to members of the Sangha to join other congruent communities that promote ethical and sustainable living. Peace groups, environmental campaigns, and the various networks monitoring the excesses of global capitalism, are all helpful. And when we join them, we take our Buddhist values and principles with us. They, too, are valuable to the world. The spiritual community is not bound by conventional values and principles. It is embedded in society, but is also distinct from it. This is a real strength as it gives us the opportunity to challenge cultural assumptions through spreading the Dharma.

ACTIONS AND THEIR CONSEQUENCES

So a plan of action could be to help build the Sangha, step out into and interact with the world, promote Buddhist vision and values, and challenge cultural norms constructively. We can know that our actions have consequences, although we may never see the results. We can, however, have confidence that we are doing this because it is important, because it comes from our hearts and it needs to be done. We need to accept that we are in this for the long haul, but strengthened by the Sangha, we can keep going. As Sangharakshita writes,

> *'It is easy to forget that the Buddhist message*
> *is a subversive one, that its values*
> *run counter to mundane or worldly norms,*
> *and that your commitment to its ethical principles*
> *may lead you on occasion to offend*
> *conventional notions of morality.''*[13]

It may not be easy, but the effects of acting in this way can be profound. Inwardly, it can increase our personal congruency, self-esteem and feelings of being worthwhile in the world. All of this releases energy and creates a sense of empowerment. We might as well act with as much integrity, as decisively and with as much kindness, generosity and clarity, as we can manage. And, accepting that we cannot necessarily predict the consequences of our actions, we just let go of the outcomes!

> *Act according to Buddhist ideals and principles.*
> *Speak your own truth.*
> *Take risks.*
> *Trust the process.*
> *Just do it! And do it with others.*
> *That is all we can do, in every moment making a difference.*
> *May these words be for the benefit of all beings.*

---

13 Sangharakshita, The Yogi's Joy

CONNECT. EMPOWER. LIBERATE

BY GUHYAPATI

This article grew out of the transcripts and notes from a series of three talks entitled connect.empower.liberate given by Guhyapati, founder of ecodharma, at Green Earth Awakening in 2014. There is an audio version on the ecodharma website.

PREAMBLE: THE WORLD TODAY

If we're listening, paying attention to the state of the world, every day we'll hear the bad news: tales of dispossession amidst growing economic insecurity, social tensions and geopolitical conflicts, and of course the statistical indicators showing, that yes, we *are* living in the time of the sixth great species' extinction and consequent loss of biodiversity. It can be hard to stay afloat in the swelling tsunami of bad news.

Though it can be difficult to see, in a certain sense, the bad news *is* the good news. The mere fact that information about the perils of our times is being made available is a crucial factor in its healing. And the listening, the hearing of those signals is the necessary starting place for any change. That the dangers are being sensed and felt, that we are beginning to identify the problems, that the bad news can be heard, is good news. It is as Thich Nhat Hahn has said:

> *What we really need to do to help the world is hear the sound of the earth crying.*

We live in a time of great peril and great promise. The nature of communication technologies and the globalisation of capital means that more than ever our individual destinies, and the destinies of those we are close to, are tied up with the destiny of the global community and the ecosystem. Living today requires that we step up to the responsibilities that entails, and find ways to share that responsibility with others, so that the same responsibilities become a support for our learning and development, and not a crushing burden.

The ecodharma project is all about this: bringing a radical Dharma approach into a creative relationship with ecological perspectives and social engagement. It is about supporting individuals and communities to be alive to our times, to face the threats of our times, to recognise the potential of our times, and to learn how to flourish in the process.

Nietzsche wrote in The Antichrist, that "Buddhism is a religion for the end and fatigue of a civilisation." Wanting to run away, to escape, seems to be a ubiquitous human weakness. The distracting mass spectacle of a world-cup, the hedonism of party culture, or the lure of growing populist right-wing politics, all show us how much of ourselves want to turn away. And Buddhism can be used to serve that turning away – and all too often it is. But I believe that the Buddha's Dharma can offer us much more than a way of accommodating ourselves to a resigned and melancholic fatalism, or of colluding with the destructive forces of late capitalism.

We live in deeply uncertain times. We face challenges on an unprecedented scale. To meet them we need a spiritual training that roots our motivation and energetic engagement more deeply than we've known before – we require a training rooted in a radical vision of our connectedness, one that offers methods for personal and community empowerment, that can liberate us into compassionate action that springs out of a state beyond both hope and hopelessness.

This article explores how committed Dharma practice can augment ecological, systems thinking, and socio-political engagement; weaving them together to support us to connect, empower ourselves and others, and discover what liberation can mean today.

Let's start with the idea "connect".

CONNECT

As a teenager, along with a few of my mates, I was gently recruited into the ranks of revolutionary Marxism through contact with the mother of one of my best friends. I gained an excellent political education. At first it was revelatory. I recall the excitement of discovering a world view that talked of the potential of a society based in the values of fraternity, equality and justice. It was an inspiring vision. We learnt how to recruit, organise, and mobilise. We learnt that through that we were preparing the way for the revolution to come.

But, I also remember the gradual dwindling of that vision. It was a vision that was perfumed by a romantic modernism and avant-garde heroism. It asked us to get on board a train, chasing the wind of progress, ridden, and even driven, by great men.

TOO LATE FOR THE TRAIN

Gradually, however, it dawned on my friends and I that we were too late for that train; that we had actually arrived on the platform of history to watch its slow crash, and to study the still smoking wreckage. Our views about who we were and our place in the world were being formed (and dismantled) amidst a landscape of ruins. As we looked at the wreckage of the beliefs that we'd been born amidst, we wondered what it meant to have arrived too late to get on that train, to be born into a time when the days of great men were over. Nihilism haunted us. It hung around us like a shadow. And I can think of many friends who got lost in the shadows. The fact is that nihilism haunts any of us who hold tightly to views. Our insistence on truths we hold fast to, our building towers of meaning and proclamations of certainties from on high, are all driven by fear of meaninglessness. Growing up amidst these ruins has helped me recognise that in fact meaninglessness is only the shadow cast by meaning.

But, while that was all screaming at my adolescent self through punk culture and deconstructivism, it took me another 30 years to really feel it in my bones. That meaninglessness is only the shadow of meaning is not an easy one to assimilate! It is a liberating koan... but I will come back to that in the section on liberation!

THE NEED FOR THE RECONSTRUCTIVE

When what we have known crumbles, when we are faced with newness, all too often what actually happens is that we find ourselves feeling unsafe. We tighten up, pull back, panic, freeze. (That's why reactionary political tendencies do so well in times of economic and social insecurity). And yet there is always something freeing when things fall apart: things get opened up, knots are loosened, spaces for the new arise. The deconstructive power of post-modern experience opened up, for me, an important space. And in exploring that space I have begun to find delight in the reconstructive power of new ideas and ways, especially the synthesizing potential of systems thinking and ecological perspectives, and the training and methodologies of the Dharma.

These new ways of seeing lend themselves to a reconstruction, one which stays open to the idea that our views are always partial and provisional, one that enables us to move from ways of acting in the world based on control to ways of acting based on collaboration, one that reveals that engaging in life need not be about aggrandising the individual self, but based instead on confidence in the creative potential of connection. And we live in a time which shows signs of such a remarkable shift, the fascinating emergence of a new vision of life. It is a shift away from the world views of modernity and the industrial growth society, an old paradigm which has been reductive, atomising and alienating, towards the newly emerging ecological paradigm, towards a world view based on relationship. At the heart of these new ways of seeing are ecology and systems thinking.

ECOLOGY

The term ecology comes from the Greek word *oikos* ('household'). So, it can be understood as 'the study of the Earth Household'. More precisely, it is the study of the relations that interlink all members of the Earth Household. The ecologist Bernard Patten has said: "Ecology *is* networks... to understand ecosystems will be to understand networks." So, it's about understanding things in relationship with each other. Rather than taking things apart to understand how they work, an ecological approach explores things in terms of connections - food chains, energetic throughput, predator-prey balances, symbiotic relationships. In biology it's been found that to understand a living thing it's not enough to chop it up into smaller and smaller pieces. Living systems need to be explored as wholes, as cells, organs, respiratory systems, immunological systems, nervous systems – and how these all function together. Similarly, where traditional biology has tended to concentrate attention on individual organisms rather than on the biological continuum, ecologists have found that sustained life is a property of an ecological system rather than of a single organism or species.

INTEGRATION OF SYSTEMS THEORY

Ecological thinking has developed in relationship to systems thinking, which arose simultaneously in several disciplines in the first half of the twentieth century, especially during the 1920's. It was pioneered by biologists, who emphasized the view of living organisms as integrated wholes, and further enriched by gestalt psychology, ecology, and, later, quantum physics, cybernetics and the study of non-linear dynamics. A system has come to mean an integrated whole, whether living organism or social system, whose essential properties arise from the relationships between its parts.

'Systems thinking' is therefore the understanding of a phenomenon within the context of a larger whole. This is, in fact, the root meaning of the word 'system', which derives from a Greek word meaning 'to place together' (*synhistanai*). To understand things systemically literally means to understand them in context, to establish the nature of their relationships, to think in terms not of pieces but of connections. For systems thinkers, the essential properties of an organism, or living system, are properties of the whole, which none of the parts have. A system is more than the sum of its parts.

While we can learn a lot about things by analysing their parts, a fuller understanding also requires that we put them back together. And when we do that many of our old ways of categorising things become problematic. We find that there are no lines of strict separation between living and non-living things, between the mind and the material, between the self and the world. A brilliant example of all this is found in the work of James Lovelock, originator of the 'Gaia Theory' and Earth Systems Science, which encourages us to see the Earth as a living planet, a single self-regulating evolutionary process in which life, mineral, biological, atmospheric, and meteorological phenomena are all bound together.

Interconnectedness is not just a vague idea, that somehow things are related. It points to the actual, concrete, connectedness of things in the world, whether atmosphere and living things, rocks and temperatures, economic systems, socio-political systems, group dynamics, personal psychology, and mind. As we begin to appreciate the complexity of all these inter-related processes we can start to see why connection is such a fundamental value. Understanding things in terms of connection rather than as separate entities can help us to understand the psyche, group dynamics, and societies better. And this implies a wide-ranging shift in values.

Honouring connection implies a shift in many values: from Reductive to Relational, from Analysis to Synthesis, Rational to Intuitive, Atomistic to Holistic, Innovation and growth to Conservation, Individualistic to Cooperative, Anthropocentric to Ecocentric, and Maximise to Optimise, among others. There is so much we could say about each of these. But right now I want to focus on the last one, a very important shift that can easily be overlooked; the shift from the value of maximising to the value of optimising.

MAXIMISING TO OPTIMISING

It is often the case that we think that if something is good, then more of it is better. But this is often not the case. Most things are useful in the right balance (like carbon levels in the atmosphere) or the right dosage. Something that is an essential nutrient for plant growth becomes a poison when there is too much of it in the soil. Just because economic growth can feed more people and generate higher material standards of living for some, doesn't mean that more economic growth is always better. In all of this, balance is crucial.

The same is true of values. We might recognise the imbalance in our culture towards the rational faculty at the expense of the intuitive. But to maximise intuition over the rational is as damaging as maximising the rational over the intuitive. Analysing things into their parts might have its limits, but so does rejecting reductionism in favour of maximising synthesis. Both have a part to play in understanding the world. And finding the optimal value for each changes from context to context.

What can look like a simple shift, from maximising to optimising, is actually very challenging. It places tough demands on us. It demands from us a more nuanced, more complex and less black and white approach to the world. Values cannot be assigned simple labels like good and bad. They need to be explored in context, to be understood in terms of their function in relationship to other factors – in a constantly shifting world.

This is an important part of what the Buddha was getting at with the idea of the Middle Way. It suggests that we need to check and adjust our approach to find what balance of method works at any one time. Not just assuming that because something worked that more of it will work better. Sometimes we need discipline. Sometimes deep relaxation. Sometimes it is a subtle interplay of both that is what is needed. In meditation we need to learn how to balance calm and vitality, checking and adjusting our approach continually. Sometimes we need strong effort, sometimes effortlessness. It all depends on the context, the moment. And to know what is going to be useful we need to be very attentive.

Often we get attached to certain approaches, certain values. We often roll them out regardless. We get stuck in habits. A developmental approach to meditation can be useful, or become a pushy attitude that straightjackets the psyche. An open awareness approach to meditation can be useful, or it can just compound a flaccid laziness. Which is right, and in what balance, requires a constant responsiveness to actual experience, not attachment to one way or the other. In a changing world, attachment to maximising one value at the expense of another can become a trap that stalls our development. The Middle Way requires that we search for the optimum balance in every situation.

RESPONSIVENESS

Healthy systems incorporate pathways of information and feedback loops. This is what enables responsiveness to change. This is also what enables self-organising systems – like us - to learn, adapt and evolve.

For many years I've been deeply impressed by the writings of Donella Meadows. In the 1970's she was one of the co-authors of the groundbreaking study *The Limits to Growth*. Its publication prompted widespread discussion about our ways of living and the non-negotiable ecological limits we live within - it was instrumental in helping us begin to wake up. As a systems thinker, Meadows helped to explain how healthy systems, biological, ecological or socio-economic, all exhibit characteristics of good feedback and responsiveness. It is through sensing what's going on (both internally and in the surrounding environment), channelling the information effectively, and responding to the feedback, that a person, a society, or an ecosystem can survive, adapt, and flourish.

In the *30 Year Update* to the original *Limits to Growth* book, Meadows and her co-authors offered a simple analogy for the industrial growth society heading on its way towards resource depletion and environmental degradation. She likened it to a car driving along a road at speed. Not far ahead on the road is an obstacle, perhaps a heavy stone wall. The road is wet, and anyway, the brakes are not working very well. Slowing down is difficult. In addition to that, the windscreen wipers just don't work. So, it's hard to see what's coming, through the wet and steamed up glass. In this analogy, feedback into the system is poorly sensed. Information of the approaching hazard isn't getting through, not arriving where it's needed to influence action. And, because of the bad brakes and wet road, the capacity for responsiveness within the system is severely compromised. That's the industrial growth society: systemic failure to notice approaching hazards, vested power interests which compound political intransigence and short-sightedness. These are characteristics of a sick system: a system that needs healing.

The application of this analogy to the industrial growth society is something many of us can recognise. What we might not always notice is how much it can also apply to the way we live our own lives.

OUR ROLE IN THE SOCIAL BODY

Each of us can play a crucial role in the healing process of society, improving its systemic capacity to receive feedback and get it to the places where responsive action can begin. We can play a role in the social body like that of the immune system in the healthy functioning of the physical body - identifying perils, flagging them up, and gathering the antibodies and resources to deal with the threat to the system. The immune system plays a role in repairing the body, and rebuilding healthy tissue, just as we can create alternative ways of living, new economics, ways of growing, ways of creating community.

But this immunological function within the social body is a role that asks a lot of us. It requires that we become good receivers of systemic feedback, open channels for the flow of information. It requires that we train our sensibility and our capacity for responsiveness. This is all about connection. How can we increase our capacity to be connected? To increase our responsiveness we need to attend to three specific facets of our own experience:

- the quality of our awareness,
- our emotional capacity,
- and our ability to become increasingly conscious of the views and beliefs which frame our interpretation of our experience.

Returning to Donella Meadows' analogy of the car in the rain, we could say that attending to the quality of our awareness helps get the windscreen wipers going again and clean the glass; attending to our emotional capacity enables us to look out of that windscreen and not turn away in terrified anxiety; and bringing increased awareness to the way our views about the world condition our experience helps us best understand what's really going on, and hence where and how to intervene to help change happen.

TRAINING IN CONNECTION: PERSONAL, SOCIAL, AND ECOLOGICAL

These three dimensions of our experience are the foundational concerns of basic Buddhist training. The greatest hindrances to a clear awareness, contributing to poor visibility, are our mental habits of distraction and fragmentation. The basic antidote is training in mindfulness, which brings brightness and lucidity to the mind. The greatest hindrances to an increased emotional capacity, to our ability to keep looking, are the heart-constricting tendencies of aversion and fear, which can be transformed through simple daily practices of cultivating skilful emotions such as kindness or *metta*. The greatest hindrance to increased awareness of the conditioning influence of our views is the grasping attachment that comes from our existential insecurity. The best antidote for this is deep reflection, grounded in both mindfulness and unconditional kindness for our self, on the impermanence and insubstantiality of things.

Building this kind of Buddhist training into our daily lives can greatly enhance our capacity to sense and respond to what is going on around us. And personal training of this sort is crucial to healing the systemic dysfunctionality of our society. Such training is essential in enabling us to recognise that the bad news is the good news, to stay open to it, get the information flowing effectively, and enable what responses there can be.

This kind of training is training in connection. There are three important dimensions to this, the personal, the social, and ecological. First however we need to understand that any given system sits within a larger system, a wider set of relationships, that systems are nested within other systems. Good systems thinking requires the agility of mind to shift one's attention back and forth between levels.

The subtlety of systems thinking not only points out the way that things are connected between each other, but also how the layers of systems within systems link between themselves, up and down through the hierarchy of layers. The cell is a whole system, but part of the larger system of an organ. An organ is a whole system, but part of the larger system of the body. The individual can be recognised as having systemic integrity, but exists within community and society. And so on. A simple way of looking at this is to think in terms of three dimensions of connection that we need to attend to:

- Connecting people to themselves
- Connecting people to people
- Connecting people to nature

Connecting people to themselves includes psychological, cognitive, and emotional dimensions and is essentially about self-awareness and emotional capacity, but also about discovering the greater depths of who we really are. Connecting people to nature includes getting ourselves out of the human-centric world we have built around us, and rediscovering the non-human world and our own ecological identity. This is not just about feeling connected, it also needs to translate into ways of living and socio-economic structures that honour our basic ecological nature. Connecting people to people involves the development of empathy, compassion, but also the basic skills of creating new kinds of social relationships.

Because of their interlinking, addressing anyone of these adequately requires paying attention to the other two. Effective training in connection requires that we address all three dimensions.

CONNECTING PEOPLE TO PEOPLE - FROM CONTROL TO COLLABORATION

When we begin to appreciate the ways that we are each part of a greater whole, it demands that we transform the way we live and work together. One of Meadows' suggestions for acting in a way that honours the insights of systems thinking is to "go for the good of the whole". And of course, because we are part of the whole, this does not imply neglecting our own needs in the process. And perhaps one of the most elegant ways of understanding how we can "go for the good of the whole" is to explore the dynamics of collaboration.

EXPERIENCE OF ACTIVIST GROUPS

The work I've been doing in recent years around sustainable activism and burnout has brought me into close contact with hundreds of activists across Europe. For many right now it's easy to feel despondent, seeing ahead of them a long uphill struggle, amidst a political climate where their values of ecological and social justice are so marginalized. But often what they find most disheartening, what really depletes their energy, are the struggles and conflicts amongst those they work with. Frequently, to meet the challenges of transforming society, it's first necessary to transform the culture and relationships within their own groups, so as to become a truly effective and sustainable force for social change.

Whenever we choose to step into action to support social or ecological wellbeing, for most of us it's going to mean collaborating with others, working together.

And working with others is not always easy. It can feel frustrating, draining, and unproductive. Meetings drag, personalities clash, both hidden and overt power struggles arise. And all this gets in the way of achieving what the group or organization started out to do. Whether at the level of grassroots and community organising, or larger NGOs, it's not uncommon to despair at our chances of making meaningful change in the world if even within our own groups we can't overcome such challenges.

One of the first things that can help is to acknowledge that, at this point in our history, our capacity to collaborate is often severely compromised.

Both self-survival and social cooperation are tendencies that have been integral to our evolution as a species. The tension between them is central to what it is to be a human animal. Within every human group, and within the heart of each individual, the tension between self and other is continually playing itself out.

But, during the recent decades of neo-liberal social development an emphasis in favour of the values of individualism and self-interest have often prevailed. This legacy, with its consequent effects of social atomization and the erosion of community, continues to exert an undermining influence on our collaborative endeavours. Many of us have grown up in the wake of the Thatcherite view that "there is no such thing as society, only individuals and their families", in a world where the skills and the values required to work well together are seriously under-developed and under-practiced. Consequently, for most of us today, effective collaboration requires a focused *re-training*.

The necessary skills include collective visioning, decision-making processes, ways of including diverse opinions, active listening, and so on. All these can help transform collaborative work from a struggle into a nourishing synergy. Nevertheless, their successful application all rest on a foundation of some basic values and qualities which are essential to reclaiming our natural capacity to work well together. And to me, one of these stands out above all others as the real secret to effective collaboration: kindness.

THE POWER OF KINDNESS

Personally, I think that kindness is one of the most underestimated virtues of our times and radically transformative of both our self and of our relationships. Don't underestimate the power of kindness! It won't solve all the problems - some of them might be unsolvable! But as a touchstone to test whether or not we are bringing our best to our collaborative relationships, laying down the most helpful conditions to support the greatest potential arise amongst us, we can ask the unbeatable question: "In this, can I be a little kinder?"

In my experiences of working with others for social change, I can see that where things failed, all too often my own lack of kindness was a major factor, and that whenever I have been able to really allow it to inform my approach, it was transformational: things worked so much better – and collaboration gained longevity, continuity, and depth.

The radically transforming power of kindness is what we call *metta*. It involves cultivating an intimate awareness of the pulse of life as it runs through our self, as it runs through others, and as it runs through the world, and letting that awareness influence our action. This quality of kindness, this intimate sensing of the pulse of life is at the heart of connection: to ourselves, to others people, to the social and ecological dimensions of the world.

- Kindness for our self supports the intimate awareness that's a key to self-knowledge and the integration of our energy with our intentions and values.
- Kindness furnishes the trust to venture beyond our comfort zone into spaces where we can keep opening gently and consistently to more and more learning.
- Kindness is the basis for the courage we need to sit amidst contradiction and diversity, to feel it unfold towards wisdom- rather than fearing the incoherence of reality.
- Kindness provides us with the nourishment that enables us to loosen our grasping onto views, and acknowledge their provisional and partial nature. It allows differences to deepen into shared understanding, rather getting entrenched in conflict.

- Kindness underpins so many other essential virtues, whether generosity, patience, or compassionate and courageous action. Kindness is a solvent which melts away the brittle dualism of self and other. The empathy it implies de-centres our world from self, and relocates our reality in the fecund world of inter-subjectivity. And even when it all goes wrong, kindness is the basis of an emotional resilience that enables us to bounce back, to forgive, to learn from experience, and to usefully share that between us.
- Kindness is a quality we can consciously develop, especially through the basic Dharma trainings of ethics and meditation. If we want to step into effective action for social and ecological wellbeing, we will need to work with others. If we want to collaborate effectively with others we'd do well to make training in kindness our radical priority.
- Kindness is a key to connection. And connection is a key to empowerment. And if we want to respond to the needs of our times we need that empowerment.

I often quote Dilgo Khyentse:

> *When we recognise the empty nature,*
> *the energy to benefit others dawns,*
> *effortless and uncontrived.*

There is an important truth to that. The empty nature he refers to is the awareness that our self and the world are empty of separateness, that fundamentally we are relationships – internal, social and ecological. When we see the emptiness of separateness, we see that we can't fall out of the web of life, that in a sense we are never alone, that the wisdom of millions of years of evolution fires through our synapses, and that the courage of hundreds of generations of our ancestors flows through our veins.

As we begin to recognise that what we think of as self is fundamentally social and ecological, acting for others flows from us with greater ease. And as it does we find that we are empowering others and that others are empowering us.

THREE LEVELS OF EMPOWERMENT: PERSONAL, SOCIAL, AND ECOLOGICAL

When we are connected we are empowered, and each of the three levels of connection discussed above empowers us in different ways. Connecting with ourselves, we discover deep resources and qualities within us. You might call them inner resources, but in a sense they are not merely personal resources or qualities. When we really connect with our depths, it's more as if we connect with a power that moves through us. And that potential can be far greater than our small selves can imagine.

Connecting with others – in community and through social action – we discover the empowerment of collaboration, the magic that arises when we come together with others. Recognising ourselves to be fundamentally social beings, we also discover within us the courage and wisdom of the many generations that have gone before us. As individuals we are formed in the context of social relations. We require community and the collective social dimension to really flourish. The complexity of human consciousness, of language, of emotional intelligence, of culture all come from social interaction. The social dimension is integral to what we are.

Connecting with nature, we open up to the support and nourishment that come from the ecological networks we live amidst. Finding that we are not separate from the ecological web we find that the power of life, flowing through countless species on a vast evolutionary journey, continues to run in our veins, to sparkle and fire in our synapses and nervous system. Also, communities and societies are all rooted in the ecological. The ecological is our most basic identity, the soil our roots have grown in and been nourished by. It remains our most basic source of nourishment, for each of us and our society – despite the way contemporary economics hides that fact.

To really unleash the power of these three dimensions of connection, we need to attend to all of them. Recognising that there is no final separation between the layers of connection at a personal, social and ecological level is more empowering than attending to any one of them alone.

Any practice that fails to stay in an engaged relationship with these dimensions of the interconnected self can also be a kind of "spiritual bypassing". Unless our spiritual practice simultaneously seeks to heal the wounds in our society and the ecosystem, (which are both integral to who we are), our practice will only lead to limited results and a simulacrum of liberation: we will be cut off from the energy and nourishment that comes from healthy connection with the wider dimensions of life. Consequently, our practice will only never have the empowerment needed to energise the process of liberation.

A THREE-FOLD PATH: CONNECT : EMPOWER : LIBERATE

The Buddhist three-fold path of ethics, meditation and wisdom is sequential. If we want insight to arise we need to attend to meditation. If we want meditation to have depth, we need to attend to ethics. The same is true with the three terms: connect, empower, liberate.

Liberation requires empowerment, and empowerment grows out of connection. Connection in turn depends on the development of an intimate caring sensibility. But healthy connection also depends on the structural aspects of our relationships - the infrastructures of society, economic relations, and community processes. We need supportive structures, relationships, communities, and institutions, as well as a connecting personal sensibility to experience empowerment.

THREE ASPECTS OF COLLABORATION: TASK, PROCESS, RELATIONSHIPS

At the ecodharma centre, I live in a community and work as part of a team. We're achieving a lot. And all of it depends on the collaborative efforts between us. When it goes well we can achieve so much more than any of us could alone. And not only do we experience the results, but also the potency that <u>is</u> collaboration. When we collaborate effectively with others it is as though our self is enriched.

Getting it right is tricky. Working well together requires us to attend to many things. A simple framework we use at ecodharma is to ensure that we attend to three aspects of collaboration: Task, Process, and Relationships.

Task: Clearly there needs to be clarity about task. What are the aims? Do we share them? What are the steps necessary to achieve them? All of this is basic. We need processes that help define task: vision, strategy, objectives, and the specific actions required to realise them. This is what defines our purpose of coming together in a specific setting with a shared vision.

Process: We also need to give attention to process. How do we make decisions? How do we coordinate our efforts? How do we evaluate what we are doing and how we're doing it? At ecodharma we put a lot of effort into our process – different kinds of meeting structures, definition of roles, careful shared decision-making when needed. These all ensure a cooperative coordination. And we also ensure a clear delegation of authority to individuals in different areas, to balance cooperation with sufficient autonomy to enable people to get things done.

But all too often what gets neglected is the third aspect of effective collaboration – which is relationships.

Relationships: No matter how good your processes are, unless you attend to the quality of relationships you will still find yourselves bogged down in power struggles, conflict, and misunderstandings. All too often people think that just by tweaking process they can iron out difficulties that are actually rooted at a deeper relational level. And often, under the pressures of the moment, when tasks get urgent, what most suffers are the relationships. But it's a false economy. Taking the time to attend to relationships empowers our groups, building trust, forgiveness, and mutual understanding. And to be effective we need that trust and understanding to underpin both task and process.

It is so important to attend to all three: task, process and relationship. To do so ensures that everything flows – as best it can.

EMPOWERMENT AS DEEP COLLABORATION

As a result of the work we've done on all these over the years, I currently feel deeply empowered. But it is not only community and team, or even them plus our volunteers and friends I feel I'm collaborating with up at ecodharma. That is not the only kind of collaboration that empowers the project. Of course, there are the other people, and so on. But that is not what I mean either. Ecodharma was set up in a remote valley in the Pyrenees. When I first arrived there the buildings were in ruins and the land had been largely abandoned for generations. I remember someone, who was obviously impressed by what we were achieving, asking me, "so, was there really nothing here when you first arrived?" I looked around at the forest, the valleys, the limestone ridges, the circling vultures, and said, "Well, actually, most of it was!"

What we are doing, as transient human animals with our little plans and projects, is only a small and momentary intrusion into much bigger processes. When I feel that humility, it opens me up to the support of the land, the majesty of the limestone, the steadfastness of the evergreen oaks, the playfulness of the streams, the exquisiteness of the orchids, and the elusiveness of the wild pigs. And I feel that both I and the project are empowered by all of that every day. And there is more than that: as we rebuild, which is hard work, we are deeply conscious of the debt we owe to the peasant farmers who first gathered the stones and dug the earth, who cleared the springs and planted fruit trees, to create their homes and terraces. Our efforts are continuous with the efforts of the historical ancestors of the place. We collaborate with them through deep time, also with the chemical and compressive processes that turned the lives of microscopic algae into limestone at the bottom of a shallow sea: each stone we place has been on a long journey and process of transformation, made deep in the earth and carried to the surface by unimaginable forces, eroded and tumbled down by millennia of weathering and erosion. We are collaborating with and empowered by all that too! When we open up to this – and to the evolutionary rhythms in our own bodies - we can feel the whole evolutionary journey empowering our efforts.

A TRAINING IN POWER

Power gets a bad press. And perhaps rightly so. So often we appropriate power to our self. We use it abusively, harming both ourselves and others. Power corrupts, they say. But it need not. It all depends on how we understand power, the training we do in preparation for using it, and the social structures we set up to keep us alive to its dynamics.

For power not to corrupt we need an initial training in connection. Mahayana Buddhism emphasizes this. It insists that the spiritual path starts with *bodhicitta*, that the basic motivation for our development on the spiritual path needs to be a strong desire for the liberation of all beings. This sense of solidarity with life is not an add-on to the Dharma. It is at its heart, right from the beginning. Otherwise we can compound our self-referential tendencies that trap us in isolation and arrogance. It therefore teaches that we first need to train in the 'ordinary preliminaries' of:

- Gratitude and appreciation of the preciousness of life,
- an awareness of impermanence – the way life is fundamentally about flow,
- a recognition that ethical acts are the basic building blocks of our experience,
- and an emphasis on bodhicitta.

After these come the 'extraordinary preliminaries' of the Vajrayana, in which we deeply acknowledge that our spiritual development is not something we do alone, that our practice depends utterly on the support of teachers and spiritual friends, and on powers that are deeper than the mere ego-grasping self. These are all required to ensure that we don't seek to appropriate to ourselves the deeply empowering methods of the Vajrayana – which would cause us serious harm.

Without an adequate ethical training, without paying enough attention to connection, power will tend to be used as 'power over' – as attempts to control others for our own benefit. Such an attempt always ultimately goes against our own self – because we are not really separate from others. Power used for control alienates us from others and, as such, alienates us from ourselves. What we do in the world we are also doing within ourselves and to ourselves.

EXPLORING POWER: POWER OVER AND POWER WITH

What I am calling "power over" is often what people think of when they hear the word power. But power is more nuanced than that. Instead of 'power over' we can learn to become proficient in using 'power with', to simultaneously empower ourselves and others.

Abusive power pervades so much of our lives – often invisibly. Mostly we are socialised to accept it as normal. But inevitably that abusive power wounds us and those around us. When we meet power in the world it can trigger some deep patterns in ourselves – we can kick against it, collude with it, try to manipulate it, confront it. Very often our responses to power or authority come from quite unconscious struggles within ourselves. Power is complex and our relationship to it can also be complex. But we can learn to work wisely with it.

If we are serious about working well with others it's very important to become more literate about power dynamics in our groups. This is necessary for working with others to be effective, to help us transform "power over" to "power with", to a position where each individual is empowered appropriately within the group. (You might notice I didn't say equally empowered, which is often an idea that actually masks actual power dynamics). Having the courage to explore power in our groups really supports the shift from control to collaboration. But if you are going to use these kind of tools – be careful to watch out that you don't use them just as a weapon in your own power struggles! As Donella Meadows says, always "go for the good of the whole".

EMPOWERMENT IS NOT AN INDIVIDUAL THING

So, to be empowered as individuals is not just an individual thing. We also need our communities, teams, and other social relationships to be empowering. In a sense it is only when we take responsibility to "go for the good of the whole" that we truly benefit from the power of collaboration. Only when we begin to help to empower each other are we really empowering ourselves.

Our own development and the development of our communities are bound up together. We do ourselves a great disservice when we forget that. We need to work simultaneously with inner process and the processes of creating social settings - teams, groups, and communities. And it is vital that those social settings reflect the values of connection and collaboration – not the values of control! Those settings need to be empowering in themselves.

Drawing on the insights of systems thinking, we see how the interconnections between the self, the social, and the ecological exert reciprocal influences in each direction, between each systemic level. To understand the self we need to attend to the social and ecological. To understand society we need to attend to individual consciousness and to the bigger ecological context. Although we can usefully talk about what's happening at any one of these levels, it is important not to forget that there is no strict separation between them, but rather a continuous flow of influence from one level to the other.

If we get too caught up with our own consciousness we run the risk of cutting ourselves off from both the social and ecological dimensions of our identity. We end up with a reduced and shrivelled self, unable to respond to challenges, or to be enriched by the nourishment that comes from these fundamental aspects of an interconnected self. Getting stuck 'on the inside' of ourselves is a developmental dead-end. And if people are getting stuck on the inside, social development suffers too, as do the health of ecological systems. The wellbeing of the individual, of the social, and of the ecological are all bound together.

Socially Engaged Buddhists are generally very aware of this interplay, and engage in a practice which honours all three dimensions. But I have found it interesting that amongst all the engaged Buddhists I know, almost all of them were already politicised or ecologically conscious before encountering the Dharma. There are very few who began with Dharma practice and then began to recognise the importance of the social and ecological dimensions. I find that curious. For sure there are exceptions – but on the whole, we can say that "if it starts on the inside, it stays on the inside".

This is why at ecodharma we emphasise the need to attend to all three levels right from the outset of our path. If there's a danger that if we start on the inside we are likely to get stuck there, we had better take extra care to guard against that danger. All our efforts to heal ourselves need to sit within efforts to heal society and ecological damage.

MEDITATION AND DHYANA: ATTENDING TO THE INNER

None of this means we should neglect the inner. Without the inner work, all our work in the world will be severely compromised. We do need to learn how to cultivate courage, compassion and awareness from within ourselves as gifts to the world.

Perhaps the most important method for this inner empowerment is meditation. Meditation is deeply empowering. Through meditation we can cultivate clear and integrated awareness and the emotional capacity, the resilience and robustness needed to keep meeting the world with tenderness and care – again and again.

A source of empowerment in meditation that seems to be inadequately attended to is the power of dhyana. Dhyana is the deep meditative concentration that is the aim of samatha meditation. Sometimes it is called samadhi or tranquil abiding. The term tranquil abiding doesn't really do justice to the sources of creative energy and joy that are integral to dhyana. It is a state of deeply integrated, clear and energised mind. Dhyana refreshes the mind. It releases a brightness and clarity which is quite unlike everyday consciousness. If we really want to offer our gifts to the world, giving sufficient attention to cultivating this in our own experience is priceless. Dhyana can often be regarded as a lofty achievement for meditators. But it need not be very distant. Dhyana is simply the natural condition of the mind when we set up the right conditions. It is just a matter of attending to them. When we do, dhyana arises, as naturally as warm air rises on the south-facing walls of a limestone cliff.

ETHICS, CONNECTION AND SKILL

As already mentioned, the principal condition for supporting deeper meditative experience is our ethics – the ability to really feel our connection with the world with an intimate care. This has to come first if we want dhyana to become part of our daily experience. We also need to be clear that meditation needs to be continuous with our everyday life. Accessing dhyana regularly is really a matter of choice about what we do with our life, how we live it day-to-day.

But then there is also the acquisition of skill. We need to approach meditation as an art, not as a chore! And like any art it requires careful perfection of the necessary skills. The good news is that there's lots of good meditation teaching in the Buddhist world today.

METTA, KARUNA AND MUDITA

As well as dhyana, another important source of empowerment from meditation comes out of the practice of the brahmaviharas. In the previous section I talked about the power of kindness, of metta. It sits within a meditation system known as the brahmaviharas. It is a four-fold practice, developing what are sometimes called the Four

Immeasurables, which consist of *metta*, plus karuna, *mudita, and upekka.* We need to practice them all. It is not enough to only practice *metta*.

Our training begins with *metta*, or loving-kindness, fostering a caring intimate connection with the pulse of life, in ourselves and in others – human and non-human. When this intimate caring is turned to face the suffering in the world, it meets that quite naturally with *karuna* or compassion. And when we turn the intimate caring of *metta* to meet the happiness and wellbeing of others, it unfolds as *mudita*, or sympathetic joyful appreciation. Together these three lay the foundation for *upekka* or equanimity.

Metta, mudita and karuna augment each other. *Metta* offers the starting point of gently opening the heart. But it is compassion, the turning of this open-heartedness consciously towards suffering in the world, that protects *metta* from degrading into mere sentimentality, and that stirs us to action. It gets *metta* off the cushion and out into the world.

The appreciative joy of *mudita* keeps us alive to the potential for joy and fulfilment in the world, it provides essential nourishment and feeds our efforts to alleviate suffering, so that we do not become overwhelmed. If we only turn towards suffering we may exhaust the nourishment we need to keep going. By consciously turning our awareness also towards the flourishing, creativity and well-being in the world (which in fact is all around us), we uplift our minds. And when we turn it not only towards everyday joy in the world, but also specifically to the deep joy that arises on the path of Dharma practice, and intentionally allow ourselves to feel within us a joyful appreciation for that, we deeply energise both mind and body. Both karuna and mudita add power to metta. Metta alone is not enough. To empower ourselves and others it is a good idea to give each of them some time in every meditation session we do.

The fourth of the four immeasurables is equanimity. It is what finally brings the other three to full fruition. But while equanimity grows out of the other three, it also needs to be perfumed with the insights of liberation.

LIBERATION: PERSONAL, SOCIAL AND ECOLOGICAL

Now I want to circumambulate the theme "liberate". I want to explore liberation in terms of the three linked dimensions of connection and empowerment already named: personal, social and ecological.

The essence of **personal liberation** is captured for me in Dilgo Khyentse's phrase, already quoted:

> *"When we recognise the empty nature,*
> *the energy to benefit others dawns,*
> *effortless and uncontrived."*

There's a simple elegance to this, weaving together both sunyata and pratitya-samutpada, both emptiness and conditioned arising. It honours the timeless heart of liberation, and yet situates it right here, right now.

The one-line definition I am using for **social liberation** is, very simply, establishing the conditions, as widely as is possible, that support people to flourish. These include factors like economic and social justice, a social balance of cooperation and autonomy, a basis for empowered participation in social process and decision-making, and opportunities for people to live useful and meaningful lives. And out of them, of course, grow opportunities for individuals to grow into the fullness of flourishing that Dilgo Khyentse points to.

And neither personal nor social liberation can be separated out from **ecological liberation**. To think otherwise is a fantasy. Healthy individuals grow in healthy societies. Healthy societies grow in healthy relationship with the environment. Ecological liberation simply means refusing the human conceit that we are somehow above and separate to nature, or that we have dominion over it. It means resisting actions that arise out of that arrogance, creating ways of living that heal us from it. It would be a ridiculous conceit to think that nature somehow needs us to liberate it. It is, and always will be, wild, with integral value in itself. We need to honour it, to stop treating it as merely something for human exploitation.

EQUANIMITY

The theme of equanimity is a good place to start. Studying the words of Engaged Buddhists over recent years, it appears many agree that one of the most useful contributions Buddhism has to offer social action is the quality of equanimity. And yet, if misunderstood, equanimity poses one of the greatest obstacles Buddhism can put in the way of social engagement.

If you've done your Buddhism 101 you'll know that, traditionally, equanimity plays an important part in Buddhist Dharma. Not only is it a quality we develop to support our on-going practice, but in some formulations it occupies a position almost synonymous with the goal of Buddhist training. It suggests a deep imperturbability, which, like the depths of the ocean, maintains a profound calm, even as the waves on its surface swell and crash tumultuously.

But the traditional texts also slap some important public health warnings on equanimity. Loud and clear they caution: Do not mistake equanimity for indifference. Indifference, they say, is its "near enemy". Indifference might have some close similarities to equanimity, but as all good foragers know, it's all too easy to pick something with a passing resemblance to a tasty and nourishing species – but which is in fact a poison. Mistaken identity is a common error. , and an indifferent, detached, withdrawal and lack of connection with the world, is <u>not</u> the equanimity the Dharma points us towards – it's a toxic pretender, a near enemy. Sadly, it offers an alluring surrogate.

The challenges of our times, with their economic and ecological irrationalities, social tensions and precarities, all too easily tip the balance in us towards a tendency to withdraw. It's no wonder that disconnection entices us - and all the more so when, mistaking indifference for equanimity, we can use Buddhism to provide the rationalization that, rather than copping out, we're actually gaining spiritual maturity! Of course it's not only Buddhists who are seduced by the coping mechanism of withdrawal: Donald Rothberg lists a range of contemporary forms of indifference, the most modern near enemies of equanimity as *denial, complacency, resignation, acquiescence, numbness, intellectual aloofness, rationalization, cynicism, dogmatism, and fear of strong emotions, particularly anger.*

Sound familiar? How often do we hear views rooted in one or another of the above, that present themselves as grounded in maturity and wisdom, when in fact they're merely ways of suppressing the heart? Denial is one of the defining psychological constellations of our times. It plays out around us all day long, becoming integral to our lives and our socio-economic systems. Denial underpins our passionless mainstream discourse – which allows statistical analysis, but gives no room to heartfelt responses. It fuels the growth economy as it leads us to consume to avoid discomfort: Denial is good for business - in the short term! And if shielded by unacknowledged privilege, it leads to a terrible life-withering complacency and superficiality. And yet, despite the perils of misidentification as indifference and denial, equanimity still remains one of the most valuable qualities Buddhism can offer us in meeting the challenges of our times. In its authentic form it offers a source of fearless compassion and incisive wisdom.

Training in equanimity begins with *metta, karuna,* and *mudita.* Training in these three protects the development of equanimity from collapsing into its surrogate life-denying near enemies. They ensure our path towards liberation is not escapism dressed up in spiritual garb. Unless our equanimity grows out of a caring intimacy, deeply alive to the pulse of life, unless it holds within it a passionate and committed engagement with the suffering of the world, unless it's illuminated by joyful appreciation, it's not the equanimity the Dharma points us towards. Equanimity is a deepening capability to stay open to the way things are, in all their heights and their depths. As equanimity grows, our capacity for compassion and joy also grow. The deep calm of the ocean does not diminish with the rise and fall of the waves on the surface. It adds a depth of context, but it doesn't turn away.

What is so deeply valuable about an integrated training in the Four Immeasurables is that it not only protects equanimity from surrogate forms of denial, but it actually provides the range of emotional skills required to attend with care and patience to the gradual process of growing beyond the old protective strategies of our self, to recognise the fear and grief that lies beneath them, to nourish our heart, and to enable us to move gradually towards a more empowered and fearless commitment to the world.

In this sense, equanimity brings together connection, empowerment and liberation. With the right training equanimity really <u>is</u> a quality that can deeply empower our efforts to meet suffering and injustice in the world with transforming and liberating action.

BEYOND THE POLITICS OF CATASTROPHE

These are especially difficult times to engage in action for social and ecological justice, for social and ecological liberation. Social change has never been a simple thing. It is complex and in a sense mysterious, rarely a simple story of winning and losing. There are times when movements are defeated, but the changes they fought for happen anyway. There are times when a struggle is won, but the outcomes are not what had been hoped for. In recent years I have seen many engaged people despair, fall into despondency, and give up. We live in deeply uncertain times, facing challenges on an unprecedented scale. To meet them we need a training that roots our motivation more deeply than we've known before – we require a vision and practice that sustains compassionate action beyond both hope and hopelessness.

Powerful social movements are slow to arise. Their causes are complex, at times even mysterious. But they *do* arise out of continuity of effort. To support on-going engagement, and the necessary longevity for movement building, we require a sustainable and motivating vision that can fully embrace the uncertainties of our times – an inspired vision not propped up by a merely hopeful optimism, but that retains its power and value whether we succeed or fail.

These are complex times. We can't know if our present actions will succeed in bringing forth new ways of living that honour our wovenness within the ecological web, or whether, in fact, we stand amidst currents whose flow towards calamitous end times is just too strong to turn. Two images come to mind: A midwife tending to the birthing of new life, and the hospice nurse, tending to the passing of the terminally ill. In our actions at this time we cannot know if we are midwives of a life-affirming future, or whether we nurse the dying process of a terminally ill civilisation. Or perhaps both!

What really fascinates me is the reflection that both midwife and hospice nurse call on the same life-affirming qualities of care and compassion. Both witnessing the first breath of a newborn child and the last outbreath of a dying parent can be met with wonder and deep appreciation of life. The value of life is not lessened for the fact of death – at times it is even heightened. What I am pointing to is the empowering attitude of the Bodhisattva, the Buddhist compassionate warrior, who trains to perfect an unwavering, vigorous effort, an energetic action grounded in compassion, amidst both birth and death. That energetic engagement is what is known as *virya*.

VIRYA AND KSHANTI: ENGAGEMENT AND PATIENCE

Importantly, however, *Virya* only matures into an unwavering compassionate engagement because it is perfected in balance with *Kshanti*. *Kshanti* is a profound patience, a radical receptivity to the way things are. *Virya* and *Kshanti* together combine to dynamise effort with a resolute energy that is like the steady turning of the sun and moon, not the mere motivational bubble of optimism.

Motivation at that depth is what can support on-going engagement with the necessary longevity for the complex process of movement building, fully embracing the uncertainties of our times. It provides an inspired vision of what is possible that is not propped up by hopeful optimism, but that retains its power and value whether we succeed or fail. To help this, I think it is useful to ask ourselves how we understand success and failure. What do these mean to us?

A DEEP SHIFT IN VIEWS

Responding to the challenges of our times requires three kinds of action. Firstly, we require **actions that resist** further on-going degradation and damage to ecosystems and society. In addition to stopping more damage, we need **actions which create** alternatives in economics, social relationships, and production. And as well as resistance and creating alternatives, we also need **actions which enable a shift** in the world views and values which have driven our society to its current point of crisis. We require a shift in consciousness.

Working for a transition from the industrial growth society to an ecological and socially just future requires us to ensure that our efforts don't reproduce the old world views that got us here in the first place. As Aung San Suu Kyi once stated,

> *"Without a revolution of the spirit,*
> *the forces that produced the iniquities*
> *of the old order*
> *will continue to be operative"*

If we want our social action to be congruent with the shift in consciousness needed for a real transition, we need to bring awareness to how the views we carry shape our social aims, political objectives and our strategizing. How we understand success and failure sets our vision. Our vision will shape our strategies. And our strategies will shape the actions we take to fulfil the objectives, actions which are the stepping stones on our strategic pathways.

LINEAR TIME AND CIRCULAR TIME

One of the most important clusters of views, inherited from the old order and often carried over into the visioning of our socio-political work, are views about time. The way we relate to time plays a key role in shaping our world. Time is so fundamental, the assumptions about it so basic, that we often take time to be a given characteristic of reality. But different cultures and traditions give very different meanings to time. They understand its structure differently. Consequently they live in different worlds and interact with those worlds in different ways.

At the heart of the dominant western world view which has underpinned the historical development of the industrial growth society is an approach to time which prioritises its linearity. Our socio-economic structures, political ideologies, and ways of living, are all influenced by assumptions about the fabric of temporality – that suggest it has directionality, that we are heading somewhere. And that that somewhere is somehow better. The core assumptions underpinning our growth-based industrial development have been that: growth will go on, technology will advance, things will get better, that increasing production consumption and population are all monuments to humanity's ingenuity and our destiny with progress.

Some of us are beginning to recognise these assumptions as part of the hallucinatory self-image that shaped modernity - a deluding and conceited fantasy which is crashing against the non-negotiability of ecological limits, its threadbare weave torn apart by mounting social tensions, the myth of 'more and more' becoming shipwrecked on the rocks of 'simply not enough'.

And yet, how much do such deep views, ideas like the myth of progress, still underpin our political and social struggles and strategies? Have we really awoken from that dream? How much do we still invest in our work for social change as a project of salvation? To what extent, seeking the new, do we continue to reproduce the old?

CIRCULAR TIME

Many older and indigenous traditions ground themselves in a different view of time. For them time is cyclical. Rather than the modernist obsession with ever unfolding into newness, time is shaped more in terms of repetitions and returns. Re-emphasising the cyclical, the passing and returning of the seasons, the waxing and waning of the moon, the passages of growing, dying, and re-growing of things, roots us here, in our basic ecological identity – a basic ecological identity that salvational programmes, both religious and political, seek to deny.

It is not that pre-modern people are unaware of the linear dimensions of time. No doubt a nomadic tribesperson erects a shelter with a clear sense that their actions will add up, progressively, to a constructed temporary home. And yet the accumulative linear steps of construction take place within an awareness of the non-progressive aspects of life, with an acknowledgement that, one day, what has been built will be dismantled or destroyed. As a simple Buddhist refrain points out:

> *the end of hoarding is dispersion*
> *the end of building is destruction*
> *the end of meeting is parting*
> *the end of life is death*

But this reminder of impermanence shouldn't be taken to imply a fatalistic, or nihilistic, end point either. Death in turn becomes the basis for life, as the darkly composted forest floor reveals.

What does this mean for our political and social projects? If there are no mundane achievements which resist the transience of things, if time is not assuredly ticking towards historical salvation, what is our politics for? Some years ago I was trying to promote more awareness and action within the Triratna Buddhist Community addressing climate change. I remember one practitioner correcting my supposedly misguided efforts by pointing out that "we cannot fix samsara" – samsara being the never-ending round of existence characterised by impermanence and suffering. At the time, and I think rightly so, I regarded that as a rationalisation for disengagement – justifying a kind of Buddhist quietism. But now I find it crucial to integrate that perspective with a passionate engagement in actions for healing our world.

Our political and social action may not offer a basis for some ultimate salvation, but they can create conditions which reduce and alleviate suffering, even that support our flourishing, at least temporarily – sometimes for generations, and in terms of ecological impacts perhaps even for many generations. Socio-political actions can and do have value. But we must be wary of over subscribing power to them that they do not have. We need to take care not to grasp after permanence in what is not permanent. If we can give up the conceited notion that there are permanent solutions to human suffering, and that somehow we are destined to get there, we can begin to fashion ways of living that integrate the incredible ingenuity of humankind with deep humility. We can stop arrogantly overreaching ourselves in projects which pit an inflated human will against reality, that seek to repress mortality, that vainly deny the limits we live within, and instead apply our creativity to living with a renewed maturity.

ECOLOGICAL LIBERATION

As well as helping us to shape a socio-political vision, the shift towards both honouring human potential and finding within ourselves a renewed and deep humility supports ecological liberation. As already mentioned, ecological, liberation simply means refusing the human conceit that we are somehow above and separate to nature, or that we have dominion over it. It would however be a ridiculous conceit to think that nature somehow needs us to liberate it.

I remember taking a long walk a few years ago, turning over in my mind and heart yet another piece of information about the ecological destruction being caused by our current social trajectory. At one point I sat on an outcrop on the high ridge of the Serra de Carreau that runs east-west above the ecodharma centre. As I looked out across the majesty of the landscape, I felt that mix of pain and numbness such reflections can give rise to. But as I sat a pair of Alpine Choughs swooped into view, playing and diving as choughs do: they are such agile and intelligent birds. And something in their play transformed my experience, breaking me out for a moment from my anthropocentric anxieties. They revealed a quality in nature not reducible to our human concerns: that in a sense nature is, and always will be, wild. That it has an integral value in itself, irreducible to our ways of understanding the world.

Nature needs nothing from us. In a sense it is complete in itself in ways we can scarcely imagine, of which we can feel only the resonance. Plum blossom needs no liberating, nor is it on a path to liberation. Liberation is only a human concern. It is only us who need to resolve our struggles with freedom.

But part of our own liberation requires us to honour the integral value of nature beyond our own views about it. And to ensure that our personal actions protect nature from our delusive ways of living, that our socio-economic systems are transformed to honour that integral value in nature, to stop reducing it to something for our exploitation. There is something about reality that is always wild. And we need to discover ways of living that are not at odds with that wildness – to stop vainly imposing our petty views on that reality through deluded action. Ecological liberation demands we make that shift away from anthropocentrism, an entirely human-centred conviction that we are special and fundamentally different from nature. It encourages us to decentralize the world, to shift the gravitational centre of meaning away from our self, to step into a world where reality no longer revolves around our beliefs and understandings, one which also takes account of the diversity, fecundity, and the irreducibility of the wild.

This shift away from the anthropocentric asks us acknowledge that we and nature are not separate, and out of that, to act in basic solidarity with all of life. Perhaps we can begin to get a sense of what the rainforest activist John Seed is getting at when he says that he doesn't experience himself as someone trying to save the rainforest, instead as *"that part of the rainforest most recently emerged into consciousness protecting itself"*.

SRADDHA: THE CONFIDENCE TO TRULY LET GO

In Buddhist terms, letting go is integral to liberation. The Heart Sutra says:

> *So know that the Bodhisattva*
> *Holding to nothing whatever,*
> *But dwelling in Prajna wisdom,*
> *Is freed of delusive hindrance,*
> *Rid of the fear bred by it,*
> *And reaches clearest Nirvana.*

And as Dilgo Khyentse has already reminded us, true letting-go does not lead to a quietism, rather to a point where truly creative and compassionate action arises. But letting go is not easy, and rarely happens all at once. It tends to be incremental: we edge forwards, we pull back. In Buddhist terms the quality we need is called *sraddha*, often translated as faith, but perhaps best described as the confidence to really let go.

Before concluding, I want to return to the social dimension of liberation, to how the social is a necessary condition for really letting go. As already noted, although supportive social conditions might be temporary, we do need to create them as a support for human flourishing.

THE SOCIAL DIMENSION OF LIBERATION

It is easy to see what happens to most of us amidst conditions of social insecurity. All too often they throw us into the panic zone. Economic uncertainty, precarity of employment, insecure housing, atomised communities all conspire to closing us down. Social insecurity breeds fear, and commonly also the fear-based politics of right-wing populism, nationalistic self-interest, xenophobia, and racism. It is as if the clubbing together against a phantasmagorical threat offers a surrogate sense of unity to replace the real sense of connection that's integral to human well-being and that's been lost.

The globalisation of Late Capitalist Neoliberalism has especially led to a corroding of the values of community and civil society, often accompanied by a withdrawal from public and political life, to a place where consumerism has replaced meaningful participation in shaping our shared social sphere. Of course, most of this can be confirmed in our own experience, and is unlikely to come as any surprise to Buddhists. The Dharma points out that human nature is conditioned. We are capable of both selfishness and altruism, and in fact both these play a crucial adaptive evolutionary function in our survival.

But basic economic justice and security, as well as empowering social settings supporting a sense of connection and community are needed to create the conditions for people to thrive. To support people to develop, to be nourished and able to step into the learning zone in their lives we need these supportive social settings. And creating those conditions is what social engagement is all about.

RECLAIMING THE POSSIBILITY OF CHANGE

But in a way perhaps we first need to reclaim the possibility of change! As Mark Fischer writes in his excellent, Capitalist Realism, *"for most people under twenty in Europe and North America, the lack of alternatives to capitalism is no longer even an issue. Capitalism seamlessly occupies the horizon of the thinkable.*"[14] We are left as spectators on the sidelines, enduring what Fischer calls a 'reflexive impotence'. This demise of an alternative vision and potency was stunningly articulated by Frederick Jameson *"It is easier to imagine the end of the world than it is to imagine the end of capitalism."*[15] But social change is possible. We can often forget the important achievements of earlier social movements, taking them for granted, or losing sight of them as they are co-opted and claimed by those in political power. Whilst we still face many challenges, it is valuable to recollect how far we have come, how many times we have won, and how much we have inherited from social movements of the past. As Ken MacLeod says -

> *"Hey, this is Europe.*
> *We took it from nobody;*
> *we won it from the bare soil that the ice left.*
> *The bones of our ancestors,*
> *and the stones of their works are everywhere.*
> *Our liberties were won in wars and revolutions so terrible*
> *that we do not fear our governors; they fear us.*
> *Our children giggle and eat ice cream in the palaces of past rulers.*
> *We snap our fingers at kings.*
> *We laugh at popes.*
> *When we have built up tyrants,*
> *we have brought them down."*

Beneficial change does happen, has happened, and is happening as people come together in collective efforts of many sorts. There is a growing movement for social and ecological justice. And connecting with that, connecting with each other, we can empower each other to support more change. We don't know what the outcomes will be, but connecting, empowering each other, and opening up possibilities for liberation are in themselves ways of truly flourishing. And for me they are integral to meaningful Dharma practice in our present time.

CONCLUSION: WHICH SIDE IS BUDDHISM ON?

When we talk about Buddhism we can often forget that it is not monolithic; that it is, in fact, a tradition of incredible richness and variety. Throughout its history it's adapted to all sorts of cultural settings, continuously evolving and reshaping itself, its forms changing to keep its basic truths and methodologies responsive to the differing needs of different places and times and cultures: the baroque feudality of Buddhism in Tibet, the austerity and simple aesthetic of Japanese Zen, the formality of institutional Thai Theravada and the shamanic aura of the forest renunciate, all reveal the creativity of the tradition. But Buddhism has also, at times withered into reactionary and stifling forms, such as the ethnic bigotry of some Sinhalese Buddhism or the warmongering of Japanese Zen in the 1940's.

And today we again see Buddhism changing its shape, applying its heart-teachings to our times. A few decades ago it might have made some sense to talk about 'Western Buddhism'. But what does that really mean in today's age of globalisation? In recent years, in most of the countries where Buddhism is newly taking root, globalisation has meant the arrival of Late Capitalism. And there is a danger that contemporary Buddhism, in its effort to be relevant to the specific historical conditions of our times,

---

14 Mark Fischer, Capitalist Realism: Is There No Alternative?, Zero Books, 2009, p8.

15 Frederic Jameson, Future City, in New Left Review 21, May 2003.

actually becomes not a 'Western' Buddhism, but a 'Late Capitalist' Buddhism. Rather than bringing its radically transformative energy as a force for much-needed change into our world, it could so easily happen instead that Buddhism becomes degenerated by its contact with the power of these contemporary socio-economic forces, in effect colonised by late capitalist society. The Dharma is not immune to the power of capitalism – which has so far shown itself to be, undoubtedly, the most dynamic and potent socio-economic formation in human history.

And we'd be naive to believe that in Triratna or Buddhafield our approach to Dharma practice is insulated from this. The ubiquitous sway of neoliberalism and consumerism, emphasising individualistic and narcissistic preoccupations, powerfully shapes our interpretation of the world – and almost inevitably colours our interpretation of Buddhism. In Buddhist circles in recent years there's been plenty of criticism of the Slovenian Slavoj Zizek's presentation of Western Buddhism, which, he claims

> *"presents itself as the remedy*
> *against the stress of capitalism's dynamics –*
> *by allowing us to uncouple*
> *and retain some inner peace –*
> *it actually functions as the perfect ideological supplement*
> *[to capitalism]."*

Zizek's critics have got a few things right (his take on Buddhism is superficial at times, and suggests a rather limited familiarity with the tradition). Nevertheless, he does highlight a distinct danger. There are tendencies within Buddhist practice that can lead us into dead ends. And in a late-capitalist world these dangers are super-charged.

There is a crucial question for Buddhists today, like the challenge that met the Catholic Church in Latin America in the 1960's, when the social injustices in their situation forced them to ask the question: "Whose side are you on?" And out of answering that question, Liberation Theology arose, which went on to make important contributions to civil society, contributing to a social landscape in which the recent shift towards more socially progressive politics in South America could take place. Similarly our times force us to ask the crucial question: "Which side is the Dharma on?"

I hope in these talks I have made it clear where we position ecodharma. We're bringing the Dharma into relationship with those aspects of contemporary culture that we can call an emerging ecological paradigm, an approach that recognises that the connection, empowerment and liberation of individuals, communities, society, and the ecological are necessarily interlinked. It is a paradigm and a vision that can help us resist the social and ecological damage wrought by late capitalism, that can support us to create alternative ways of living that are in solidarity with life, with nature and with each other – and which can support us to truly flourish as the human animals we are as we discover our deep potential for authentic liberation.

STRIVE ON!
FIVE WAYS TO STAY SANE AND TRUE AND SURVIVE GLOBAL MELTDOWN

BY AKUPPA

We seem to hear a lot about survival nowadays. Now that things like climate change and peak oil have seeped into our consciousnesses, our egos have needed to find ways to defend themselves against what's going on. It starts with denial or ignoring, pretending it's not happening or that it's someone else's responsibility. But this has got more difficult as time goes by and as evidence has mounted up. So it seems that the next strategy is to think, "Right, I will survive! How am I going to survive whatever comes?"

We cannot assume that there is going to be global meltdown - we don't know the future. But there seems to be a lot of fear around in peoples' consciousnesses, part of which is that there may be a breakdown in our ordered, civilised society, a breakdown in our very means of survival. The fear is present, and we wonder, "How am I going to get through this?" When fear arises, however, it can be instructive and healthy to look at it and ask ourselves, "How would I cope if things really fell apart?"

To help us think about this, we can draw upon the experiences of people who are really up against it. What does happen to human beings in very extreme situations? What does it mean to survive, and how do people survive? And, more to the point, how do people survive with their humanity intact? One of the survival fantasies we might have is to imagine oneself holed up in a bunker somewhere with 3,000 tins of beans, and hopefully a tin opener. But what would be the point of surviving if we're going to be completely cut off from the rest of humanity? The act of separating oneself off like that would have an effect on us, on who we are. It would be a very isolated, defensive state of being. Could we honestly say, even if that strategy worked for us individually, that that would really constitute human survival? It would be physical survival of the body, but would it really be the survival of the human being?

So this article is not just about physical survival, but what it would mean to survive fully; it is about keeping one's humanity as we confront the challenges of survival. In order to do that, I offer five ways or strategies to survive global meltdown, drawn from the five ethical principles (precepts) of Buddhism:

- Don't lose sight of the unity of humanity
- Give yourself to community
- Don't get tied in to harmful lifestyles
- Speak out
- Keep the broadest possible perspective

The foundation that underpins these five ways of surviving, however, the first thing we need to survive global meltdown, or any extreme circumstance, is discipline. That might seem an odd word to choose. What is meant by it? Perhaps it can best be illustrated by the story of a friend who is facing life imprisonment for a crime he didn't commit. It seemed the only prospect of his getting out would be to admit to a crime which he didn't commit. In order to deal with the challenges of his false imprisonment, the advice that he'd been given by other people in the prison was "gym, library". That meant getting down to the gym to keep himself in good shape physically, and going to the library or education classes to keep his mind active. In his case, he added a third – meditation. He says that he wakes up every morning in his prison cell, realising firstly that he's still there. Then he realises that if he doesn't keep the initiative with himself, he'd sink into a downward spiral of bitterness which would completely consume him if he gave it energy. Another danger would be to lapse into complete lassitude, or institutionalisation, drudging round the exercise yard. Through 'gym, library and meditation' he's doing exactly what he needs to do, keeping the initiative with body, mind and heart. He's not allowing the system to take him over. And he does it with real discipline. It's helping him to survive with his humanity intact, rather than sinking into a spiral of bitterness or numbness.

The Buddha, in his last words, said, "With mindfulness, strive on!" The word that is translated as 'mindfulness' is 'apramāda', which means something like being vigilant, or on guard. It is mindfulness in the sense of keeping the initiative with yourself, keeping a locus of control. We can't control the world 'out there' but we can, at least to a considerable extent, learn to better control the world 'in here', and to be aware of the dangers of negative states of mind. So the Buddha's final exhortation is to keep the initiative with ourselves, because he knew that that is really the foundation of everything. Without it, we're lost.

Two and a half thousand years later, if things unfold the way they seem to be unfolding, it could be that peak oil and climate change bring about some sort of global crisis or collapse. That means it's the Buddhists of this and following generations who will be endeavouring to 'strive on', taking the Buddhist tradition forward into this crucial time in history. It's down to us how we survive, how our community survives, and how the Dharma survives. And this could be extended to include all of the great spiritual traditions. Whatever spiritual tradition we're from, we are the ones who will need to dig deep enough within it to meet whatever crisis is to come. And the foundation we need is a sense of discipline, keeping the initiative.

FIVE WAYS OF SURVIVING WITH HUMANITY

1. DON'T LOSE SIGHT OF THE UNITY OF HUMANITY

There seems to be a direction in which history is going in our privileged societies, the development of a certain 'fortress' mentality. We hear the phrases 'Fortress Europe', 'Fortress North America' or 'Fortress Australia'. We live in a society where unfair economic relations are bolstered by huge arsenals of armaments. It's very tempting to rest in the sense of security that gives us, here in one of the more privileged countries of the world. We might easily entertain the subconscious thought that "we're alright here, aren't we, because we've got Trident (or whatever)". It might be very deluded thinking, but there's still a temptation to give in to that sort of false sense of security. The question we have to ask ourselves is, do we assent to that state of affairs? Maybe we do through the electoral process and who we vote for. But perhaps the main way we assent tacitly to the prevailing state of affairs is through our silence, through doing nothing. It's what we don't say rather than what we do.

Furthermore, we need to hold dear to a universal perspective, for the sake of our humanity. If we're going to survive as human beings, it's simply impossible to do that while cutting off great swathes of the human race. Sangharakshita, the founder of the Triratna Buddhist Order and Community, links this universal perspective to his very identity as a Buddhist:

"This is one of the reasons why I am a Buddhist.
I believe that humanity is basically one.
I believe that it is possible for any human being
to communicate with any other human being,
to feel for any other human being,
to be friends with any other human being.
This is what I truly and deeply believe.
This belief is part of my own experience.
It is part of my own life.
It is part of me.
I cannot live without this belief,
and I would rather die than give it up."

That's a very strong statement! Perhaps it resonates with many of us, and maybe it's one that might be tested at some point - or is it already being tested?

The Dalai Lama uses the phrase 'universal responsibility'. He believes that what we need to cultivate in the world is the sense of us all being responsible for each other, more of a family. We all need to think beyond just our own security, or our own country's security. There needs to be more thinking on a global level, of us all taking universal responsibility.

The unity of humanity is part of our experience. In a way, it's a very ordinary thing. If we think about how we feel in ourselves when we act either ethically or unethically towards somebody else, we might find that our own deepest happiness is really a mirror of how we treat other people. That simple experience is pointing to the very profound truth of interconnectedness. It's pointing to the truth that human beings, and all life, are intrinsically one. That is part of our experience.

So let's not lose sight of the oneness of humanity, whatever fear might be provoked in us. When the powers that be try to provoke that sense of fear in order to justify the production and sale of more arms, or to further threaten and curtail our freedoms, we need to resist this provocation and maintain a vision of the unity of all humanity.

2. GIVE YOURSELF TO COMMUNITY

Another strategy for survival is to organise ourselves into community in one form or another. One of the roots of the problems of the modern world is the 'atomisation' of society into ever smaller consuming units. We need to break out of that, and not just for an hour a week; we need to take action that, as it were, breaks down the walls of our individual houses on an ongoing basis. We need to break out of the idea of ourselves, or our households, as the basic consuming building blocks of society.

Why is this so important? We might again draw here on lessons from people who have been in extreme situations. In a study of American soldiers who survived the Vietnam War[16], some lived on as isolated, traumatised individuals, their humanity not fully and healthily intact. Others, though, apparently managed to reintegrate themselves successfully back into society after their return home. The research looked into what was it that allowed some to survive happily and some not. Part of the answer was the soldiers' young age; many 19 year-olds just didn't have the means or maturity to deal with their experiences effectively, and a lot of them consequently didn't adjust well on their return. Of the rest, however, there were found to be three ways in which the soldiers had behaved in Vietnam which subsequently influenced their survival.

---

16 "Trauma and Recovery: The Aftermath of Violence - from Domestic Abuse to Political Terror" by Judith Lewis Herman

Firstly, there were those who just gave up and went along with whatever was happening. A second group went to the other extreme – they were the 'Rambos' who completely hardened themselves and did whatever they needed to do to survive, including getting involved in atrocities against the Vietnamese. Members of both of these groups, if they did survive physically and get back to America, were most likely to experience trauma and not reintegrate themselves back into society.

But there was a third group who did manage to survive more happily. Their behaviour while in Vietnam had followed particular patterns. As a rule they took responsibility for others as well as themselves, and were willing to challenge orders they believed to be ill-advised. They had a realistic sense of the danger they faced; they had fear, and accepted that they had fear, and did what they needed to do to work with the fear. They kept some sense of initiative around their fears. At the same time, they avoided getting into rage, realising that rage and anger were dangerous in themselves and weren't going to help them survive. Likewise, they didn't get into hatred of the enemy, despite what they were encouraged to do by their superiors. Finally, they were lucky!

Their stories are fascinating and moving. In taking responsibility for others, it seems they didn't close off from their humanity; taking responsibility for others is central to the notion of giving oneself to community. It also seems that this is essential for individuals to survive extreme circumstances with their humanity intact. It's an integral part of being human. If it's worth surviving, it's worth surviving together.

Similar observations have been made about people who survived disasters at sea, and the subsequent effects on their lives and behaviour.[17] There were those who just gave up in the face of the disaster, those who took action but went off by themselves, and a third group who cooperated with and helped others. One man who survived the sinking of the Estonia managed to clamber out of the ship by himself. But he still lives with the trauma, haunted by the fact that he hadn't taken the simple step of looking behind him and reaching out to help one or two other people.

So there seems to be something of a universal pattern here in the face of adversity, that we can go passive, become aggressive and individualistic 'Rambos', or take the middle ground of reaching out to those around us. And it is this latter response that we need to develop before things start to fall apart. If we're going to prepare for a world in which things are going to get more difficult, then we need to build community now. There is no better action we can take than that.

3. DON'T GET TIED IN TO HARMFUL LIFESTYLES

We're all, to varying extents, implicated; we're all part of a consuming economic system which is founded on global inequality and an unsustainable relationship with the natural world. There are all sorts of ways we can endeavour to reduce our impact, such as buying 'fair trade' goods and organic food. But there's something else we can do which is very simple but fundamental, which is to resist the ideas and images put out by the mass media defining what it is to lead happy, material lifestyles and encouraging us to strive to achieve them. We need to walk away from that. We can choose to consume less and to stop buying literally and metaphorically into the whole system of supermarkets, long-distance food, and exploitative relationships.

Changing lifestyles is not going to be easy. Perhaps it needs to be a gradual progressive process rather than a sudden radical shift. But it's worth considering just what's going to happen when the supermarket lorries stop turning up, realising how

---

17 Ibid.

dependent we are on these transport systems and how delicate those systems are. The more we start to take steps now and find other ways of meeting our needs, the more robust our lifestyles will become and the better prepared we'll be for the day the supermarket wagons stop rolling.

4. SPEAK OUT!

One way of viewing the world is as a big complex of interlocking systems in which everything affects everything else. And this includes our voices, our faculty for communication in whatever way it might be - speaking, writing, playing music, or the visual arts. Life on the planet is a system that's said to be out of kilter at the moment, and our voices are part of that system. Life on Earth needs feedback mechanisms within the realm of human activity. And we are it! Who else is going to speak out about the visible signs of distress on the planet and within humanity? If we find ourselves amongst those who are sensitive to those things, if we have a feeling response when we see the pollution of the oceans or the great inequalities in human society, then we need to speak. In whatever way we have available to us, we can speak out, whether through radical political activism or simple conversations with friends, through writing articles or singing songs. We need to give expression to it, and not out of a dry sense of duty. In doing so, we affirm and strengthen our own connection with life; to speak out is itself truly life-affirming.

And yet sometimes we find ourselves not speaking out; why is it that we don't give expression to the pain we feel about the state of the world? It could be fear - a lack of confidence or the fear of not fitting in, of going against the grain. Maybe we feel that we're ill-informed, and that we have to understand everything about economics or whatever before we can express a legitimate opinion. But in fact we don't need to worry about that. If we speak from what we see for ourselves, and how we actually feel about it, no-one can argue against that. Our own experience cannot be denied.

It's not just a question of speaking out, but learning how to speak out in a way that will be heard. It's quite easy when talking about these kind of things to speak gloomily, or full of anger. Then all that we're doing is adding to the sum total of pessimism, anger or anxiety in the world. Again, we need to keep the initiative with our awareness in order to be able to communicate effectively. We need to speak honestly, but not in a way that spreads gloom or anger. If we do that, people either get gloomy or angry themselves, or they just switch off and discount what is being said. Giving voice to what we see and how we feel with self-awareness, honesty and clarity, is a clean and effective way of communicating.

5. KEEP THE BROADEST POSSIBLE PERSPECTIVE

It's very easy in a time like ours to lose perspective on our sense of humanity, of who we are, where we've come from and where we're going. This is one of the regular themes of the activist and writer Joanna Macy. She says we need to have a sense of ourselves within a much bigger story. If our basic mindset is as isolated individuals endeavouring to confront all the great problems in the world, then of course we'll often feel overwhelmed and powerless. The resources 'in here' seem to be a mere drop in the ocean compared to what is needed to bring about the scale of change required 'out there'. But the root of the problem is actually that story, that basic mindset. We can change the story and develop a sense of ourselves as something bigger. We're part of an ever-emerging human story. Look at how people have coped in previous crises in history, how they've brought about change in quite unexpected ways that might not have been predictable at the time. We need a sense of openness to new possibilities and confidence that we, too, can make a difference.

The story, however, must include the future, remembering that what we do now bears fruit in future generations. Take, for example, the Buddhafield Festival. It comes about through the efforts of a huge number of people – those who work to put the site together in the days before the Festival and those who organise it and get everything together in the weeks running up to its opening. There are all the people who have decided to turn up and join in. Going further back, there are the people who started Buddhafield in the 1990's. And going further back, there are those who have carried on the Buddhist tradition from one generation to the next throughout the centuries. Without any of these, the Festival wouldn't happen. Everything we do is creating the world for the next generation, and it's important what sort of world we create today - it really matters. Every positive action today builds something that will make it easier for people in the future, including ourselves, to survive.

We can take an even bigger perspective from Buddhist teachings, and look outside of time and space altogether. This takes some training, it's not something that can just be taken on. But from this perspective, positive actions that affirm life need no justification because they are seen as intrinsically precious and worthwhile. Even if things don't seem to work out as expected in the short-term, those actions aren't lost and will manifest in positive outcomes sooner or later. There's something adamantine, diamond-like, about any action that connects us with others. It might be difficult to rationalise, but this perspective is one of the things that we're trying to awaken through Buddhist practice. We act how we act because it's intrinsically beautiful, not solely that we want to bring about a certain result in time. This is a truly liberating, deeply radical perspective.

In an age where there is talk of global meltdown, and of a worst-case scenario in which humanity doesn't physically survive, how do we keep ourselves going in ways which are realistic and meaningful? The answers lie in our ordinary, everyday experience. Simple acts of kindness are beautiful in themselves. They are what the Buddha called the 'deathless', because they transcend life and death altogether. How and why this is the case is difficult to know, but great inspiration can be drawn from faith in this description of the ways things really are. Whatever we do, we need to broaden our outlook from the narrow mentality of 'me, myself versus the world', to include other people, to include a bigger time perspective, ultimately to have a perspective that is outside of time altogether.

So those are the five ways to stay sane and true. The foundation is discipline, keeping the initiative in body, heart, and mind. We need to keep a vision of humanity, give ourselves to community, avoid being implicated in systems that cause harm and division, speak out, and keep the broadest possible perspective. In doing those things, we survive in the deepest, fullest sense of the word, and in our survival what is most precious about our humanity will not be lost.

MYTH, POETRY AND THE GODDESS: ANOTHER WAY OF IMAGINING

BY DHIRAMATI

My glance is clear like a sunflower,
I usually take to roads,
Looking to my right and to my left,
And now and then looking behind me.
And what I see each moment
Is something I've never seen before,
And I'm good at noticing such things.
I know how to feel the same essential wonder
That an infant feels if, on being born,
He could note that he'd really been born..
I feel that I am being born each moment
Into the eternal newness of the World.
I believe in the world as in a Daisy
Because I see it. But I don't think about it
Because thinking is not understanding.
The world was not made for us to think about
(to think is to be eye sick)
But for us to look at and be in tune with.
I have no philosophy: I have senses.
If I speak of nature, it's not because I know what
Nature is
But because I love it, and that's why I love it,
For a lover never knows what he loves,
Why he loves or what love is.
Loving is eternal innocence,
And the only innocence is to not think.
Alberto Caerio (Fernando Pessoa)

I remember a Buddhafield retreat a few years ago on beautiful piece of land in Devon. I spent several days wandering the woods thinking a lot about Tara as nature and as a nature goddess. I was looking to experience her as something real and alive in the world around me. There was a genuine longing for something. I was wanting to have an experience and yet nothing seemed to be happening. At least, not in the way I wanted.

I remember sitting down in the forest and relaxing a little. Laying down I looked up into the canopy of trees above me. The light was like a fire of brilliant silver shimmering and dancing between the leaves which were illuminated from within and glowing. The trees were swaying and whispering as the wind breathed. It's hard to describe but in that moment I knew Tara. I wasn't thinking but rather sensed directly something there in that beautiful place. An unfolding, a presence, alive in nature, singing and calling to me, to my body, my breath, my senses. There were no words or thoughts, just this being with something mysterious yet very present. And there I was lying on the earth, held by the earth, breathing with the earth. Simple and wonderful.

143

I reflected later that I had started by wanting to have some experience. Wanting to add something to my sense of self. As I did this it felt that everything had a familiar feel, a sameness to it. I was not allowing anything new and immediate into experience. By opening, and unconsciously relaxing into my body and senses, there was space for something unexpected and magical to happen. This was a feeling of yielding, a letting go of my consciously directed self-will, a making an offering of myself. I learned that to be open is really not to know, to have no idea of what is going to happen. It is a willingness to face new experiences. A willingness to die into the moment as it unfolds. As Padmasambhava says " I do not know, I do not have, I do not understand".

This made me wonder about awareness itself. That awareness has this quality of interest, curiosity, care, attention, patience, receptivity, freshness, a sense of "essential wonder". Paying attention, noticing, allowing what's there to reveal itself. In that space I had noticed that everything was flowing, and changing. That whoever I am, I am always changing moment to moment with it. Sometimes especially in the midst of nature I experience this as the call of the Goddess. She is something immediate, dynamic, fresh, and vividly present. Calling me to be present. Tara's voice is the bird song, not as an afterthought or idea but as it is experienced directly in my breathing, sensing body.

> *"The Five Elements are Tara,*
> *Abiding in the nature of all things."*

Sangharakshita has said, "to be truly pagan is to sense nature as peopled with living forces, animating every stream tree or mountain... paganism is a good foundation for being a Buddhist" (*Precepts of the Gurus seminar*)

Every culture has its sacred places and animals, rivers, wells, trees, hills, and groves, where the material and other worlds meet. Where the human imagination comes alive and resonates with its environment or with animal powers. These were very deeply rooted within the local landscape and experience of nature. This was very much the case with the Celts.

In the Irish story of Cormac and the silver branch, Cormac, the king, is searching for his family and becomes lost in a great mist and when it clears he finds himself in a strange new land. He hears the bubbling music of a stream and follows it and comes upon a deep pool of water. Surrounding it are nine hazel trees that drop their nuts into the pool below. Five salmon swim in the waters and eat the fruit of the nuts. And from the pool five streams flow, making a melodious and beautiful music as they weave away. Cormac drinks from the pool and experiences the world as a web where everything touches everything else, suddenly he can remember deep into the past and has knowledge of the future. He knows that the nine sacred hazels are dropping the nuts of inspiration into the well of wisdom where they are eaten by the salmon of knowledge. And that the five streams are the five senses flowing out into the world.

These beautiful images give a sense of the sacred within nature, and within our bodies. The bull, the crow, the hawk, the hawthorn, the hazel, the horse, the moon, the owl, the pig, the raven, the ivy, the mistletoe, the rowan tree, the salmon, the snake, the swan, otter, wolf, willow, yew and many other natural forces were all rich with meaning and significance for our ancestors and appeared in many myths, in stories, poems and songs.

So it seems to me that we need the sacralisation of the familiar rather than any escape into some other reality. Seeing with new eyes, like the poet. Seeing non-literally. There is a deep imaginative possibility within our natures. To imagine is to see things from another perspective, there are many ways to see the world,

"What I see each moment
Is something I've never seen before...
I feel I am being born each moment
Into the eternal newness of the world"

As Taliesin the 6th-century Welsh poet-seer says,

"I have been in many shapes;
I have been a narrow blade of a sword;
I have been a drop in the air;
I have been a shining star;
I have been a word in a book;
I have been an eagle;
I have been a boat on the sea;
I have been a string on a harp;
I have been enchanted in the foam of water.
There is nothing I have not been"

The poet enters the life of what he or she senses, feels, sees, hears, touches. Like the beautiful, entrancing Celtic spirals, carved in stone and painted in manuscripts, everything flows into everything else. In zoomorphic images we see men and birds and beasts emerging from and entering into each other. Everything is united in a web of life.

The poet shapeshifts into the soul of things. Awareness becomes tree, star, stream, earth itself. We are intimately, deeply part of this world, forever linked, touched, and moved. The elements of the universe are what we are, and this universe is alive. Where better to feel this than within our own bodies and senses?

Where I live, in Devon, there is a small mound-like hill with a solitary oak at its top. At its roots are badger setts, a network of tunnels dug into the side of the hill. Often a buzzard sits in the tree, watching, waiting.

I visit the tree regularly, throughout the year. I have seen it in full leaf, in sun and rain, bare and naked, with snow at its feet. I have stood beneath it with friends and alone, when I have felt sad and angry or down, and when I've felt joyful and content. I've felt seen there. I have lain down and felt the earth hold me and stared upward into ever-opening space, watching birds of prey circle and hearing flocks of wild geese passing overhead. I love this hill, I love the land I live in. I feel blessed.

"If I speak of nature, it's not because I know what nature is
But because I love it"

When I was thinking about this I was reminded of another old Irish story. Finn MacCool, leader of the wandering forest dwellers the Fianna, is in the forest looking for a man called Derg Corra when he sees someone sitting in the top of a tree. The man had a blackbird on his right shoulder and in his left hand a white vessel of bronze, filled with water in which was a skittish trout and a stag at the foot of the tree. And this was the practice of the man, cracking nuts; and he would give half the kernel of the nut to the blackbird while he would eat the other half himself; and he would take an apple out of the bronze vessel that was in his left hand, divide it in two, throw one half to the stag that was at the foot of the tree and then eat the other half himself. And on the tree he would drink a sip of the bronze vessel that was in his hand so that he and the trout and the stag and blackbird shared together.

This gives the sense of the body and our senses as a source of wisdom. Also of our deep intimacy with nature, with life in all its forms. When I feel connected to the earth, my breathing, and feeling embodied, there seems to be a natural sense of presence,

145

sensitivity and aliveness to the world. I'm in and with the ever-changing world. It's not something I need to add to experience or something to do more a relaxing into what's there. Sometimes in this way just gazing at trees or bushes I've seen faces and presences emerge from the green. I've felt clouds gesture and articulate. I've heard voices singing in the stream.

To the pagan, gods and spirits are found in the things, places and animals that surround them. The world is full of "sensuous presences of archetypal significance" (Hillman). We can take things as literally real or as a dynamic interplay of which we are part. We are arising together with the world and that has something innately mysterious and magical to it.

In the story above the Tree is the Centre of the world, through it the shaman (Derg) journeys upward to higher realms or downward through the roots to the underworlds. Through it he connects to all life. The tree nourishes all life, being home to bird, stag, fish and man.

This is what the Buddha does as he sits at the Vajrasana, the Place of Enlightenment beneath the Bodhi Tree, the World Tree. He is recognising his intimate relationship and connection to all that lives. He touches the earth gently with his fingertips and the earth goddess rises in response. He is telling us that we are always part of the world. To exist is to be in relationship, this what the Buddha is saying, this is what the world is saying to us all the time.

"The Earth is my body,
the body of the world,
ever changing and universal.
From the womb of the earth I was born,
into the body of the earth I shall return.
What I receive, I shall yield.
Stone upon stone,
drop after drop,
flame within flame,
breath after breath,
space within space"

In our relationship to the elements we dance with the world. Consciousness dances in space with the ever-changing elements. We dance with the dakini in that great space of liberation. We dance with the Goddess who animates and brings to life our experience.

Recognising the cycle and dance of the seasons I see a pattern to my life, I can sense the presence of the archetypal. There is life and growth and death. I feel this in my changing identity, as I become older, as I move into new areas of life and leave behind old ones. Life asks me to grow, change, to shift, and to die with it. Like the different sides of the goddess. With her I can descend into darkness and rise again with the spring. The goddess flows with the seasons, spring (maiden or virgin) to summer (mother/queen) to winter(crone/hag) and spring again. The goddess has all three aspects, the maiden, the mother and the crone. These relate to the three phases of the moon, the new moon, the full moon and the dark moon. The goddess herself, like the moon is constantly renewing herself. This mirrors the three phases of our lives (youth, maturity and old age) and also the cycle of birth, life and death. I feel very strongly that these patterns in nature deeply reflect the most important and vital aspects of my life both psychologically and spiritually.

Living in the countryside this winter I have sensed this very tangibly. The trees and earth are bare and darkness deepens. Everything draws into itself. It is colder, darker. It is a time to go inward, to descend, to dream. A time to walk the land and to feel the chill wind blow through my senses, to let my feet sink into the mud. To feel myself naked as the trees. It is a time of waiting, and patience. Where I have a strong sense of both the light and dark sides of the Goddess. Winter is the old crone, the hag, the dark Goddess. She laughs harshly, and in her wrinkled wizened face I see her faded, lost beauty. She challenges me to be more honest, to accept loss, grief, to embrace change, to meet pain, to acknowledge limitation, to listen to the voices of death in the dying land. I think of friends, of family, of my hopes past and gone. I feel myself fall to the earth to rot like Autumn's leaves. It is a time to weep with and for the world.

Out of this darkness and death regeneration occurs. One November day I watched from the hill as a farmer ploughed the broad back of a field below. The red earth turning to embrace the low golden winter light. The earth yielding, awaiting the seed. I felt such a deep love of her then. I felt tears flowing in my heart. This eternal giving, this eternal sacrifice.

Our ancestors would build burial mounds deep in the earth. Places of death that were also wombs of new life. At the site of the great burial mound at Newgrange by the river Boyne in Ireland, each year the sun is reborn at dawn on the winter solstice as its rays penetrate to the womb of the earth and lights up the stone altar at the end of the passage. That seed of light slowly grows in the darkness until the spring. Then the first snowdrops come to life as they are in my garden right now. The catkins on the Hazel trees and the new born lambs herald a new spring. The great mother is reborn as the maiden: out of death, new life.

I remember the myth of Persephone, her abduction and descent into the underworld of Hades, Lord of Death. How her mother Demeter was mad with grief and anger at losing her beautiful daughter. How the land became barren and how Persephone ate six seeds of the pomegranate in the underworld. How she returned to the world in Spring and returns to Hades each Winter. I remember how this story nourished me again and again and held something very deep, valuable, and mysterious for me when my sister died. When I had to make that journey down and inward too and began to feel for myself how universal this journey into grief and loss is. Not as an idea or sentiment but deeply felt. I also remember sitting by the coffin of a good friend recalling his vitality and beauty. Sitting there with all his friends and family sharing this loss. Giving my waters for him. Releasing my pain with others. And knowing he had reflected long and deeply on death, reaching out his arms to embrace it, living a life of meaning and love. So for me this, the dark side of the Goddess, has to be embraced, I have to journey into darkness over and over to live life to its fullest.

One day five brothers were out hunting and became lost in the forest. They lit a fire and ate but had nothing to drink. In turn each of the brothers went alone in search of water but each encountered the same hideous, disfigured hag who was guardian of the well and would let none drink unless they embraced her fully and kissed her. In turn they all fled. Lastly Niall came to her and agreed to kiss her and lie with her. But when he held her and kissed her to his wonder he held a beautiful woman, soft, slender and gentle, her eyes brilliant blue, her skin white as snow. He asked who she was and she replied "I am the land. The wind is my breath, the rivers my blood and the rain my tears, this earth my body. My name is Sovereignty and I bestow it on who I choose and I choose you because you did not fear my darkness and ugliness and so you are worthy." And so Niall became king. The king is wedded to the land.

The Celts seemed to have thought cosmically, mythically, ritualistically, poetically rather than literalistically (a mode of thinking where there is just one way of seeing things). So the king is seen not as one imposing order on nature and the world but as one who is working in harmony with natural forces, as the one who dwells at the centre as a living giving sun, providing abundance, fertility, allowing the flow of seasons, day and night. The world turns and the King maintains the balance, often between opposing forces. The King and the land are one.

We can see something similar to these stories in the Buddha's life. At his awakening the Buddha was sitting beneath the World Tree. The Buddha was born, gained enlightenment and died beneath a Tree. The Tree that links heights and depths, spirit and soul. Its branches in the sky, the plane of earth from which it grows and its roots reaching into the lower worlds. Snakes coil at its roots, birds sit in its branches. It is the world's axis, it is the centre.

Mara, embodiment of craving, ignorance and hatred, has claimed the throne where the Buddha sits for himself. He wishes to be at the centre and challenges the Buddha. Should he win, the world would be turned into a wasteland. The centre turning around our own wants, our own selfish desires. However in response to the challenge the Buddha does not speak, he does not talk to Mara. He just touches the earth and as he does so the Earth Goddess rises up, she responds, she is always there. She bows to the Buddha and she witnesses the Buddha's centrality, his right to claim the Diamond Throne. The awakened and compassionate one assumes the central place. For at the centre, he is connected to all worlds, to all existence and there the hub of the Wheel of Life is transformed into the Wheel of the Dharma.

Following his enlightenment the Buddha remains within the circle of the tree of awakening. He sits there for a week. Then, rising, he stands facing the tree, and over the next seven weeks, journeys round the tree, following the path of the sun.

He then sits again beneath the Tree. For seven days the monsoon rains fall and a great storm rages, and the serpent king Muchalinda emerges from the deep in the earth at the foot of the tree, wraps his coils seven times around the Buddha and extends his hood over his head.

Sitting beneath the Tree the Buddha has ascended to the sun door, the source of light. He has encompassed all directions of space in circumambulating the Tree. He has descended into the underworlds by being wrapped in the coils of the chthonic serpent. All of these he now embodies within himself. The Buddha and the world are one.

There is a deep resonance within me to the Buddha's journey. He sits, he meets, he experiences everything there beneath the tree. His heart is boundless, his mind free. He touches earth. He walked this earth, he breathed this air. When I visited Bodhgaya, the place of the Buddha's awakening, I felt this very strongly. I circled the tree, I made offerings.

I bowed before the Tree. With others, many others. All of us orientated toward the Centre together. There beneath the Tree with the sound of blaring Hindi music, hawkers, screaming beggars, tourists, monks in red and yellow robes, Tibetans, Koreans, Japanese, Indians, Westerners. People prostrating, chanting, meditating. There I was in the world with awareness, devotion and love. With suffering, anguish, madness, greed and confusion. The Sacred Tree rising up beautiful and majestic. Beneath it, at the centre, the Buddha like a sun radiating compassion.

The Tree is the Centre of the world, and through it the shaman journeys upward to higher realms or downward through the roots to the underworlds. The wild man Derg Corra sits in the tree and shares his life with bird, stag, and fish just as the Buddha sits beneath the world tree recognising his intimate relationship and connection to all that lives. We are always part of the world. So once again, to exist is to be in relationship, this what the shaman says, this is what the Buddha is saying. This is what the world is saying to us all the time. This is where Tara calls to me, Tara the divine soul in cosmic matter. She is there playing at that edge of self and world. Where I recognise through my senses that who I believe I am is not separate from this world. I am not separate from what I perceive.

Tara calls to me saying everything is shared. Out of the Lake of Suffering she rises. She calls to me when I feel my grief and loss as it is. She calls to me and I can feel for the suffering of others too. There she is always present. There Tara is, inseparable.

Some years ago I was about to lead a Padmasambhava retreat at Buddhafield. My sister had just gone into intensive care. I arrived in the field in turmoil. I went up a small hill to a spring surrounded by hawthorn trees. Some people had made a small shrine there. I sat quietly. Slowly a voice began to speak in my heart, singing out of silence as a feeling rather than words. Something calling to me with love. I knew I had to leave to be with my sister and my mother and father.

Six months later trekking in Nepal I was high up in the snows of the Annapurnas one night when I had a dream. A beautiful white dakini spontaneously appeared before me. She said she was very glad I had given up everything I was doing to be with my sister and then said "I love you" before dissolving into a brilliant moon reflected in a the waters of a beautiful lake.

Returning later to Kathmandu I went into a friend's thangka (Tibetan painting) shop where he was showing someone a lovely thangka... as I looked I knew right away: "It's her! The one in the dream!" Fortunately, the other person didn't want the thangka and I was able to buy it. Not long after on the same trip I also found a beautiful statue of her dancing, graceful, poised and strong. The figure was Machig Labdron, the great 11th-century yogini. Since then I have read about her, practiced her teachings, done puja for her, sat with her image for a long time. I'm aware now as I write with tears in my eyes that I love her deeply. I'm incredibly moved by her life and example. Her boldness, her intense and passionate love for others. There is a lovely story about her I'd like to tell...

Machig had visited a certain teacher for initiation and in the course of a long ritual she suddenly rose up into the air and danced and then passed through the walls of the temple and flew up into a tree above a lake outside the monastery. Now this lake was the abode of a powerful Naga, a water spirit, a nature spirit. A naga can cause disruption and raise all kinds of obstacles if disturbed or ignored or they can act as treasure holders or protectors. This particular naga was well known locally as violent and terrifying. But Machig, when she landed in the tree, just sat there quietly meditating. The naga was very angry but also a little fearful so he called up his army of demons and phantoms to overwhelm her. Machig instantly transformed her body into a food offering of nectar and in the words of the story, the demons "could not devour her because she was egoless". Their aggression and fear dissolved and they committed themselves to her, promising not to harm her or others, vowing to protect her and her teachings.

By facing the demons and giving herself as an offering with love instead of fighting them, Machig turned them into allies. Machig does not kill or fight the dragons, she does not polarise into good and evil. She doesn't seek to dominate or control. She meets the demons and feeds them what they need. She radically embodies her own understanding of emptiness. In the flow of impermanence, that she lives and feels, the demons of ego clinging are liberated.

This story has given me great courage personally to face and meet my own demons, especially my fears, my anxieties and anger. It can be very hard to acknowledge and face these but I have often found I am held there with loving kindness by something far bigger and wiser than myself which I can only call Love. So I feel this immense gratitude to her, the Great Mother, Machig.

There is something similar to this story in the life of Padmasambhava. The King of Tibet was trying to build a monastery to establish the Dharma in his lands and was being hindered by the Nagas who resisted his attempts by each night destroying what had been built during the day. Eventually Padmasambhava says that the King must ally himself with the King of the Nagas. He then meditates by a great lake for three days, toward the morning of the third day a beautiful woman appears asking him what he wants: he says an alliance between the king and the Nagas, for their help in finishing the monastery. This message is passed on and a great serpent appears two days later, stirring up the water so that a golden sand floods onto the shores. With the help of the Nagas the monastery is built. Shortly afterwards the king marries, not to a noble woman but to a common woman of the country, a peasant woman, symbolic of a union between the King and the land.

There are a number of different levels to the story. Because we are part of the world what we do has an immediate effect upon it. Building a monastery effects the land, it needs to be done in harmony with the land. The king has a plan, an idea on the conscious level, to establish Buddhism in Tibet but there is resistance, there are deeper unconscious forces at work. These need to be met but without conflict.

There needs to be some shift in attitude, a responsiveness to changing circumstances when something is not working. So there is a questioning. Padmasambhava asks, "What's happening here then? What lies deeper and unseen that has to be included?" He knows that the quality of awareness affects how the world and others are perceived, that they arise together. So he decides not to fight the Nagas. He meditates and meets them with compassion, and they change, they become allies.

I find it is very important just to stay with these images and let them sink in allowing them to affect me. The language of myth, poetry, symbol, and dream speak to the unconscious and larger parts of ourselves. They have to be lived, felt and experienced in our bodies, in our senses. Dwelling on the images with an open heart they speak very deeply to me. They move me. Chanting the mantra of the Great Guru, and reflecting on his life, I feel myself unfolding within a world of myth. A world that brings such rich treasures to my life I feel blessed and I long to share that with others as much as I can.

What comes to me now as I come to a close is another memory. A few years ago I was in Patan, Nepal, looking for Buddhist statues and found something that took my breath away. It was a statue of Tara sitting beneath a tree with a serpent-dragon coiled by her feet and rising up into the branches over her head. She was smiling and held a vajra (diamond of truth) to her heart. Here was a beautiful symbol of Tara as earth goddess, as goddess of the forests and goddess of wisdom. But also it reminded me so clearly of Eve and the serpent in the garden of Eden. I had also recently read a book by Jean Markale on the Goddess where he puts forward the following view:

Eve breaks the prohibition proclaimed by God the Father and listens to the serpent, an age-old symbolic figure of the goddess. This he says was a clear and simple return to the cult of the ancient mother goddess. So this original sin is the first act in the long struggle of God the father against the mother goddess. We know what followed. The serpent was cursed and Adam and Eve and so mankind, punished. The curse against the serpent, and so also the mother goddess, extends to women, suspected of being followers of this deity. And so the church fathers issued warnings against women, leading to their banishment from priesthood and active participation in the church, and in a more violent form seen so cruelly in the witch hunts from the thirteenth century onward.

So this is what he says. Woman is body and sex, sensuality, instinct and feeling. All to be feared because they cannot really be controlled, or understood, by the patriarchies that followed - only felt and experienced.

And so Eve loses her innocence, that sense of oneness with nature in a natural, healthy way, by being expelled from the garden. Nature begins to lose its creative voice.

The Goddess is banished. The daemons and spirits of the land become demons to be exorcised. There is a loss of soul.

This is just one reading, even a mythical one, but it certainly resonates for me. We cannot exclude the goddess and all she represents. Climate change and ecological crisis confront us. We live in a world losing touch with itself. Fundamentally the real challenge is in our underlying attitudes and beliefs and how we experience the world. Is the world just matter to use as we wish? Is it just an ideas or series of ideas, is it just made up of objects? Or is it a vibrant, open and alive field of being? Something we are intimately inseparably involved with which? Something with which we participate and engage in in a ceaseless dance? Something we feel for ourselves, to be respected and cared for? Something to be loved? Seeing Nature as Mother or the Goddess is an imaginative, concrete and real way to do this. Kneel down now and touch the earth. Give up having so many ideas and bow to the tree. Stop thinking so much and make an offering to the stream. Pay attention and yield your step to the earth. She has given to you since you were born, she is your body, she is all bodies. She has supported you every step of your life. She has nourished you, you have drunk from her cup over and over. She has witnessed you without judgement. You breathe her, she fills you. Sing to her. Learn to love her.

"Loving is eternal innocence."

For myself I have been up the mountain. I have strived for the peaks. I have been led by ideas and thoughts. I have turned away from what is right before me and within me. I have tried to go beyond the world I sense, see, and feel. And I have been burned by flying too high. I have crashed down to earth. I came to Buddhafield from a high, beautiful but dry desert valley in Spain. I came down the mountain because my heart had dried up. Because I had denied myself and others love in striving for my ideals. I came to a rich green field in high summer in Somerset where a small festival of 500 or so people was being held. I was greeted by two friends who hugged me and tumbled me to the ground. I felt seen, I felt loved. I sang, danced, drummed, chanted, sat in hot tubs under the stars, laughed and played. And each night I gathered with others in the tribe by the great sycamore tree, sat atop the hill and watched the sun set over the Vale of Avalon. The waters began to flow again, new life had come to the wasteland. I was home. I had heard the call of the Goddess.

Om Tare Tuttare Ture Svaha

THE BUDDHAFIELD FESTIVAL

The Buddhafield Festival is an annual gathering of up to 3,000 beautiful people — a joyful and unique creation of community. Ritual, song, dance, arts and crafts, yoga, tai chi, meditation, and play all blend together in a drink- and drug-free environment, unique among Britain's alternative festivals. The Festival is for people from all traditions — and none — coming together in a mindful and family-friendly space, allowing hearts and minds to open.

It's held today on a beautiful site in the Blackdown Hills, in an Area of Outstanding Natural Beauty, about 7 miles out of Taunton, near the tiny hamlet of Culmhead.

It offers a full programme of activities, including the teaching, discussion and study of Buddhism and meditation in the Dharma Parlour and Meditation Space. If it's relaxation you're looking for, take your ease in one a number of vegan and vegetarian cafés, whilst waiting for one of our extensive range of workshops to start. There's a full programme of music and cabaret performances. There's a set of specialist Areas and Spaces including Permaculture, Social Change, Women's - and a terrific Kids Area. Amongst the delights of healing and bodywork on offer you could learn or practise Yoga, Tai Chi, Chi Gung, book a massage or investigate one of the dozens of other treatments.

Opening Ceremony, Buddhafield Festival 2009

THE VISION AND PURPOSE OF THE FESTIVAL

The Buddhafield Festival launched as a tiny 350-person festival in 1996, on the well-known 'Teddy Stone's Field' near Shepton Mallet, which remained its home or the next five years. At the time this was a very ambitious project for the tiny Buddhafield team, being five times the size of any gathering they'd put on before. By the early 00's however, it had grown to a couple of thousand people and was in urgent need of some 'professionalising' and a clearer vision: what, exactly, was it there to achieve? The following are notes from a 'Brainstorming Meeting', held at the London Buddhist Centre in early 2003, exploring exactly that. It opened with two questions: "What is the overall purpose of the Buddhafield Festival?" and "What do we want to define as success?" These were the answers:

CONTACT:

To put Buddhist ideas into the festival-going sub-culture.
To make people outside the FWBO aware of Buddhafield and the FWBO as a spiritual community they could join if they so wished.
Introducing Dharma to a different constituency.
Encouraging encounters between different kinds of people.
It is a crossover event so can't impose the Buddhism too much - lest people react.
Many Buddhafield Festival people aren't joiners but say "if I had to choose anything it would be Buddhism...".
We are creating a Buddhafield: people can enter it & experience it & think 'Buddhism is wonderful, magical...' - leaving the details for later.
Buddhafield creates a porous world.

RITUAL:

Giving meaning to art, music &c by underpinning them with the sacred.
The Festival is a unique context for Buddhist ritual/dance &c.
In trying to manifest the Dharma, the effect will always be mysterious.

THE WIDER FWBO:

Develop more conscious connections between Buddhafield/other FWBO centres.
Centres could send teams to train for a season. then go home & replicate.
Buddhafield could draw more on the Movement's assets - manpower, skills, etc.
Make people inside the movement more aware of environmental/ ecological issues
Encourage them to come more into relationship with people active in those areas.
Challenge them more!
Buddhafield complements the experience of city Buddhists: A bit funkier, more on the edge.
The Movement is saying "thank god for Buddhafield".
The FWBO needs reinventing, much more experimentation: that's something that's easy in Buddhafield.

THE BUDDHAFIELD SANGHA:

To have fun doing it (in a spiritually productive kind of way!): a positive experience of Right Livelihood/teamwork.
And we're trying to make some money for Buddhafield.

THE DHARMA PARLOUR

After 10 years, in 2006 Buddhafield introduced a new element into the Festival mix: the Dharma Parlour. This was a collection of venues right in the heart of the 'Village Green' area, each dedicated to one or another style of Buddhist teaching - talks, debates, workshops, children's activities, poetry and more. It consciously included a variety of Buddhist teachers from within Triratna and beyond - an unusual innovation at the time for an FWBO Centre. Buddhafield was able to do this by drawing on the extensive network of contacts it had built up, inviting teachers with whom it had personal relationships to come together and build up a 'Dharma Parlour community' of teachers that could reconvene every year, slowly expanding as the network grew.

Regular faces today include the Pure Land 'Amida Trust', the secular 'Oxford Centre for Mindfulness', the inter-Buddhist 'Network of Buddhist Organisations', the activist 'Network of Engaged Buddhists' teachers from the 'Work that Reconnects', visiting Burmese Nuns, and Christopher Titmuss' ever-popular 'Dharma Enquiries'.

The Dharma Parlour, Buddhafield Festival 2012

BUDDHAFIELD FESTIVAL FIELD GUIDELINES

Below are some Field Guidelines from an early Buddhafield Festival, held on the Shepton Mallet site, when Buddhafield was still learning how to put the necessary conditions in place to give rise to a successful Festival. Connoisseurs of festival management may spot a certain amateurishness in what follows! It's followed by some later Festival literature, especially relating to the ever-contentious topic of drink and drugs at the Festival. Buddhafield realised very early on that making the Festival both drink- and drug-free contributed greatly to its unique atmosphere – but also realised that Festivals were very difficult things to police and rules very difficult to enforce. How then to balance the need for clear, respected guidelines with the pragmatic necessity of 'light-touch' enforcement? The answer gradually emerged, being a combination of stating very clearly Buddhafield's vision for the Festival, developing a body of regulars who appreciated exactly that vision, and creating an experienced team of invisible 'Peace-Keepers' to complement the more visible 'Festival Security', whose job it was to spot potential troublespots as early as possible and enter into dialogue with the people there in a friendly and non-confrontational manner. As a last resort, and an option only very occasionally invoked, it's always possible to tell people we're very sorry but they won't be welcome back next year.

WELCOME TO THE FESTIVAL and to this beautiful field. By following these guidelines you can help us leave it as we found it - ready for next time!

FIRST AID - first aid points are at the main gate and in the Buddhafield café. Report any emergencies to the site crew at the main gate.

TOILETS - the compost toilets are designed to create compost from solid waste - if possible pee in the hedges (as deep as possible) or straw bales rather than into the compost toilets. Cover your deposit with a handful of sawdust (stops smell and flies). Soap and water are provided to wash afterwards. At night each toilet will have a lantern by the entrance - please do not remove it. If any toilet needs attention, please see one of the site crew (by the main gate)

FIRES - please keep all fires to the prepared fire pits. Do not cut wood from the hedges, firewood is provided.

RECYCLING - please be sure to use recycling points for your litter. Bags are provided at the main gate. We recycle everything we can, when you bring your litter to the recycling point please sort it into the bins provided.

MEADOW - the meadow area is a seed bank for the field's wildflowers, so please do not walk in this area. Please also respect any 'keep out' and 'private' signs.

HOT TUBS - please do not alter the taps in the hot tubs as this can be dangerous. Report any problems to the site crew.

MUSIC - please observe the midnight drum and music curfew to respect the peaceful and meditative nature of the festival (as well as local residents). Dogs are not welcome - sorry, but the field's owner runs a cat sanctuary! No vehicles on the main field, and the field gets very muddy if wet which may make all vehicle movements impossible for the duration.

DRINK and DRUGS - please observe the Buddhafield policy of no alcohol and no drugs on site.

DOGS - this is a no-dog festival because of the very many local cats and they don't mix with dogs. Any dogs you see will have been agreed with the farmer in advance.

If you have any questions please ask the gate crew. The festival ends after the closing ritual on Sunday. Have a good one!

DRINK AND DRUGS ON THE BUDDHAFIELD FESTIVAL

In a Pure Buddhafield the Dharma can be heard on the breeze, in the song of the birds, seen in the flowers and the trees. It is the perfect environment to hear Dharma, it is always being taught and everyone is receptive to it. The Buddhafield festival is not however a pure Buddhafield - but we aspire to create a reflection of such a place. Every workshop, cafe, performance space, every campfire circle, every group of people working and every hot tub could be perfumed by the scent of the Dharma.

The Buddhafield festival is hosted by Buddhists and we attempt to have Buddhists involved in all aspects of the festival, but it is of course, a festival open to all. Therefore many people at the festival will not know what Buddhism is, and fewer will consider themselves as attempting to practice Buddhism.

One particularly contentious issue at the festival has been people drinking and taking drugs. We are very clear that we want to have a drink and drug-free festival, and that by doing so we are creating a place where people can have a good time at a festival and also be receptive to each other and to the Dharma. So our principle is that our festival is drink and drug-free. However a principle is one thing and putting it into practice is another. Not only will some of the people at the festival have no intention to try not to drink or smoke, but some may find it hard not to do so even if they wanted to. Some people may want to try to not drink or take drugs but may find it hard when others around them are doing so. I think we need to empathise with each other and be kind to each other.

We are clear that we do not want any selling of drink or drugs at the festival, and that we do not want people drinking at the festival. So if you see people not keeping to these rules do feel free to talk to them about it. But only do so if you feel confident to do so, and please be sensitive to the people you talk to - try to talk to them about it rather than confronting them.

If you do not feel confident in talking to such people then do come and talk to security - they will arrange for someone from the security team to talk to them. But please bear in mind that we cannot solve all the problems - and we do not want to, nor do we feel it is appropriate to, use force to resolve such situations unless it is absolutely necessary. If there are any other similar issues you feel we should know about at the festival then please let security know.

Perhaps the best thing that you can do to help our festival become a pure Buddhafield is to exemplify what it means to be a practising Buddhist by trying your best to practice. This is surely by far the most effective way of creating a positive festival - in which people will naturally be ethical and friendly to each other.

Satyajit
'Buddhafield festival security'

THE FIVE 'C'S FOR HOSTING AND SURVIVING A FESTIVAL
Composed during the Buddhafield Festival set-up retreat, July 2001

For a serious Buddhist to successfully host and survive a festival is a real test and challenge to our practice. In so many ways it is the anathema of what we are recommended to do! How can we stay happy, mindful, and friendly in such a busy, confusing, and unpredictable situation? Here is a list of five ingredients that may help. We came up with them on the working retreat before the 2001 Buddhafield Festival, and offer them to you in case they are useful.

Commitment to practice Unless we take personal responsibility for maintaining our daily meditation practice, we will gradually become frayed and worn down. This is crucial if we are to sustain ourselves through the festival.

Communication and co-operation We need to know where to find our friends if things get difficult, and to be in good and co-operative communication with the others in our teams. If these links are maintained we will always have resources to draw upon if we need to.

Confidence in the Dharma We are not just inviting people to come and have a good time on the Festival - we are offering them the Dharma, which is of inestimable value to the world. Each one of us and everything we do embodies this to some degree, and from this comes a great confidence in the value of what we are about.

Cosmic hospitality As Shantideva says, the Bodhisattva invites gods, antigods, and all to a 'festival of temporary and ultimate delight'. We need to prepare ourselves so that when the festival starts we are able to welcome all comers, and, most importantly, to see the potential - the Buddhaseed - in all who come.

Cheerfulness It is all too easy to lose our perspective and become distressed by the many things that don't go right. Cheerfulness is not a superficial cheeriness: it comes from maintaining a deep insight and broad perspective on the whole situation - that however serious the business in hand it, it is not so important as to be worth us falling into negative mental states.

If we are able to successfully keep all these 'ingredients' in mind, we'll not only be able to help many beings encounter the Dharma, we may find ourselves embodying Hakuin's 'lotus that blooms in the fire'. As he says,

> *because the lotus that blooms in the water withers*
> *when it comes near to fire,*
> *fire is the dread enemy of the lotus.*

> *Yet the lotus that blooms*
> *from the midst of flames*
> *becomes all the more beautiful and fragrant*
> *the nearer the fire rages.*

Or to quote Festival Eye,

> *"The marriage of the Celtic dance*
> *and Buddhist serenity*
> *creates heaven on earth"*

Expect Chaos
Allow Chaos
Have Faith in Impermanence
See one another with Eyes of Kindness
Get It Right First Time

Wicker Buddha, Buddhafield Festival 2013

BUDDHAFIELD FESTIVAL REVIEWS

Here's a selection of reviews of the Buddhafield Festival spanning the 20 years of its life, 1996 - 2016 (and counting!) Some are longer and more in-depth, some social-media-style soundbites, some written for circulation within the Triratna Buddhist Community, some for a more general readership. We've attributed them where possible and attempted to seek permissions.

As the reviews came in year after year, it became increasingly clear that one thing people especially appreciated about the Festival was its clear no-drink-no-drugs ethos, probably unique in the UK festival circuit. In particular it was much-loved by families with young children and people in recovery, both of whom found it a 'safe' environment.

In 2013 Buddhafield conducted its first systematic research on who was coming and why, asking respondents to say what they especially loved about the Festival. Here's some of the answers, followed by the year-by-year reviews.

Meeting like-minded people who I never knew existed. Saunas, ecstatic dancing, awesome range of workshops and yoga classes, 24-hour meditation area, sitting sessions and classes in meditation. And all in a drug and alcohol-free environment — just awesome. It has been life-changing for me and I'll be back as long as there is a Buddhafield to come back to.

It's longer than other festivals, gives the opportunity for community to form.

I loved the way it's completely chilled out yet there is a sense that people are very passionate about the Dharma, the environment, meditation, Buddhist ethics.

The energy, the vibe, the friendship, it's like stepping from the crap world of everyday life to a joyous nurturing world of bliss.

I love the free wild beautiful vibe that is laced throughout the whole event. And the pure energy feeling that comes from a drink and drugs free zone. I love just how many things there are on offer. And I especially loved the opportunity to dance in the huge dance tent nearly every day, and to sing African rhythms. But the warmth of the people, I feel largely which emanates from the crew underpinning the whole event, is also glorious.

You can learn a lot, meet people that you could never imagine, find quiet spaces, watch a permaculture film at 9pm. feel happy to be myself, try new challenging and exciting workshops :) the first time I went, many years ago, it was an early introduction to meditation and a new experience.

I love being surrounded by positive energy, how everyone smiles when they catch your eye. And there is always some good music in the background, way too many cool things to do and people to talk to, and amazing chai and food!

It is the only festival I'd ever feel comfortable going to on my own.

I've been coming for 10 years because it's safe peaceful place where I'm accepted and loved just as I am.

The fact that there is a Buddhist ethic that pervades the atmosphere (even though I'm not Buddhist), the fact that it is drug and alcohol free (even though I do drink!), I love the fact that there is a great mix of workshops and entertainment — I can be serious all day in the Dharma Parlour one day, and spend all day dancing the next. I love the fact that there aren't tons of food outlets to choose from, but there is a defined sense of 'mealtimes' (unlike other festivals that can feel to me to be like consumerist feeding frenzies!). I like the way that because of these things Buddhafield feels very different from other festivals.

A thoughtfully held festival that allows people to grow and meet each other and be creative and curious about themselves, others and the world.

I can be travelling down on the train on Wed afternoon in 'normal clothes and a normal life', and by the evening I am in Buddhafield, with a feather in my hair and a smile in my soul, dancing half-naked under the moon... It is a space where we can be free.

Seeing old faces, some I see only at buddhafield. I love having no pressure to drink it always feels like a mini personal journey going to the festival, it can be transformative.

It was great; I even bought a notebook at the station and spent the whole journey back to London writing down my experiences and revelations before I got back to the crowds — even when I got to Paddington Station I just plonked my bags down and carried on writing for an hour to get down my experiences. (When I had finished and looked up there were 3 security guards wandering around checking out the Hippie!) Highlights for me were SAMs Sauna, the Permaculture and Social Change area (especially workshops by Mac from Embercombe and Thomas from Trackways). I also thought that the Parallel You-niversity was inspired and I spent a lot of time there. Pachamamas was also superb as ever (the world may be anicca but Pachamamas breakfast pancakes always hit the spot!).

The singing was brilliant, the dancing and play and children's areas were incredible. The food was amazing and the general safe and fun atmosphere was fantastic. I was also blown away by the jazz — such talent abounds!

It was pretty much one of the most beautiful experiences of my whole life.

Buddhafield for me is one the very best festies of the year and would recommend it to anyone from any walk of life.

It's a beautiful lovely festival! My boyfriend said yesterday that he thought about it every day and was counting the days to the next one like it was Christmas

Buddhafield Festival feeds my soul and after ten years of attending just to bask in the love, I have finally started to 'get it' with the meditation and am going to regular classes in London. I love the fact that the festival connects up people and groups from all over the country for an AGM like no other!

ten years coming... that's only in reality ten weeks of a 50-year life and yet it has touched me and changed me and it of HUGE importance to my life. I come with a three generation family group and it is special beyond words. xxx

I love festivals but it is definitely the non-alcohol/drugs that makes Buddhafield the best for me.

The no alcohol/drugs, the love and trust and open friendliness, the kid-friendliness, the laughter and acceptance and non-judgement, the craziness, the food, the stalls, the peace and harmony...been 10 times and will come forever! love you all xxxxx

You have managed to create a warm, friendly environment where it's easy to meet new people and make special friendships. I met my partner at Buddhafields about 2 1/2 years ago and we've hardly left each other's side since. We are expecting our first baby any day now!!! Thank you Buddhafields xxx.

The delight of being able to be with and connect with such a variety of good hearted people. Fun, laughter, kindness and conversations ranging from a smile with the eyes, to deep dharma. The joy of seeing others having space to express different ways of being, at ease with both themselves and others.

BUDDHAFIELD 2014 - A BREAK IN THE CYCLE

In 2014 Buddhafield decided not to run the Festival, the first time it had taken a break since it started in 1996 – meaning it had had a 17-year-long unbroken run, pretty impressive in the festival world. Many on the core team wanted a year off, and the project as a whole needed some time and space to reflect on where it wanted to go next. Here's what it put out at the end of 2013, explaining its decision:

"Buddhafield has been able to continually reinvent itself because it's a collective. We've been able to seamlessly adapt to changes in personnel because, as one person's inspiration has naturally moved on, another's has flowed towards us. This has led to a series of cycles in the shape of the collective that have occurred naturally and steadily, keeping the project fresh and fluid.
We're now at the end of one of the biggest cycles in our evolution, but this time the transition can't be seamless. For the first time in 17 Festival years, we feel the need to pause, get back in touch with who we are and what we're about, and from within that space invite a new generation to join the collective. In order to achieve that, we think the wisest move is to not run our Festival in 2014.
Buddhafield only exists and functions because of the ongoing generosity of hundreds of people. Many of the Festival organising team annually give up considerable amounts of their spare time to plan and organise their Area, even going so far as to work at the Festival in their own holiday time.
Clearly this is done from a great love – a fire in the heart – for Buddhafield and we'd like to thank everyone who's given so much, especially the crew and workshop leaders.

BUDDHAFIELD FESTIVAL 2012: THE MUD-BATH

Buddhafield 2012 was... wet! In fact, seriously wet. Everyone knew it was going to be, and it was. It wasn't easy, and the Café flooded and had to be closed temporarily for emergency overnight repairs (installing a complete raised plywood floor!) But everyone survived, and here's what people said:

I think you all do an amazing job, having worked on festivals of all types for many years you create what is very difficult: you create community, an alternative culture and spirit. You create a place to call home and a place which feels safe on so many levels. You 'fight' the elements quite literally and I'm sure endure much moaning and indecision. Know that it's absolutely worth it. I LOVE Buddhafield. I know myself and many of my friends see it as an uncompromised central social occasion on the calendar. I particularly love the drug+alcohol free ethos. Thank you and really well done.

There is nowhere else I want to be in July than at Buddhafield festival. The sum of its parts is so much greater than people simply living in a field together. The potential for healing and transformation for individuals and for the planet is ENORMOUS when we gather in this way in a spirit of co-operation and good will. I love you!

Buddhafield is the best festie ever! Such a beautiful energy is created by all those lovely people. Even if it is a swamp, it will be a swamp full of love! X

Two happy survivors from the 2012 Festival mudbath

Triratna's ClearVision crew made a great documentary of the 2012 Festival which you'll find online at vimeo.com/51225683.

BUDDHAFIELD 2011: AN AMAZING FESTIVAL!

I expected Buddhafield to be good but I didn't expect the experience to completely blow my mind and leave me feeling totally and utterly blissed out and in love with fellow man. And that's not half of the profound effect that it had on me!

When we arrived the site seemed quiet and peaceful and I was pleased to note the many trees surrounding each field. This gives the whole place a really alive and grounded feel and it felt really good. Once we'd pitched our tent, we went to explore and discovered proper thunderbox compost loos. Brilliant! These were clean and didn't smell (unlike the compost loos which all feed into same pit, and don't even get me started on portaloos!) and were also kept well stocked with recycled loo roll throughout the festival.

Arriving in the festival field, it's clear how much love and care has been put into setting up – the ritual space holds a huge gold buddha surrounded by plants and crystals. And so, begins a magical weekend of discovery. Our daughters discovered the saunas first under the guidance of a friend, preferring the cold plunge pool over the heat of the sauna. Then they were off, meeting people, playing with the other children on site and generally turning the whole beautiful space into their playground. As they get older, it becomes more and more possible to give them this freedom and it is a pleasure to watch them fly with it.

So J. and I found ourselves in the Ecstatic Dance workshop with Jewels Wingfield. A mindblowing way to start the festival – we walked out with hearts and minds wide open and proceeded to have lots of fun! We met loads of people over the weekend who are involved with the magazine, a whole community of readers, writers and contributors. We also met lots of people doing incredible inspiring things who will feature on the pages of The Green Parent in the future.

The food was amazing, lots of organic, wholefood options, the vibe was incredible, the people gorgeous and the selection of workshops fantastic. We sang with Mahasukha, danced with Jewels, played didgeridoo, practiced yoga, meditated, listened to poetry and song and much much more. We all had an amazing festival and my eldest said it was the best she had ever been to. When asked why, she explained that "People here are really happy; they aren't just pretending to be. That's what happens when people don't drink." And I think this was a key factor to such a beautiful heart-wide-open experience, there was no alcohol or drugs so nothing to hide behind. People were who they really are. And on that scale, watching a community in action it was quite something to witness. So, we'll definitely be booking tickets for next year's festival. And for those who are looking for something magical and inspirational over the summer, Buddhafield holds various retreats, each with a different focus. I love the sound of the Gandharva Music Retreat in September. Many of the retreats are held at Frog Mill, a wildlife-rich space in Devon. Buddhafield are working to raise money to pay for this land to regenerate areas of woodland and enable them to keep holding events here, such as the Family Friendly from 30th July to 6th August.

M. C., originally published in www.thegreenparent.co.uk

'Dancing Buddhas' is an in-depth look by Daniel Dobbie of angelfishfilms at the crew setting up the Buddhafield Festival 2011. It's at youtube.com/watch?v=tv_oiqpPwqE

BUDDHAFIELD FESTIVAL: THE WORKSHOPS, 2010

Instead of a review, here's the workshop list for Buddhafield 2010: an extraordinary collection of opportunities squeezed into a single weekend! The list was compiled from the collected 'workshop cards' posted on the daily noticeboards: they don't of course include all the spontaneous happenings and meetings that make the Festival so special...

*Opening Ritual - Planting the BuddhaSeed
     followed by...*
Adult Games - daily at 2pm
Advice to the Zen Cook
African Kora Drumming
Aikido
All-night Puja by Dhiramati
Amida Trust
Animal Magic - Touch and Connect
Aromatherapy

Awareness Through Movement

Bach Flower Remedies
Back Massage made Easy
Belly Dancing with Live Drumming
Bhajans
Bhangra and Bollywood dance workshop
Bindoo Babas
Biodanza
Bollywood Dance

Book Binding Made Simple
Bowen Technique
Brazilian Forro - sensual partner dance it's wild...
Breton Dance
Buddhafield East
Buddhafield Retreats Stall
Buddhafield's 6th Annual Poetry Slam
Buddhafield's Got Talent - the Final!
Buddhawheel board game
Buddhist Action at Copenhagen
Building and Maintaining Sustainable Communities
Building Buddhafield - a talk by Satyajit
Building the Buddhaland - Transformation of Self and World through Work

Cabaret Extravaganza
Can Violence Ever be Ethical for Buddhists - a Debate
Capoeira
Chalk-Carving
Children's mindfulness, daily
Comedy Improvisation
Common Loaf Christian Cafe
Compost and Compost Toilets
Conscious Communication - stepping away from the Flames of Anger
Cranio-Sacral Therapy
Creating Grace - using the Arts to Connect
Creating World Peace
Creative Word Games

Dance of Life - delight and thanksgiving
Dances of Universal Peace
Dancing 21 Praises of Tara
Dancing the Rainbow
Dedication of the Shrine
Dhamma Revolution in India, with Bodhidharma
Dharma Inquiry with Christopher Titmuss
Dharma Parlour
Direct Action - explore ideas with climate campers
DIY action: make the change you want to see...
Dowsing and Meditation
Dowsing for Earth Energies
Dream Workshops with Maharatnajyoti
Dressing-Up Dome

Earth Heart Guided Dance
Earth Oven Bread-Making
Eco-Dharma Design
Ecstatic Dance - daily
Education Otherwise
Electric Beats with DJ Clarabelle
Embracing Your Shadow
Emotional Freedom Technique
Envisioning a UK Permaculture Festival
Essentials of Meditation

Evolutionary Parenting with Devapriya

Feeding your Demons
Finding the Courage to Face the World's Troubles
Five Rhythms Dance
Fluid Druid - contact juggling - with crystal balls
Forest Gardens with Tom
Fraser Clark Tribute Talks - the Rave-o-Lution
FreeBuddhistAudio
Future-Friendly Living

Genetics, Plant Breeding, and GM Crops
Green T-Shirt Stencilling
Group Vortex Healing
Having Fun, Making Money, and Helping People
Healing Dance
Healing Garden workshops
Heart-to-Heart Tantra
Hedgehogs
Homeopathy

Indian Head Massage
Indigenous Democracy
Introducing Buzzcomic.com
Introducing EcoDharma Retreat Centre
Introducing Stewards Wood community
Introduction to Buddhist Psychology
Introduction to Men's Work (all welcome)
Introduction to permaculture

Japanese Buddhist Poetry
Karuna Trust

Living Love Tantra for Couples
Living Presence Agata
Lost Horizons Cabaret
Love Angels Temple of Delights at Rupadarshin's Water World
Low Impact Building

Making a Home for Friendly Bugs - children's workshop, in cafe
Making hemp milkshakes
Mandala Making for Children
Martial Arts Bodywork
Matrix Re-Imprinting and EFT - the Freedom Fairy
Meditation No Teaching Just Bells
Meditation Posture Workshop
Meeting the Buddha - story-telling
Metamorphic Technique
Mindfulness of Breathing
Mindfulness, Science, and Well-Being
Mindfulness-Based Stress Reduction
Mitra Ceremony 3pm
Monogamy - past its sell-by date? - a Parallel YoUniversity Debate

Musicians welcome...

Native American Dance
Native American inspired Movement and Voice Ritual
Natural Bee-Keeping
Nature Spirits: How to Talk to a Gnome
Network of Engaged Buddhists
Non-Violent Communication
Non-Violent Direct Action - Lokabandhu

Orchards - their Planting and Management
Padma Pancakes
Padmasambhava Dakini Puja
Permaculture Cafe
Play for the Day by the Buddhafield Children's Theatre Company
Poetry Slam
PolyAmoury - the Way Forwards?
Puja
Q&A with members of the Triratna Buddhist Order

Radical Routes
Rasta and Gospel Songs
Reflections on Zen and Working in the Buddhafield Cafe
Reflexology
Reiki
Releasing Negativity trapped in your DNA
Rites of Passage - Coming of Age in the Wilderness
Ritual art making - making prayer flags
Romantic Love through Buddhist Eyes: a Debate
Roots Reggae Dub Dancehall

Sacred Sexuality
Sacred Sound Meditation
Sakyadhita Buddhist Women's Organisation
Salsa Dancing
Saunas - Saunas - Saunas
Shamanic Journeying
Shamanic Trance Dance
Shambala Warriors - Tales from the Front Line
Shiatsu
Singing in Harmony
Singing with Bee
Small World Solar Stage
Sonic Incense
Soulful Singing with Mahasukha
Sound Bath Journey
Sound Bath Journeys
Sound Healing
Soya or Dairy - Ethics and the Environment
Steve's J's Quality Tat Stall

Story-Telling around the Fire
Sunseed Wholefoods
Swamp Circus circus skills
'Stupa Stomp' Danceitation with Jayagita

2012 Paradigm Shift
Taiji Chi Gung
Talks by and for Young People
Tamalpa work
Taoist Tai Chi
Thai Massage
The Adventures of Perseus, by Vajradaka
The Art of Taking Yourself Less Seriously
The Poet's Way
The Rights of Mother Earth - community video
The Work that Reconnects
Theriaca Anti-Parasite Tea
Toddler Space
Transcendental Dance
Tree Walk
Tribal Trance and Old Skool Beats
Tuning in to the Buddhafield - talk by Kamalashila
Twelve Step Recovery Dome
Uplifting Psy-Trance
Using the Arts to Connect with Ourselves
Veronique's Healing Dance

Walking Meditation
Water and Forests for Life - Reforesting the Himalayas
Web 2.0 - the Community Web Revolution, with Candradasa
What Hippies can Learn from Business
What is a Retreat?
Wild Food and Medicine Walk
Wind turbine demonstration
Wolf at the Door - writing as awakening
Women's Space
Yin Energetic Movement

Yoga, including -
Beginners Yoga
Hatha Yoga
Iyengar Yoga
Laughter Yoga
Pregnancy Yoga
Scaravelli Yoga
Sivananda Yoga
and Yin Yoga

and finally
Zhineng Qigong

and of course the
Closing Ceremony

And the legendary Brian Viziondanz created his own take on the Buddhafield Festival 2010, released shortly before his untimely death the following year. It's still online at www.youtube.com/watch?v=2hWIzlwXyFE

BUDDHAFIELD 2009: REAL FLOWERS

> *Come, see*
> *real flowers*
> *of this painful world*
> - Basho

In 1996, a group of FWBO[18] members, inspired by the *Dharma*, environmentalism, music and ritual set up a fledgling festival. They named it 'Buddhafield', reflecting their aims to make the festival an ideal place to discover Buddhism, to celebrate the Dharma and to explore it in new and innovative ways. In its first year it attracted around 300 people, Buddhists, environmentalists, musicians and individuals.

Over a decade later Buddhafield is now the biggest event in the FWBO calendar outside of India and has firmly staked its place in the British festival circuit. Taking influences from India, gatherings ancient-old and the Buddhist teachings of compassion, awareness and generosity, Buddhafield is like - and unlike - any other festival.

For just under a week in July, it nestles in the green Somerset countryside, not far from Glastonbury town, a small village of fluttering flags, tipis, yurts, gaily painted gypsy caravans and solar powered tents. For many it is a reunion: people stride through the damp grass to greet each other with open smiles and warm hugs. For others it is a chance to see the world they want to live in, alive and thriving, if only for a week.

Officially opening the festival, a parade takes place on the first evening. With red hearts printed on grin-rounded cheeks people sing, dance, drum and cavort their way around the three main fields. Archways, twisted out of bamboo or willow are adorned with brightly coloured flags: red for love, white for mindfulness, blue for truth, yellow for generosity and green for contentment. They mark the openings between the main fields and extol the five Buddhist precepts. They are also points for impulsive art - at the blue point signs celebrating truthful communication are plastered with photographs of Bob Dylan cut from magazines.

The parade ends with singing and dancing in the ritual space, a large circle pegged out with bamboo poles. Each morning and every night a ritual is observed here, celebrating the Dharma and artistic expression. In one, men dressed as skeletons – like characters from the Mexican Day of the Dead – leap around the circle provocatively. In another a play is performed by actors in black lace and top hats.

As night gathers in the corners and shadows of the festival, candles and lanterns are lit and warming braziers glow darkly. The scent of cardamom, cloves and sweet honey encircles the chai tents and it's hard to walk past more than one without being tempted in for a hot mug amongst cushions and laughter. Music jingles and twangs and voices chatter and sing, there are slam poetry events and gigs taking place across the festival: if you have words in you there is a place for them. In one tent, as rain falls coldly outside, folk singer Martha Tilston holds the crammed in crowd rapt with stories and bell-like melodies.

In the morning a mysterious chai woman picks her way through the tents with a thermos calling, 'chai, buy my chai', in a sing-song voice. It's the gentlest wake-up call

---

18 The FWBO is now known as the Triratna Buddhist Community

and people emerge slowly, sleepily from their tents to smile at one another, cupping the warm fragrant tea in chilled hands.

> *"The bird a nest,*
> *the spider a web,*
> *man friendship."*
> - William Blake, Proverbs of Hell

The history of festivals and markets as reunion and gathering points goes way back in many cultures. Historically, they have always been a place where people meet, trade and set deals for the coming year. There is music, food and laughter, more than anything there's connection.

Joanna Macy, the eco-philosopher and Buddhist famed for her 'Work That Reconnects' teaching, repeatedly emphasizes the need to build a sustainable society, a society within the one we live at the moment where each unit becomes more and more connected. In many ways this is what Buddhafield is about, a deep reconnection with each other and with nature. Buddhist and environmentalist Akuppa echoes Joanna Macy's sentiments, arguing that, 'living in harmony with nature is inseparable from living in harmony with each other'. This is perfectly illustrated at Buddhafield: proximity to nature – to darkness, damp and cold – pushes people to find warmth in one another. But this is also where Buddhafield's uniqueness lies. Many festivals are billed as places to escape the daily grind, to forget your worries and fears and party. Connection is natural and friends are made, and lost, easily. At Buddhafield though, there is a sense that things are slower, with no drink or drugs allowed, and with this request largely respected, the edges of experience are not blurred or fuzzy. There is a sense of honesty, nothing can be blamed on the booze, and a deeper connection is allowed to arise.

This is fostered in a variety of ways, cafes are furnished with large tables surrounded by cushions or long benches and people scoff spicy vegetarian thali or fresh, stone baked pizzas alongside one another. Sharing food space breaks down barriers of reserve easily. There are also dance workshops – you can learn Bollywood bhangra or simply shake it in the ecstatic dance tent. Start the day with a singing workshop or get up early and join the tranquil group in the meditation tent. In many ways people are encouraged to do things, not just in the same space, but actually together. There isn't a lot of encouragement needed.

A natural result of this is a kind of freedom, innocence and unrestrained, immediate joy. Most festivals encourage and allow a kind of freedom that is not usually possible in everyday life (ever tried dancing on your desk at work because the sun just came out?) Immediate acceptance breeds spontaneous expression and in the warm atmosphere and gusting rain of last year's Buddhafield people leapt into gleeful dance when the sun momentarily stretched a warm beam down to the soaked earth.

> *Let us reflect on what is truly of value in life,*
> *what gives meaning to our lives,*
> *and set our priorities on the basis of that.*
> The 14th Dalai Lama.

Even the toilets are something special. Buddhafield's aim is to, 'promote greater environmental awareness, mindfulness and loving kindness', creating a community for a week that many people would like to see last all year. Within this community a new, but actually ancient, way of existing in the world and with each other can arise. One of the five precepts that the festival is built around, as well as a central Buddhist principle, is that of generosity. Waste is the first concept to be challenged.

In much western society, waste is to be flushed, thrown or cast away. In Buddhafield's compost toilets it is saved, effluent becomes not waste to be disposed of but a resource to be gathered. In the most basic and unavoidable way festival-goers give back what was taken. Waste becomes compost - useful and valuable.

Where the toilets at most other festivals I've been to are chemical hell boxes or filth pits, the toilets at Buddhafield are clean and open to the air. Neither do they stink – they exude a faint sweet sawdusty scent. This reveals another kind of generosity. The organisers recognise how horrendous an experience many festival toilets are, yet how inevitable their use is. In providing clean, natural and stench-free toilets they are providing a huge kindness to the people who have to use them. This is the kind of community Buddhafield is; grounded in awareness, common-sense and kindness.

These ideas are not new. They are ancient, and not so much ideas as instincts. For centuries people have drawn together as the night gathers over the land. With costumes, music and dancing they tell stories and foster bonds. In England pubs used to be the hub of the town. Now tribes, or families and friendship groups, are often stretched over wide expanses of land or sea. There is global community online but there is something deeper that the Internet hasn't yet been able to provide. A connection stripped of distraction, something akin to that found in music. The sensation of dancing wildly with, not alongside, a group of happy, open people is, at its best, like a twirling, mischievous, brazen answer to death. Music transcends barriers, uniting people with rhythm, it is a wonderful antidote to the human condition of loneliness and fear and its strains pervade the festival.

> *Singing waka, reciting poems, playing ball*
> *together in the fields -*
> *Two people, one heart.*
> Ryokan

It's not only Buddhists at Buddhafield (though all guests are requested to respect the ideals of mindfulness and compassion, to be nice to people and not get drunk!) The sign outside the women's space, colourfully painted and decorated with flowers reads, 'Welcome all women: Dakinis and sisters, grandmothers, witches, fairies, girls, mothers, wise women and wild women, whoever you are - WELCOME'. There are herbal healers, masseurs, people who will tell you about your past or paint a picture of the future. There are Dharma talks and writing workshops. It has been described as a 'marketplace at which we (the FWBO/Triratna community) offered our wares and an atmosphere.' In the end it matters not so much how you define yourself, what matters is that you are there.

Sarah Ryan, previously published in Urthona

BUDDHAFIELD FESTIVAL 2008

The Festival was WONDERFUL! I was only there for the setup, having missed it totally last year, but found myself deeply moved reflecting on what an extraordinary exercise the whole event was in positive relationship building and maintenance. That probably sounds a bit boring but actually it's magic - which means, it enables ordinary people to do extraordinary things. There's perhaps a dozen or so on the Buddhafield core team; by the time the Festival proper starts there must be at least 500 people present, all there entirely for love (and a few free meal tickets!), all there specifically to contribute in some way or other, anything from tractor driving to vegetable chopping to rainbow healing. Which, all put together, adds up to... a festival! And one that by the time I left had sold over 2,000 tickets (more than ever before) and was clearly as much-loved as ever. Buddhafield's field of positive relationships is massive and a joy to witness and be part of.

Lokabandhu, Shabda August 2008,
reproduced with permission

BUDDHAFIELD FESTIVAL 2007

Here's two reviews of the 2007 Festival, both from Festival Eye 2008:

Buddhafields began on the M5 with my guitar and big bag, my hat adorned with all the gifts of special people over the past years and my thumb stuck out into the road.

I was in Birmingham and Buddhafields was in Devon and it was 4 in the afternoon. Many distractions, many faces. Only three cars later and three very happy smiling faces ending with a beautifully simple country couple who only knew how to help people I arrived at 8 o'clock, almost quicker than if I'd driven myself, I was dropped off at the gate. "I'm a journalist"...I never tire of saying that. My ticket in was a handmade clay pendant... the first simple touch of magic that Buddhafield's gives as standard. I pitch my tent next to Sam's Sauna, my second home.

I see and greet the ever-present festival faces that appear in each field that I live in each year and I never tire of them either. The Small World chatters folk into the night behind the hedge that grows between my home and my playground for the next days. It lives next to Moon Beams and Beth, three of my favourite festival things.

Buddhafield's is as close... so far... as you are likely to come to a perfect community of beings living and celebrating the way we all know we should be. We all know how and at Buddhafields we are reminded of that. No drugs and drink leave the air and the smiles as clear as crystal. Add countless children, the Chai Chapel, a lost horizon with a sauna in it, a tribal Tent called Triban, some mud, but also a lot of green grass (very rare in 2007 as I'm sure you are all aware), a community notice board, some pirates, some fairies, some horses, many meditations, many dances and dancers and many naked people including myself and I think you understand. I love it, totally.

Its small, it's pretty, it's clean, and laying back in the Cafe of the festival I look towards the opening in the tent and set against the turbulent blue skies were the special green eyes of a dream-like memory from the Small World early hours of Glastonbury's grey skies. I don't have a choice, I'm already walking towards her and before the cushion I was sitting on could resume its shape I was holding her deeply. Thank you Buddhafield, from the bottom of my heart for giving me this gem again. I could carry on with more description of how the magic in this field left me gleaming and in awe but it's not needed, just go. Don't ever rely on second-hand descriptions of anything, rely on your own experience of the love that is so obvious in Devon and everywhere else, all the time.

J. C-W, Festival Eye

A magic place, only a few fields, only a few hundred people, has the feel of a post-cataclysm community of survivors, living in harmony with nature, practicing rituals to thank mother earth, to thank the universe, a community of earth children practicing all forms of meditation.

No drugs, no dogs.. but a lot a lot of love. Loving interactions, very loving and not sleazy. No, people were loving me like one loves a child.. Buddhafields is such an invitation to play, dress up, dance until you sweat so much you want to take off your clothes, till the earth vibrates so much under your feet that you want to cover yourself with it... dance till sunset, dance till dawn.. in silence.. the whole site turns silent at night... you can hear the fairies breathe.. the earth children gather in tents, or go to their nests in dream land, warm up in Sam's sauna or around the fire of Lost Horizon.. tell stories, have funny competitions, better be a nudist, a pirate or an earth woman...

At the top of a hill, some bells, some shrines and meditation tents.. that's where non-stop, someone is in meditation. It is Buddhafields.. the fields where you're invited to be as playful as a laughing buddha, playing with appearances of this world...

I arrived a little sad, a little lonely.. my landlady smuggled me in. No she just found a job for me as a maid, a maid making sure this land stays clean, green and unspoilt, I was a recycling fairy, like Yvonne, like Maisy and like Peter. You might have met Peter, he's an African man, every festival is his village, he shares countless treasures of songs, he can sing all night, and we all sing-along... 'because the night is made for lovers'

He's an angel, a gem, when he's around everything & everyone seems to shine, because he paints a smile on their faces. Yes in Buddhafields, people seem to like to hang out. We love Peter's and each and every person's company. New souls old friends to meet and connect with, that's what buddhafields is about, a bit of a sorcerers', prehistoric gathering.

Walking around the site, checking out the scene, I was hoping to find the warm silhouette of a special special person - who told me he'd be here. I was hoping to see that man-child again...the one who drummed behind me in Small World stage, two weeks before, on that unforgettable Sunday late late night.. where someone painted my face blue. I danced and sang my way through that night, told stories about how Glastonbury turned me into the Mud Bra Girl... watched the site be dismantled and the earth re-appear under the structures that made a weekend party, the dismantling of a city.

Buddhafields is a tiny village compared to Glastonbury monster, it's a nymph's paradise, a microcosm, you might discover under a droplet of dew. I'm not the mud bra girl here, it's too clean. No I'm the recycling fairy. Each festival made me into some new character, a new game to play.

I walked and found many happy faces, a flock of naked people, running on the green grass. Yes Buddhafields was green. Mmhhhhhhhhhh.. I found many dustbins, but none was full enough to be dragged all the way to the recycling 'bennes'. My guide and colleague Maisy knew the job, She said we have to have a chai break. We stopped at buddhafields cafe and gazing through the huddled crowd I meet warm, surprised, welcoming, embracing eyes, like a dream come true. I don't move - they come closer. They're blue, I don't move, they're diving deep inside my green eyes and as I close them I melt into the embrace of a healing hug. It's like coming home - Now you'll think I say Buddhafields is full of love because I was filled with loving eyes when I've been. Maybe. Maybe it's just the place that's magic, and people fall in love there.

Spent the next days following butterflies, dancing in the mud, dressing with leaves, dancing at late hours with umbrellas like in 'parapluies de cherbourg', singing made up and memories of Russian and French songs to an accordion, against tasty crepes, running about and sliding in the mud down the only slope with excited munchkins, hugging and humming with a crowd of hundreds, discovering wonder stars and galaxies in the tent and coming out all smiley, and the smiles passed on very fluidly, dynamically through the whole site...and I kept on doing my recycling fairy job....

C.S., Festival Eye

BUDDHAFIELD FESTIVAL 2006

2006 saw the launch of the 'Dharma Parlour', a new space in the Festival designed to give the Buddhist element of the Festival a much higher profile. It was also planned to open up opportunities to more consciously include Dharma teachers from other traditions to Triratna. Here's a report from Akasati, followed by reviews from Padmavajra and Kavyasiddhi. Akasati says -

This was the year we gave the Dharma a higher profile - it's always been there but you had to work a bit to seek it out. There's a whole discussion happening about our relationship to other teachers / groups. Briefly, Christopher Titmuss coming (as well as some others from different Buddhist groups) and being a dynamic presence in the Dharma Parlour was overall a positive experience in the view of pretty well everyone who was involved this year. I felt we in the Order rose to the challenge and presented ourselves clearly, confidently - and dynamically. And undefensively - people pick up on these things. Christopher seems to have been a kind of catalyst, & I'm grateful to him, Jenny and his other friends & colleagues as well.

Mandarava flowers & general rejoicings...

Shabda August 2006,
reproduced with permission

Dear Friends, I have just attended my first ever Buddhafield festival and I want to salute the team of order members, mitras and friends who run Buddhafield. They are doing incredible work and deserve all praise.

Some of my friends expressed surprise when they heard that I was going to Buddhafield and, I have to say, that I was bit surprised myself! But Akasati asked me if I would come and give a talk in the Dharma Parlour. As I like to respond to any request to communicate the Dharma, I just said yes! And I am very glad that I did.

Buddhafield is a quite extraordinary event. I think there were about 2000 people there doing all sorts of things: ecstatic dance, different kinds of healing, cabarets, slam poetry etc etc. There's loads of things for children - it's a paradise for them. I tended to wander around taking things in, talking to people - lots of old friends.

You end up in some strange spaces, like seeing an insane and hilarious Buddhist game show in The Lost Horizons Tent, in which Padmapani (who had only gone to the place for a late night sauna out the back) ended up a joint winner. It involved some extraordinary natural, spontaneous creativity from Padmapani, which left me in tears of laughter and admiration. The game show came after some deeply stirring singing by an astonishingly beautiful Sephardi woman singing in Ladino songs of longing for the Beloved! And the Buddhafield atmosphere. Perhaps, above all, the atmosphere. It's just so easy and friendly.

Which seems pretty remarkable to me, that so many can come together, doing such different things in such an easy friendly way. That atmosphere flows from the Buddhafield Team. Out of the corner of your eye you see them working away with great dedication and friendliness.

It's said that one of the ways a Bodhisattva benefits beings is by providing festivity, opportunities for people to come together in a festive way - a skilfully festive way. Well, I think the Buddhafield Sangha are certainly doing that. And a lot of Dharma teaching goes on as well. In the midst of the drumming, the dance, the music, the children's processions, there was a lot of Dharma teaching and discussion, meditation and puja going on. I was very pleased to sit in the Dharma Parlour listening to order members communicate the Dharma so clearly, so well and with their own voice. I had a go at it myself and I hope that I get another chance to do some more of it in the future.

So, big shouts of Sadhu to the Buddhafield Sangha. You are doing great work, may it grow and thrive.

Padmavajra, Shabda August 2006,
reproduced with permission

Hello all, I want to say how much I enjoyed being in the Dharma Parlour at the 10th Buddhafield Festival. The Parlour was an area with half a dozen spaces of various sizes, offering a mix of activism and Buddhism: people packed the place out - to find out about deep ecology [thanks Akuppa and Guhyapati], about The Work That Reconnects, and to hear talks by people who practice the Buddha-Dharma day in and day out, who try to live in accord with How Things Really Are.

A theme – a celebration! – emerged: wherever or whoever you are, now is the perfect place to practice. Tim Malnick.said this on the first day and then everyone, memorably Karunagita and Amaragita ("I want a baby! Just a small one!") in their talks on parenting demonstrated that you *can* practice anywhere.

Hearing such diverse and mundane ways to apply the teachings was fantastic. All nine speakers reminded me, in their own way, that trying to apply the Dharma is the most important thing to do with my life.

And yet something so important can be expressed and received lightly – with humour and affection. Kamalashila pointed out, when he and Padmavajra spoke so beautifully and passionately on Sunday, that the Bodhisattva offers festivity. For which I am heartily relieved and deeply grateful.

I've heard a bit of chuntering over the years - mostly to the effect of Buddhafield being an unwashed nest of feel-good hippies - and I wonder if this is one of the last polarities in the F/WBO: 'They are like this, I am like that'. True, there is drumming, but there are also hot showers and regular meals. Shaving is permitted.

I was nervous when I first went on a Buddhafield retreat, fearing enforced nudity and tent fascism, but they're very welcoming. This time I turned up with a suit carrier and feather duster and no one batted an eye.

During the Festival I'd sit in the field and watch the beautiful slope of green, peopled by an ever-moving stream of kids, circus folk, shamans, healers, Dharma teachers and people on their holidays: the whole spectrum of 'Goa meets the Village Fete' which is the Buddhafield Festival. The joy and acceptance really touched me.

And it is definitely a branch of the FWBO tree. A playful, hard working, idiosyncratic and collective branch. At the risk of sounding like a big fat hippy - albeit one with a linen wardrobe - thanks to EVERYONE who cared enough to make it happen: the speakers, the painters, the makers of tea and washers of cups. Especially to all those on the Buddhafield Team who took the risk of putting the entrance to the Dharma at the entrance of the Festival.

You built a Buddhafield.

Kavyasiddhi, Shabda August 2006,
reproduced with permission

BUDDHAFIELD FESTIVAL 2003: PEACE AND LOVE? YOU BUDDHA BELIEVE IT!

It was back to the days of peace and love at last week's Buddhafield event on the Blackdown Hills when 2,000 people, most of them young, got together to sing, dance and learn more about their religion. From Wednesday to Sunday the 30-acre site at the Gallop near Clayhidon was taken over by friends of the Western Buddhist Order for their annual outdoor festival, which took the theme of Touching Earth.

But unlike many other outdoor festivals, this one had a policy of no alcohol, no drugs and no dogs. There was hardly any loud amplified music and, unusually, the police said no crimes had been reported during the five-day event. The licensing authority, Mid Devon District Council, was also pleased with the way things went.

People in Wellington may have wondered about the weird and wonderful folk they saw walking around the town during the event, so the Wellington Weekly News decided to see for itself what was going on.

When we visited the site on Friday afternoon, someone told us it was rather like the early days of the Glastonbury Festival before it became such a giant commercialised event.

The calm, non-threatening atmosphere was certainly impressive - unlike the centre of Wellington on a Friday or Saturday night.

There was a lot of opposition to the holding of the event by some local people and the organisers made great efforts to ensure any disturbance to neighbours was kept to a minimum. Representatives of the Devon and Cornwall Police, the Devon Fire Brigade and Mid Devon District Council were on site to see that the many conditions imposed before a licence was granted were complied with.

Although the atmosphere was very laid back, a lot of work had obviously gone into the organisation of the event with loos, showers, a sauna and a vegetarian cafe all provided to meet the physical needs of the festivalgoers.

Their spiritual needs were also well looked after with a beautifully decorated worship tent and areas for healing and meditation - very important aspects of the Buddhist religion.

Altogether, around 600 people were involved in running the festival, which must be one of the biggest such events to be held in the area.

The busy programme included classes in dance and music and a whole range of workshops ranging from nanotechnology to compost making. There was also plenty to occupy the many children at the festival with trampolines and swingboats, and plenty of opportunities to dress up and take part in plays and processions. The main aim seemed to be to encourage the children to be creative and be aware of and care for their environment.

One of the organisers, a "gentle" man with the name of Lokabandhu, told us that Buddhafield was the outreach branch of the Western Buddhist Order which has 20 centres throughout the country offering teaching and retreats.

"We are a community which does things out of doors and we visit various festivals around the country as well as have our annual Buddhafield event, " he said.

"This is our eighth event and the second at The Gallop. Our strict no alcohol and no drugs policy is important as a lot of people who come have suffered from both in the past.

Lokabandhu stressed they tried to buy as many supplies as possible in the area around the festival site to help the local economy and aimed to leave the site as they found it.

"We are keen to have good relations with our neighbours and cause as little disturbance to them as possible, " he said.

We also met the owners of the field, Steve and Margaret Lee, who were pleased with what they had seen as they walked around the site. "We see this as a way of bringing town and country together, " said Steve.

On Monday a spokesman for the Devon and Cornwall Police told us: "There were no crimes reported during the festival - everyone seemed to be very well behaved. If only that would happen at every similar event."

That sentiment was echoed by Marjory Parish, Mid Devon's licensing officer. "We have been on site and found nothing to complain about, " she said.

"We have had just one complaint about noise, but we were monitoring noise and found no evidence to substantiate that complaint." Mrs Parish said the organisers had been very co-operative.

"The atmosphere was very relaxed and everything came together as we had hoped."

From the Wellington Weekly News:

But it wasn't an easy ride getting permission to hold the Festival in 2003! Here's three more articles from the same paper describing some of the dramas in the lead-up to the event. You have to admire their headline writers' talent for punning...!

DOZENS WANT FESTIVALS NIPPED IN THE BUDDHA

16 April 2003

Many residents in the Clayhidon and Hemyock areas have written to Mid Devon District Council objecting to the staging of two summer festivals near their homes. Today (Wednesday) the council's licensing committee will consider applications to hold the Buddhafield event between July 16-20 and another by the Tribe of Doris from August 20-25.

Following similar events last year the council received a number of complaints about noise and general disturbance - and already this year the council has received 25 letters objecting to Buddhafield and 17 to the Tribe of Doris event. There have also been nine letters of support, however.

A leaflet calling on people to object to the Tribe of Doris application has been circulating in the area, claiming that "summer in Clayhidon could again be disrupted by incessant drumming".

The theme of this year's Buddhafield event will be "Touching Earth" and it will include Buddhist practices, yoga, meditation, debates, workshops, musical performances and children's activities.

The organisers say: "As Western Buddhists, our focus will be on non-violence, meditation, creation of real community and living in harmony with the local environment. There will be a no drugs, no alcohol and no dogs policy on site." This application is for 1,900 people - as opposed to 1,400 last year - and the organisers say it will finish each evening at 11pm except for the Saturday, when they want permission to go on until midnight.

The Tribe of Doris says it runs "a rich programme of culturally diverse workshops in order to foster the aims of our organisation". These are to promote friendship and understanding between people of different cultural backgrounds through participation in the arts of drum, dance, song and ceremony.

They say the event is acoustic, there is a "no dogs" policy on site and they "do not condone the use of illegal drugs".

The application is for 1,000 people, 300 more than last year. Organisers have requested a finish time of 11.30pm except for the Sunday night, when they want to go on until 2am.

In her report on the applications, council licensing officer Marjory Parish says: "Such events are not silent, although the music at the Buddhafield event last year was quiet and barely audible at the boundary.

"However, the drumming from Doris was clearly audible and on some occasions carried some distance." She said some of the fencing of the site was less than satisfactory, but fears about pollution had been unfounded, and the fact that the site was in an Area of Outstanding Natural Beauty had no bearing on whether such an application should be granted.

Mrs Parish concludes: "These events, and now these applications, have aroused strong feelings and do intrude, no matter how sensitively they are managed, into what is normally a very peaceful part of the countryside.

"When one is used to almost total silence, any kind of noise could be felt to be a violation."

Among those objecting to the applications to hold the festivals is Clayhidon Parish Council, which believes the site is unsuitable for such events. The council is particularly against the Tribe of Doris event, which it says will produce "very intrusive noise over a period of six days".

Councillors at Hemyock are also concerned about the festivals and at their April meeting they agreed that if they do take place, Mid Devon District Council must enforce any conditions imposed on the organisers.

One of the organisers of Buddhafield, a man called Lokabanghu, has written to Mrs Parish after reading some of the objections.

He says: "Reading them, I have to say I did find the language used in several cases to be rather intemperate. What concerns me more objectively, however, is that the facts of the case were often misrepresented; what is alleged to have happened, simply did not.

"I hope they won't stand as a record of historical fact. What comes to mind is the famous comment on Lady Macbeth: 'Methinks the lady doth protest too much'."

LOCALS ALREADY BIDDING TO STOP 2004 FESTIVALS
19 June 2003

Clayhidon villagers have launched a campaign to stop two new age festivals being held near their homes next year - well before this year's events have even taken place. Permission has already been given for the Buddhafield festival from July 16-20, while a similar event staged by the Tribe of Doris is scheduled for August 20-25.

Both events were given permission to party in a field known as The Gallop by members of Mid Devon District Council's licensing committee in April, despite 45 letters of objection.

Now opponents are busy rallying the troops in an effort to prevent similar events being given permission in 2004.

The fight is being led by Clayhidon Parish Council, which believes the disturbance caused by an estimated 3,000 festivalgoers is intolerable for people more used to the peace and quiet of the countryside.

Councillors have sent leaflets to villagers, urging them to act now to prevent repeat performances next year.

And they left members of the district council in no doubt of the strength of their feelings when they lobbied them at a committee meeting last week.

But they could have a hard battle on their hands as neither the police, the fire service nor the Environment Agency lodged any objections to this year's licence applications, while nine letters were received by the council supporting the festival plans.

Parish council vice-chairman Michael Hudson said drumming sessions staged by Tribe of Doris followers were particularly distressing for local residents.

He said the tribe brought an estimated 100 drums which could be heard several miles away.

Cllr Hudson added: "We are anxious that these festivals should not become established in the parish.

"They cause considerable disruption and are spread over several days, with a high production of noise." District council officials have already slapped noise curfews on both of this year's festivals in the hope of minimising disturbance.

All festivities must cease by 11pm each night, although festivalgoers will be able to party until midnight on the last day of each event.

Tribe of Doris organisers had asked for permission to party until 2am on the final Sunday of their festival.

While the tribe runs workshops in drumming, dance, song and ceremony in order to promote friendship and understanding between people of different cultures, the Buddhas practise yoga and meditation, hold debates, organise children's activities and stage musical performances.

This will be the second year running that the two festivals have been held at The Gallop.

FESTIVALS GO AHEAD AFTER FOUR-HOUR DEBATE

23 April 2003

After more than four hours of debate Mid Devon District Council's licensing committee has agreed to grant public entertainment licences for two summer festivals in fields near Clayhidon. Despite many objections from local residents, the Buddhafield event will go ahead from July 16-20 and the other by the Tribe of Doris from August 20-25.

The five-member committee heard from those opposed to the events, but also from council officers who gave a full report on the background including some of the problems faced following similar events last year.

Objectors claimed that last year they suffered noise, trespass and disturbance. Many felt such events should not take place in an Area of Outstanding Natural Beauty.

But the committee was told in the report from officers: "Noise from these two events last year did not give rise to statutory nuisance and neither the police nor fire service are objecting to this year's applications." Both groups of organisers said there would be a no-dogs policy on the site and the Buddhists added there would be no drugs or alcohol.

The Tribe of Doris said it did not "condone illegal drugs".

Although the committee approved both licence applications, members did lay down a number of conditions which will have to be complied with by the organisers.

On Buddhafield, the committee insisted that all three fields on the site should be made available for the event and that all activities connected with the festival should adhere strictly to the dates applied for and not several days before.

All tickets will have to be pre-sold and all ticket holders will have to be off the site by 6pm on July 21. No more than 1,900 people should be on site during the event, which will be restricted to between 11am and 11pm, except on Saturday July 19 when it will be allowed to continue until midnight.

All security fences must be installed before the event and approved by the council's head of environmental health, who will also be authorised to deal with all other licence conditions.

The conditions for the Tribe of Doris event will be similar, except that the number of people will be restricted to 1,000. Tickets holders will have to be off the site by 6pm on

Tuesday August 26 and activities will be restricted to between 11am to 11pm, except on Sunday August 24 when they will be able to continue until midnight.

The committee also insisted that "drumming activities should be held at the bottom of the top field".

BUDDHAFIELD 2002: BUDDHAFIELD'S BEST YET

The Buddhafield Festival was improved by a move to a new site in 2002 which is situated a few miles from Taunton, on the Black Down Hills. The site was on high ground in two fields and sheltered from the road and breezes by high hedges round its perimeter. Car parking and camping was at the top end of the site. Moving away from the gate you soon came to the main festival area where you found 'shanty style tarpaulin structure's and tepees selling organic fruit and veg, colourful ambient chill-out lounges and workshops where you could do everything from dream-catcher making to tie-dying and lots more besides. The two main marquees had stages with 12v systems, powered by people, wind and sun. These hosted entertainment from many different styles and cultures.

Jazzy-Folk, Tribal Rhythms. The general running order went something like: Mornings-Song, dance, spiritual yoga and musical workshops. Afternoons- Folk and Country singing with guitars and violins etc., leading on to the evening with acoustic bands playing jazzy-folk, tribal rhythms and ambient dance music.

Cafe Society. A few small Chai-Tea bars were dotted around and another marquee for yoga and meditation was next to a spiritual healing garden and created a really nice area to be in. The second field was quieter and more open and Buddhafield Café did a grand job here, supplying different choices of appetising platefuls daily. The 'kids area' was well organized, busy & arranged the daily procession, around the site. A play, following a Buddhist theme, was put on by the children, coordinated by Helen & Amanda of magical youth.

A Fine Show. There were spaces too for healing and discussions, candle-lit shrines and creativity in abundance, all brought together in a caring sharing environment, with a happy energetic vibe. Several compost toilets were built around the site and kept clean throughout.

The event was a fine show of Buddhist principles in practice and the people who attend benefited from a policy of 'No Drugs, No Drink, and No Dogs'. All in all Buddhafield festival was one of the most peaceful, friendly and beautifully sited events We've had the pleasure to attend. The organisers deserve a meddle!

A.S., D&L, Festival Eye

BUDDHAFIELD FESTIVAL 2000: WHEN RURAL ENGLAND MEETS BUDDHISM MAGIC HAPPENS...

The marriage of the Celtic dance and Buddhist serenity created heaven on earth at the most sublime one-off gathering of like- souls in 2000. Held at Shepton Mallet's back- door overlooking the delicious green pastures of Somerset, the setting for the BuddhaField Festival was truly spectacular

The space had been spiritually attuned in the weeks prior to the camp and this energy was strongly felt and sustained for the duration. Extremely well-priced, Buddhafield provided more than enough facilities to go around: a spacious, sing-songy sauna; a hot NB; a hot and cold shower; well-placed compost toilets; the famously delicious and nutritious Buddhafield Cafe; Helen Hat's crazy Kids Area; meditation spaces; a Healing Area with a diverse range of healing; a Chai Tent and more, more, more... It was a Festival for Every Age.

The only challenge was choosing in which of the many workshops and activities to indulge, though that's hardly a negative! Among the abundant selection were Five Elements Dance, Afro-Caribbean dance, African Drumming, yoga, sound baths, a myriad of other singing and dance workshops, and too much more to list! Yet again there was great abundance in the evening entertainment which ranged from Bristol's Samba collective, singer extraordinaire Juliet Russell leading the Buddhafield Choir (comprising over 200 festival-goers) and favourite group, Earthsong, on the mainstage, to chilled-out DJ's in the Chai Tent.

Catering for every age and with a strict no-drugs or alcohol policy (it's Buddhist, remember!), Buddhafield is a Festival for all. Groovy dance areas contrasted wonderfully with spiritual practices. A great variety of choice In idyllic camping areas made the stay even more perfect (as if it could have been...

The Buddhafield Festival is co-ordinated and run by the Friends of the Western Buddhist Order (FWBO). Watch for details their 6th Buddhafield Festival 11-15 July 2001, and various retreats and events on their website http://www.buddhafield.com

If you can go to only one camp this mid-summer, make it this one!

Festival Eye

BUDDHAFIELD '99: PAGANS MEET BUDDHISTS AND PARTY!!

Given that this small festival was on my favourite site in the West Country - nay - one of my favourites in the whole country - it was off on a winner for me immediately. The weather was glorious and the quiet, lushly green sight was clean and open, with 2 magnificent Oak trees towering over the clear spaces between the camping and holistic areas.

Water was reasonably well provided, but if the participants hadn't been so mellow and friendly, disputes might have grown over the wait for the taps, as I personally only discovered 3 water supplies, although that isn't to say there weren't more in other parts of the site. Loos were a bit of a problem too as there weren't very many compost bogs on sight, although those that were provided were solidly made, provided with good supplies of sawdust and even toilet paper. In addition, at night (a nice touch this) lanterns lit the way into the edge of the wood were the toilets were to be found. Unfortunately, some scummy people decided to shit in the woods and not cover it up rather than queue for the toilets like the rest of the VERY civilised crowd who attended.

Stewarding was well organised, friendly and mellow although organisers were strict about no vehicles on site which meant the walk up to the top of the camping area could be a bit of a drag if you had loads of tat to set up. There was actually a site wheelbarrow to aid in this job, but unfortunately I didn't notice it till to late. However, there were loads of friendly people around who appeared willing to help carry gear up the field, and we even had offers of help to set up the tent and fill the water container!! I can't remember when I last attended a festival when that happened!

So, having set up, and become on friendly terms with the neighbours, (many of whom were Buddhists from Brighton or previous attendees of the festival who had come back for more) it was time to explore. Although not a very large site it had everything one could want - a number of very reasonably priced tat stalls - particularly good clothes and even notices up for two fairly yummy vehicles which I checked out enviously in the car park! Food was good and reasonably priced 'cos the Buddhafield cafe is of course a staple of many festivals, workshops were abundant most of which had a Buddhist or ecologically responsible themes. As an unreconstructed pagan, I did not however feel excluded or unwelcome in any way. I soon managed to find a large contingent of fire dancers/swingers and jugglers with whom I hung out for most of my time at the site, all coming out to play as soon as it got dark.

The kids workshop and entertainments were superbly organised, and a brilliant strap-in gyroscope kept both adults and kids enthralled. Solar /wind-powered energy kept the main stage going which had a variety of good bands until quite late in the evening. A second, smaller acoustic stage also kept the music coming and there was definitely a nostalgic feeling reminiscent of old style small festivals around the site! This was particularly noteworthy in the fact that people felt perfectly relaxed walking around with little or no clothes on and knowing that they would not be leered at or objected to. In all a glorious, relaxing few days with time to talk to people, lay around in the sun, practise that fire swinging/juggling or whatever it was you've been meaning to do for ages. Meander down to the stage and catch a band and straggle off to bed after another long conversation on the meaning of life...

Oh yes, and the hot tub was good too ...

But for me one of the highlights of the entire festival was the appearance of the brightly innovative LIBRARY!! This was a supremely chilled Out space away from the heat of some of the hottest days of the year, with books on every subject you could desire, from motor mechanics to obscure theological doctrines, astrology, tarot, herbalist, sci-fi novels etc. No books could be removed from the library and no bags in the space just in case, but you could lay back and read drink a cup of home-made elderflower cordial or ginger beer, or even a cup of tea and smoke a roll up whilst debating on this and that with your other bookworm neighbours! I even went to sleep in there one afternoon nice one you people who lent your personal books for the common good - it made everything so civilised!

Finally, this festival is very realistically priced and, whilst deserving to become better known, I hope it does not change the character too much as a result of growing to a larger size, as it inevitably will! Speaking personally, we'll be back.

Festival Eye

BUDDHAFIELD 1998: AS FLUFFY AS IT GETS!

Buddhafield festival is nestled cosily on a hillside, which hosts a variety of events, including the Tribe of Doris. This site is quiet, green and perfect for a Buddhist festival. The organisers of the event had just finished a ten-day retreat so the gate crew were dishing out 'big love' as well as wristbands to new arrivals.

This is a fairly new event in the festie calendar but I think it's set to stay as it has all the right ingredients and a lot of good karma. It's organised by a group of Buddhists based mainly in Brighton. A lot of the crowd, there, were also from Sussex and had gone the year before, so most people seemed to know each other. But the warm, openness extended by everyone there meant no one was an outsider

There were the usual elements of any festival: kid's area, healing area, workshops, and cafes The Buddhafield organisers do catering at other festivals so the food was tops, varied, vegetarian and reasonably priced. If you're not shy try the open-air, mixed hot tubs. Not much live music was planned but there were spontaneous bursts of music during the camp, the best being a wake-up call from a soulful saxophone one morning. Blissful notes echoed around the site, symbolising the whole theme of the camp.

But this wasn't the sort of event where getting a copy of a programme was important, or even necessary. The emphasis was on being social rather than active, so most people just sat and talked to each other. I mean really talked to each other. None of your banal, bland chitchat, this was about caring and sharing, loving and living, laughing and crying, feeling at peace with yourself and the world. I know that sounds like an advert for a bank, but it really was like that.

It's the place to go if you want to spend a few days wrapped in a virtual duvet. But they do need to sort out their loos, a problem the organisers are dealing with in time for the next event.

Festival Eye

BUDDHAFIELD FESTIVAL 1997: PILTON BECOMES THE BUDDHA'S LAND

Buddhafield heads to Buddha's Land. Mellow as Glasto is hectic and only a stone's throw from Pilton's famous swamp bash. This was the second innings for this beautiful little event where rain didn't stop play, not that it had either when it poured at Pilton Mega City, the fortnight before.

Buddhafield was a stark contrast to Glastonbury Festival and was more like a camp than a festival. Lots of happy faces, sorted utilities, pleasant friendly crew, reasonably priced vegetarian/vegan food, children well catered for, I can't actually think of anything bad to say about Buddhafield. All in all I think the event was well planned and the organisers got the balance just about right. If you are looking to go to a safe, enjoyable, children friendly camp/festival then you would be pushed to find a better one. Attendance under 500.

A.S., Festival Eye

And here's two reviews for the first-ever Buddhafield Festival, held in July 1996 on Teddy Stone's field outside Shepton Mallet. The first is from Festival Eye, visiting Buddhafield for the first time (well, it didn't exist before!) Some of the details aren't quite right, but Buddhafield was delighted to get such a positive review, delighted also that it'd pulled it off at all, especially that it had succeeded in its core ambition: to draw together a rich and interesting mix of Buddhists and activists from around the UK...

BUDDHAFIELD FESTIVAL 1996

The 1996 Buddhafield Festival took place at Shepton Mallet in August. It was organised by Lokabhandu from Friends Of The Western Buddhist Order, and originally set up as a movement to teach meditation at festivals and camps across Britain. Around 400 people gathered together for one week.

The previous week there had been a Buddhist retreat, and many of those religious folk remained camping on the site for the festival. However, I am not a Buddhist and many others were not, and although there was the odd person who tried to encourage you to join the movement, you could more or less do what you wanted to.

The activities there ranged from hourly debates on... guess what? Buddhism, protests, drugs, society, etc, as well as creative workshops (eg. lampmaking), spiritual workshops (eg. Tai chi, Reiki Healing etc), acoustic music workshops, sweatlodges, conscious cinema showings (footage on protests and festivals) etc. You get the general picture?

There were various provisions and workshops for children, who put on a play for everyone which explored deforestation. There were a few clothes stalls and food stalls which were fairly cheap for a good veg stew in the evening, but during the day there was a choice of veggie sausages and veggie sausages. Firewood was provided and you could always cook your own food this way. If you wanted to sell, cook, protest, teach or perform music, then the site was all yours to play with. The field was situated in beautiful countryside and it was at the peak of the hot weather. Everything, I seem to remember, was golden.

The most interesting part of this festival was the diversity of people apparent in the hourly debates, held in one of the tents. It seemed to be a positive centre for spiritualists and environmentalists to meet up. Towards the end of the week, a gathering of people from Newbury, Tepee Valley and the Buddhist movement swarmed the tent arguing the best ways to combat capitalist greed (which seemed quite ironic to me).

If you couldn't afford entry then Lokabandhu was pretty willing to sort out something so that you could come and join the festivities and the arguments. The last night of the festival, Parallel YoUniversity put on a rave which was very enjoyable and was, incidentally, advertised on the flyer. However, many were surprised and angry by the noise of techno and they created such a fuss that I doubt there will be a sound system this year. At the same time, there was a large tent each evening with lots of drum beats, guitars and acoustic sounds, so it wouldn't really matter.

Overall this was an immensely enjoyable experience, one not to miss. Despite all the debates, the general spiritual vibe showered a degree of respect on most people, and when I left the festival I felt as if my energy had had a thorough clean out. There was abundant love, peace and smiles, stemming from the many rituals performed in that glorious field.

On the last hour the entire group of 400 or so met up around the tree and performed a ritual of thanks to the Universe. For me, this was not a festival, but a retreat and marriage between the spirit and the environment.

E.O., Festival Eye

ClearVision, Triratna's own in-house video production company, had also sent a crew to cover this strange new event in the Buddhist world, which had been boldly billed, *pace* Shantideva, as "A Festival of Temporary and Ultimate Delight". Released as part of the 'FWBO Newsreel 11', it's now on YouTube at youtube.com/watch?v=lzhYffdPtw4

BUDDHAFIELD'S THEMES YEAR BY YEAR

For many years now Buddhafield has chosen a theme for the annual Buddhafield Festival and in some cases its carried over into the rest of that year's programme. As time has gone by and the project has matured the annual themes have become more central to Buddhafield's whole approach over the year, informing its Dharma talks, rituals, retreat themes, artwork and more. Collected here for the first time are all its themes going back nearly 20 years; where possible together with the 'blurb' used in that year's publicity - some, sadly, have faded into the mists of time, and we can offer only their titles.

Often there will have been a story behind why exactly the theme was chosen that year. In 2001, for instance, the Buddhafield Festival had moved to a new site in the Blackdown Hills and built a set of very beautiful 'living willow' compost toilets which it planned to use again and again. The local planners, however, decided that these, despite basically being just trees with chicken wire netting around them, constituted "permanent structures" and ordered their removal. Buddhafield appealed, and chose "Are you Vacant or Engaged?" for its theme for the year as the appeal process ground slowly on. And in 2014, in order to give the core team space to envision a new way forwards for the project, the Buddhafield Festival took its first break in over 15 years, the team choosing 'Dreaming the New' as their theme.

2016 - COURAGEOUS COMPASSION

It takes courage to open up to suffering, whether our own or that of others. Our habitual responses towards suffering tend to be to ignore it, to withdraw, to react with anxiety, or to engage in compulsive activity. Within the Buddhist tradition, the archetypal figure of Tara exemplifies opening up to suffering with courageous compassion. She has one leg folded up in the posture of profound meditation, and the other leg firmly in the world ready for compassionate action. Her sublime meditation informs and motivates her compassionate response. Only a heart that is tranquil and liberated through compassion can see things as they truly are, and take action accordingly.

Tara exemplifies the genuine compassion, born of wisdom, that, although often obscured, is natural to every one of us. This year we will explore how to cultivate the courage to open up to the suffering we see in the world in this moment, as well as to the suffering of future beings who are affected by our actions now, and to respond with wisdom and compassionate action.

2015 - AWAKENED AWARENESS

By awakening our awareness we can engage in the world with a deepened presence and can begin to mindfully sustain ourselves in our daily lives, in community and in the wider world. By feeling the benefit of sustaining all life, we can become empowered to thrive.

The whole of Buddhist practice rests on awakening our awareness, coming awake to our present moment experience: the practice of Mindfulness. Everything flows from this: compassion, ethics, Insight and freedom. Through it we can transform ourselves and our world.

2014 - DREAMING THE NEW

Experiences are preceded by mind,
led by mind,
produced by mind.
The Buddha

Buddhism teaches that all experience originates in the mind and that our skilful intentions lead to positive change. The image of the Buddha itself is a vision of the positive intention to awaken. To find new sustainable models for living, rooted in an ancient relationship with the natural world, we must first envisage the world we wish to see. Together, we must dream the new.

Go Confidently in the direction of your dreams.
Live the life you've imagined.
Henry David Thoreau

2013 - FIRE IN THE HEART

2012 - DOORWAYS TO FREEDOM

2011 - FINDING ABUNDANCE

The theme this year is ABUNDANCE - as in the richness of nature and all that we have around us and within us without needing material wealth. So cultivating gratitude, generosity, non-clinging, and an awareness of the rich inner life that is available to us all at all times.

The theme doesn't refer to material wealth or material possessions. It is not about that craving we all get for something shiny that costs an arm and a leg. It refers to celebrating the bountiful world around us, thanking the earth for her treasures, thanking each other for the love and support that we all receive in one form or another. It refers to the warm fuzzy feeling we get when we make someone laugh. It's about our inner goldenness and not about desire for a lump of yellow rock!

2010 - A FORCE FOR GOOD IN THE WORLD

2009 - TRUTH & BEAUTY: SKILFUL LIVING IN A CHANGING WORLD

2008 - DANCE OF THE ELEMENTS

2007 - A LIVING MANDALA: THE MAGIC OF COMMUNITY

2006 - DHARMA WARRIORS TRANSFORMING SELF & WORLD

2005 - INTERCONNECTEDNESS: THE JEWELLED NET

Far away in the heavenly abode of the great god Indra, there is a wonderful net which stretches out indefinitely in all directions. At the net's every node hangs a single glittering jewel; since the net is infinite, the jewels are infinite in number. There hang the jewels, glittering like stars...If we select one jewel and look closely, we discover that in its polished surface are reflected all the other jewels in the net, infinite in number. Not only that, but each of the jewels reflected in this one jewel is also reflecting all the other jewels, so that the process of reflection is infinite.......

We think of ourselves as a separate self. But by doing this we chop the net or web of life into separate pieces and obscure our true identity. Our true identity is much bigger:

it reflects and contains the whole web. Experiencing our true identity is freedom.....we naturally become kinder to ourselves, to others, and to all life......we come home.

2004 - BUDDHA-NATURE: THE LOTUS UNFOLDS...

We are part of each other. We are part of the earth and the earth is part of us. There is no gap or seam between ourselves and the whole of the phenomenal universe. The natural world mirrors back to us our own, true, Buddhanature. Can we still be that Buddhanature when standing in the fire of what most challenges us, in the demon fires of ignorance, hatred, injustice, greed? Can the lotus bloom in the fire? Let the Lotus of our True Nature unfold, releasing joy, compassion, acceptance and wisdom.

The Red Lotus is associated with Amitabha, the Buddha of the Western quarter, of love and compassion, and also Padmasambhava, the Lotus-Born, the great magician of transformation. The White Lotus is connected with Avalokitesvara, the Bodhisattva of Compassion. His mantra is OM MANI PADME HUM. When we chant this mantra with good intent we help bring compassion into the world.

2003 - TOUCHING EARTH

Today we desperately need to restore Right Relationship with the natural world. If in gratitude we give her honour and respect, our human lives and spiritual struggles will be supported – if not, we may all perish.

We call upon all to reflect on our own earth relationships: celebrating the positive, as we become more conscious of our interdependence with Nature; enjoying the beauty and freedom of living lightly; discovering new skills and myths and magics through which to acknowledge and transform the negative in ourselves and in the world; connecting to the mythic and magical dimensions hidden within us.

Come, listen, learn, share...

> *"Touching Earth,*
> *I contact all life.*
> *Contacting all life,*
> *I ask it how to change my own"*

2002 - VACANT OR ENGAGED?

The 7th Buddhafield will be radically different to previous years. Last year we celebrated the 'Mythic Journey to a Sacred Space': this year the world itself becomes that sacred space. Whatever our personal vision, without engagement with the world it will come to nothing. Whatever our vision for society, without engagement with ourselves it is doomed. So we ask - are you vacant or engaged?

This year Buddhafield will be hosting a gathering of Britain's most passionate, skilled, and effective exponents of change to present a rich variety of workshops, debates and performances - with the emphasis on participation. There is no room for passive spectators: as Rilke said - "Here is no place that does not see you: you must change your life."

Come and learn and share spiritual practices, techniques and rituals, come and work with us in cafes, on site, and with children, come and participate in debates and workshops, come and learn what it means to be truly radical in today's world: come and engage with the real-life challenges that face us all. For we must engage or die.

This process can and must include social AND individual change: activism AND meditation, our own body speech mind AND society. Too often people live only on one pole of this Zen paradox: this year Buddhafield will especially encourage cross-fertilisation through debate, ritual, and direct confrontation. Yogis - are you engaged? Eco-warriors - are you?

Buddhafield is a travelling collective of Western Buddhists: naturally, our own loyalties are broadly Buddhist, focussing on non-violence, meditation, and the creation of real community. But we know well that no one has all the answers and we are therefore actively seeking contributions from others, especially in the areas of performance, community creation, and land use, the emphasis being very much on participation and education. Musicians are also warmly invited, please note that this year the event will be largely acoustic-only. As always Buddhafield will have a strict no drugs no alcohol no dogs policy on site. Please respect this.

Free tickets are available to contributors, total numbers are limited and advance booking strongly recommended.

2001 - MYTHIC JOURNEYS TO A SACRED SPACE

We are engaged, all of us, in a Journey to the East. We shall not cease from exploration - and the end of all our exploring will be to arrive where we started, and know the place for the first time. We invite you to pass through the "unknown, remembered gate" into the 2001 Buddhafield Festival; to make the mythic journey to a sacred space. The Festival is a place where everyone - from site security to ritual leaders to the café crews to you and I - are engaged in the same one enterprise: building the Buddhafield.

And what is the Buddhafield but a field of living beings, a field of high resolve, and an ever-growing network of practice, friendship, community, and social transformation? 'We' are not putting it on for 'you', 'you' do not come to consume at 'our' expense. We are all co-creators of the festival, co-beneficiaries.

Here is no place that does not see you. You must change your life. Let us know how you can contribute.

with thanks and apologies to Hesse, Eliot,
the Bodhisattva Vimalakirti, and Rilke.

2000 - VISION AND TRANSFORMATION

Before 2000, we have no records of any specific themes for Buddhafield.

BACKSTAGE AT BUDDHAFIELD

Buddhafield isn't just about meditation and sunbathing! Every event both starts and ends in an empty green field, with home, workshop, and often, shops, a long way away – meaning that everything, but everything, that will be needed has to be carefully loaded in advance onto one or several vans; even the smallest thing forgotten is likely to cause extensive ripples of consequences and inconveniences further down the line. That's a long-winded way of saying that it takes a prodigious amount of mindfulness to put on a Buddhafield event. Here's a selection of glimpses into Buddhafield's 'backstage' procedures, starting with the Café. We're delighted to include a couple of Buddhafield recipes, published for the first time and a possible precursor to a long-dreamed-of Buddhafield Recipe book...

THE BUDDHAFIELD CAFÉ

Putting on a Festival Café in a field is difficult. It's in a highly regulated and meticulously inspected environment, and one in which operators must be prepared for any kind of weather from scorching sunshine to unremitting downpours – and Buddhafield has had both, many times!

Pretty much all the Buddhafield café kit has been made by Buddhafield, from the enormous 'aircraft hangar' tent (known affectionately as the Parthenon) to the stainless steel cooking tables to the café decorations to the wood-fired hot water system (which doubles up as a secret sauna for the crew!)

Here's some of the Café's promotional material, working procedures, and recipes, written by the Café team:

The Buddhafield Cafe's Menu Board

WHAT WE COOK

We are well-known for our full, cooked vegan breakfast, soups and the Buddhafield Coconut Curry — a lightly spiced vegetable curry served with brown rice. There is often a roast dinner available on Sundays.

Thanks to the brilliantly creative cooks who join us, the menu changes daily: it depends on what we have and what we feel like cooking! So our Daily Special might be Baked Marinated Tofu with a Bulgar Wheat Pilaf, or Indonesian Stew with Satay Sauce. We always have a variety of salads, generous with toasted seeds, olives and tasty dressings. Our soups are also interestingly different each day and there is usually fresh, homemade soya yoghurt to go with fruit salad and organic muesli as an alternative to our full, cooked breakfast.

We ensure there are always wheat-free options available and can give assurances on other ingredients such as yeast or nuts where relevant. We order a wide range of organic vegetables, salads, herbs and fruit, as much as possible from local organic growers, to make sure there is an exciting selection for the cooks to choose from. Wholefoods, other cooking ingredients and our wholly biodegradable cleaning products come from the Essential Trading Co-operative, based in Bristol, are GMO-free, organic and fair-trade whenever possible.

Our food and drink is usually served on ceramic plates, bowls and mugs with metal cutlery, all of it bought from public recycling centres in Devon. This eclectic design standard may result in a your mug, bowl or plate proving itself a novel talking point!

We can also offer hot tubs, a sauna and domes. Contact us for more information about hiring these.

OUR TENTS AND STRUCTURES

Our tents are custom-made by Buddhafield. Canvas covered, they are based around an extendable Parthenon-shaped aluminium frame. The standard sized version is 25m x 8.5m, with the busy open plan kitchen completely on view behind a colourful and inviting counter. The seating area is light and airy with low-level seating at beautifully painted tables. Colourful rugs cover the floor. A canopy of billowing, sail-like fabric, in blues, oranges, golds and pinks, creates a warm and cosy, yet spacious feeling. The outside is decorated with prayer flags, painted banners, bunting and large colourful flags.

We have a smaller tent which we run as a takeaway café for use at smaller or one-day events. This is more versatile, quick and easy to erect and does not require the large teams we need to run the full shebang (as few as seven people per shift). The menu is simpler, with crêpes, veggie burgers and baked potatoes served all day.

We can also adapt our set-up to offer a spa garden — complete with sauna, hot tubs, showers and chill-out space — and a cinema.

Café Recipes

Here's two classic recipes from the Buddhafield café. Note that the quantities are café-sized, that a 'box' is a 15-litre Tupperware container, and a "big serving spoon" is roughly equivalent to 3 dessertspoons.

SHEPHERDESS PIE

Prepare:

15-litre box onions
15-litre box mushrooms
1/2 box celery (optional)
15-litre box carrots, chopped small
15-litre box other green veg (broccoli, cauliflower, courgette, chard)
15-litre box cooked green or brown lentils
4 bulbs garlic (finely chopped)
900g tomato puree
Mushroom stock cubes or bouillon to make 2 ltrs of stock
cup of Tamari
Herbs of choice - 1/2 cupful (rosemary, thyme, sage, marjoram)
60 litres of potatoes/swedes for mashing
cup of mustard
1/2 tub margarine or 1 cup olive oil

Heat 2 cups of oil, and fry:

6 dessertspoons onion seeds
6 dessertspoons poppy seeds
3 dessertspoons caraway seeds
optional cumin, or celery seeds

Add onions, cook till soft, add celery and garlic, cook till softening, then add mushrooms and other veg, Stir fry long enough to coat in oil before putting lid on to cook veg in their juices, adding tomato puree, tamari and stock if getting dry, making sure it's all added before veg is cooked.

Stir in lentils and herbs and spread in baking trays, leaving 1/3 of the space for mash on top

Make mash with mustard and herbs in, oil or marge and vary by mixing with swede or parsnip or celeriac (when in season) or finely chopped chives, spring onions or cooked leeks.

BUDDHAFIELD CURRY

Prepare:

1 box onions

1/2 box carrots

1/2 box potatoes

1 box green vegetables (cauliflower, broccoli, cabbage etcetera)

1 box cooked beans

4 bulbs garlic (finely chopped)

Fist-size lump of ginger (finely chopped)

6 blocks of creamed coconut

optional box of courgettes or similar to add near end of cooking time

1 cup of oil

Heat the oil and fry for a few minutes:

2 big serving spoons of cumin seeds,

2 big serving spoons of black onion seeds,

1 big serving spoon of brown mustard seeds

2 big serving spoons of crushed coriander,

1 big serving spoon of crushed cardamom seeds.

Add onions and fry until soft and then stir in:

6 big serving spoons of ground cumin,

3 big serving spoons of coriander,

2 big serving spoons of turmeric,

1 big serving spoon of fenugreek,

4 big serving spoons of medium/madras curry powder,

1 big serving spoon of bouillon,

1/2 big serving spoon of chilli powder,

2 big serving spoons garam masala.

Allow all this to cook gently in the oil for five minutes.

Add 2 jugs boiling / hot water (if the carrots have been par-boiled first then this water can be used) and half a tin of tomato puree.

Add the cauliflower and any other vegetables that take 20 minutes cooking, then the others

Add cooked carrots, potatoes and beans and more liquid if required (soya milk is good).

Add chopped creamed coconut and any extra seasoning such as garam masala, black pepper, lemon juice. If the consistency looks a bit thin then add tahini, soya milk and lemon juice.

KITCHEN SECRETS

DESIGN AND LAYOUT

The Café layout is designed on an event-by-event basis to respond creatively to the size, shape and geography of each pitch. It aims to ensure that:

- There is plenty of room to work and move about.
- The cooking area is separate from other general areas.
- The urns are positioned between the washing-up and tea-serving areas.
- The prep tables are in the centre of the kitchen, allowing easy access to the vegetable stores, to the exit for washing and to the cooking area. This also allows the Shift Coordinator to oversee good practice around the kitchen.
- Floor surfaces are as level as possible, anti-slip, easy to clean and disinfect.
- Firefighting equipment is well displayed and accessible.
- Fire exits are kept clear and accessible and signs are well displayed.
- The carpeted seating area is as clean as possible.

WORKPLACE HYGIENE AND SAFETY

All volunteers are asked to arrive by 4pm the day before the event begins to receive a comprehensive briefing on hygiene and safety practices. We display a copy of the basic rules for food handlers at the handwash station.

FUEL AND ELECTRICITY

The Café cooking appliances use LPG gas. A number of checks are in place to ensure the safety of the appliances and the gas cylinders.

- Cylinders are kept outside firmly secured in an upright position and always closed off at night.
- Only trained staff have responsibility for changing over bottles.
- Gas spanners are stored near the bottles for quick use.
- Hoses (pipes) and regulators are checked each time a bottle is changed.
- Each appliance is connected to a rigid gas pipe fixed beneath a stainless steel table. Isolator taps are mounted at both the point of connection and at the end of the rigid pipe, allowing a choice of places to shut down quickly. Should a leak occur, each appliance, it's piping and cylinder will be closed off and checked.
- All gas appliances are checked and certified annually by a Gas Safe registered engineer, and checked by the managers between events.
- As far as possible all LPG is purchased on site and used up before we leave.
- A maximum of 45kg of gas will be transported per vehicle, secured in an upright position. All appliances are dismantled for transport, and thus never connected to a supply.

At most events we run our own purpose-built, wood-fired hot water system from a self-contained trailer, situated outside and to one side of the kitchen. The system is supplied by water from the event's system, heating and storing it in a cylinder. A wood supply (usually a combination of hardwood off-cuts and softwood pallets) is stored neatly near the trailer, but away from LPG cylinders.

All electrical power (used for the Café's lighting and stereo) is supplied by a 12v battery system, recharged by our own solar panel rig. Wiring is installed by trained staff members.

WATER

We expect to be supplied with mains water from a spur outside the Café kitchen. At most events we plumb this into a set of complete wash stations (including running hot and cold water). Grey-water drainage is either plumbed into a displacement container supplied by the event organisers or run off to a suitable soakaway. There are separate washing areas for:

- Handwash — Depending upon layout, handwash water is either kept at ideal temperature in an insulated container, or by supplied by running hot and cold taps. In either case, the station is situated by the kitchen entrance and supplied with bacterial handwash, nailbrush and paper towels.
- Vegetable washing — a table is set up outside for cleaning vegetables before they come inside to the prep tables.
- Dishwashing — a complete dishwashing area is fitted with sinks and supplied by running hot and cold taps.

A substantial volume of cold water is stored as an emergency/backup supply behind the cafe tent.

WASTE DISPOSAL

We are obliged to accommodate ourselves to the waste management policies of the event we are attending, but we aim to:

- Recycle as much as possible, i.e. glass, metal (cans), paper and cardboard, plastics and food waste. If facilities for recycling are not provided at the event (we aim to recycle tetra paks for example, which aren't usually included in site policies) we take what we can away with us.
- Collect food waste in buckets and transfer it to lidded containers or plastic sacks outside the Café, raw and cooked kept separate when required.
- Transfer all grey-water waste to containers supplied or to a soak-away.

- Provide recycling bins and compost bucket in the seating area for customers' use.

FIRST AID AND WELL-BEING

We carry a fully stocked standard First Aid kit as well as a non-emergency Secondary Aid box (which includes items like sun lotion and alternative remedies). Both are kept at the handwash station. All members of staff are made aware of their location.

At least one geodesic dome will be erected and available as a private, dedicated Café crew area.

- There is always a trained First Aider, usually on each shift, but if not then at least quickly contactable.
- Any serious accident will be recorded in the incident book by the shift Co-ordinator. The incident book is kept in the shift coordinators box and used for recording anything the managers need to know about.
- Guidelines for manual handling are given during the training session at the start of each event.
- Each shift meets for half an hour before starting work in order to report in on any health or well-being issues or anything the coordinator needs to know.

FIRE SAFETY

At every event there is a water extinguisher in the seating area and another beside the trailer. A dry powder unit is at each end of the kitchen (near the exits) and a CO_2 unit at the central (prep) area.

Fire blankets are distributed evenly between cooking stations.

All compressed fire-fighting units are checked, maintained and certified annually by a suitably qualified service provider.

All canvases and hangings are fully treated to be fire retardant.

FOOD STORAGE

We have two storage areas. A fresh fruit and vegetable store is at the back of the kitchen, raised off of the ground on pallets. A dry food store is kept in a customised truck outside and behind the kitchen space. Any foodstuffs at risk of attack by pests are kept stored in plastic bins with well-closing lids. All stores are regularly checked by the managers and rotated as necessary to ensure freshness.

Vegetable preparation in the Cafe

WORKSTATIONS IN THE CAFÉ:

COOKS AND SHIFT CO-ORDINATORS

Each shift usually has a cooking team of two and a coordinator. Given that these are key roles, they are usually recruited from amongst core team members. The lead cook usually focuses on the day's Special dish, whilst the second cook makes standards like our coconut curry and vegan chilli recipes. There's training documentation for General Staff and Supervisors in the Café section of the Buddhafield website.

COUNTER STAFF

The Café can get quite busy, so this can be a high-energy job. It is vital to remember that, in this role, you are the public face of Buddhafield and therefore should behave appropriately; remain calm and polite. Don't stress if there's a big queue: focus on the person in front of you.

There may be up to three people on the counter at busy times. Communicating and working together is very important, work out a system that works well between yourselves, usually it can be best to have one or two people serving and one person taking money — money should not be touched if you are serving food (health and safety).

Sometimes (particularly at the end of an event), customers may try to get free/reduced food, whilst remembering the spirit of generosity also remember the food is very expensive! Counter stock costs the Café a lot of money and must not be sold at discounted prices to anyone apart from Café staff.

Always keep the counter clean and tidy and ensure food being served is hot. Presentation and care is very important.

VEGETABLE PREPPERS

Vegetable preparers are to consult the cooks about what vegetables need preparing. All prepared vegetables should be stored in square plastic tubs, always with lids on, on the rack (usually at the end of the prep tables at back of Café).

No unwashed vegetables are allowed in the kitchen — All veg is to be washed outside — taking particular care to wash potatoes/muddy vegetables separately.

Generally it is good to have two different salads being served, (usually one leafy, one grated). When it's busy there always needs to be at least one or two salads ready to be served waiting on the rack. Always check with the cooks what can be used in the salads — sometimes things need to be used up/saved for something.

A fruit salad needs to be made at breakfast time.

Always clean your workspace as you go and whenever you start a new task. Compost goes in buckets that need to be emptied regularly (usually into IBC container or compostable bags). When giving sharp knives to the washing up team always inform them.

BURGER MAKERS

Shape burgers using round Barleycup lids and make a few trays, cover in cling film and store on rack.

Always keep plenty of burgers and onions on the griddle (turn down gas when quiet to warm rather than cook). Use the times when quiet to prep more burger mix/shape more burgers & prep onions in long thin slices.

Keep an eye on what's happening at the counter and keep the counter supplied with hot burgers and onions.

WASHING UP

The Buddhafield Café uses a three bowl washing up system: 'Scuzz', 'Hot Wash', and 'Very Hot Rinse'.

When the water needs changing the wash water is poured into the scuzz bowl, the rinse water is poured into the wash bowl and the rinse bowl is refilled from a hot urn. The water moves but the bowls stay in the same place.

The scuzz bowl is for the initial rinse/soak and can get quite cold and dirty, when it needs emptying it gets poured into an IBC container (usually outside the back of the Café).

The washing up bowl should always be fairly warm and clean with plenty of washing up liquid.

The rinse bowl should always be hot, clean and bubble free, add a few drops of tea tree oil (natural antibacterial) each time the water is replaced. Refill from the urn adding a little cold — it is best to use washing up gloves to avoid burning hands. Never let anyone else put their hands/dirty objects/cloths in the rinse bowl before using the first two bowls.

Work together in a team to make an efficient system, always try to keep on top of things to ensure the Café will not run out of plates/mugs/cutlery and the cooks have plenty of pans, etc.

Never leave sharps in washing up bowls, always inform your co-workers when washing sharp things.

Sometimes people will volunteer to do an hour of washing up in return for a meal, welcome them and make sure they know what they're doing — either integrate them into your system or set them off on their own task, often pans can be scrubbed outside if the weather is nice.

End of the night: if you are on the night shift no one finishes until all washing up is done and the Café is cleaned, this is a time when everyone has to really pull together and help each other in order to get out as quickly as possible whilst leaving the Café lovely for the breakfast shift.

Be inventive and create new washing up systems — find extra bowls or use large tubs/saucepans, organise yourselves into pan scrubbing/cutlery rinsing/etc — find something to clean. When everyone helps it doesn't take long, particularly if washer uppers have worked consistently throughout the shift.

Additionally the hob, counter and front of house all need cleaning and the floor needs sweeping and sometimes mopping.

URNS AND FIRES

Always ensure urns are topped up and there are always at least two boiling at a time. Never let an urn boil dry. Top up regularly, particularly watch out for when one is used to refill washing up bowls. Gas can be turned up if an urn needs to be brought to the boil, but always remember to turn it down again when it reaches the boil.

Morning: ensure the counter has a supply of fresh hot tea and coffee to serve with breakfast.

Keep the urn and tea area clean and tidy.

BUILDING A BUDDHAFIELD DOME

BY RUPADARSHIN

A guide to designing, building and erecting basic geodesic domes for camping or similar uses, written by Rupadarshin. As used by Buddhafield!

This is the **Standard Pattern** diagram for all 'two pole length' or 'two phase' Domes. The Long Poles are in solid black, the Short Poles - are the other ones. Copy this diagram, take it with you - and *keep it dry* until you *know* the pattern.

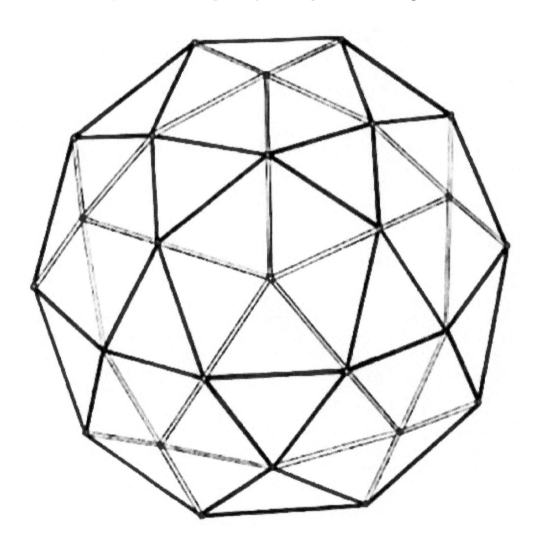

WHAT SIZE DOME?

Anything less than 5'6"(1.6m) tall is a waste of time and effort. The upper limit depends on your transport - what length poles or weight of canvas you can carry. The diameter is twice the height of the basic dome. My 6' 6" high dome sleeps four or five easily - with the ground diameter being 13 foot (4m).

DESIGNING THE POLES

The standard 'garden' dome (properly known as a 'two phase' dome) has 2 pole lengths: A+B. In the illustration above, the long (B) poles are the solid-coloured lines. The short A poles all form 5 pointed stars – remember this. To work out the lengths needed, these poles have a standard 'pole factor'. (aka chord factor, where the chord = the line between two points on a circle.) For pole A, this is 0.54653, for pole B, this is 0.61803. **Accuracy of pole lengths is important.**

The pole length is calculated by dome radius (= dome height) X the pole factor.

So, for a 6'6"(2m) high dome the pole lengths are:

Pole A. 78"x0.54653 = 42.63" (or@1.093m) = Short pole.

Pole B. 78"x0.61803 = 48.21" (or@1.236m) = Long pole.

You will need 30 short poles and 35 long poles.

WHAT ARE THE POLES MADE FROM?

For a camping dome, the choice is between wood or metal. Coppiced wood poles of hazel or ash, de-barked, are ideal (and free - if you can find them). Broom handles are good - though 1" wood dowelling may be cheaper. 15mm aluminium tube is light and works well, though steel tubing is better for strength. Wood needs treating - I use hot linseed oil - in the winter every year - to stop it drying out and becoming brittle.

JOINING THE POLES (SIMPLE METHOD)

The simplest method is to flatten the ends of the poles, drill the ends, then bolt the poles together. For metal this method is simple. Wooden poles need sleeves of tough plastic, or metal pipe, flattened and drilled. Plastic sleeves need to be heated in hot oil until soft before the ends can be flattened and drilled (top left in this diagram). The ends of the poles should be at an 18° angle, the ends of the short poles at 16°. (Don't worry too much about precision, just get close..) The absolute simplest method is to screw ring bolts into the ends of wooden poles (pre-drill these holes) and just tie the rings together (top right in the diagram).

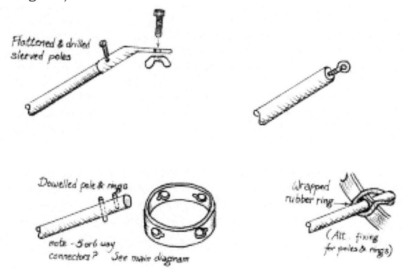

JOINING THE POLES (TRICKY METHOD)

Another popular method is the 'rings and poles' way (The bottom two in the diagram). The appropriate number of holes are drilled into rings of tough thick plastic typically cut from @8" yellow gas-main plastic pipe. The poles have 'stops' of doweling glued through the pole ends that hold the pole in place when twisted after passing through keyhole shaped ring holes) or alternately with rings of motorbike inner tube, wrapped over the ring the pole has passed through then back again. Another variation of this one is string passed through a hole through the pole - and knotted in place inside the ring (where the dowel stop is in the above illustration). The string end goes over the ring then through another hole in the pole to tie – or even hangs loose, as the pole cannot pull out of the ring while the string is in place!

THE KEY PRINCIPLE OF ERECTING A DOME:

At the top of the dome is a 5 pointed star of short poles. Attached to the end of each star 'point' is the point of another 5 pointed star of short poles. In all, you have 6 stars of all of the short poles. Everything else is a long pole. If you get stuck, just work out where the '5 stars' are and backtrack.

Another way of looking at it is as five pairs of equilateral triangles, paired vertically point to point, with five pointed stars between each pair and completing the top. The five remaining long poles fill the gaps under each five point star. See - The Diagram.

ERECTING THE DOME

'Top Down' method

The key principle is vital: follow The Diagram - lay out all of the short poles first - a central star of five poles, then five more five-pointed stars linked to the end of the poles of the central star. Then place a long pole between the outstretched arms of the five-pointed stars. Five long poles are left over. These go between the five pentagrams just laid out to complete the base ring.

Then tie, bolt or - rubber strap - it all together! OK, unfair! In more detail:-

Fix the centres of all of the five-pointed stars.

Then fix the five junctions around the central star (6 poles to each junction). (Each short pole runs straight to another short pole).

Then fix each of the 6 pole junctions between the outer five-point stars. (The centre will start to lift as you pull these together.)

Stand the dome on its 10 points (help needed)

Fix the last ten long poles between the poles of these 10 points.

Cover.

Move in.

Designing the cover

Briefly, Use medium grade – or marquee–grade canvas – buy second hand from a marquee hire firm. This should be water proof. 5 years after manufacture it will <u>not</u> be fire proof. Beware. The simplest method is to wrap 2 marquee walls around the dome, tie these on to the dome poles, then throw a square of canvas - with metal grommets fitted for ropes - over the top and peg it all down. **OR** if looks don't bother you - use the big green plastic tarps (3m x 4m) that DIY stores sell - that have grommets fitted.. With these I'd buy three - two act as the side walls (doubled over) then one as the roof sheet, roped to strong ground pegs. Also note – **a groundsheet is essential**, due to dew, then carpets can be used.

Doors

The jury is still out on this one. A square door is simple to build of poles and inserts into the space of a 5 point star. Note that it is vital for stability to steady the door by linking the door posts to the adjoining joints with bolted short poles. The lintel, short poled to the joint above, can be stabilised with wood or even rope braces.

SECRETS OF THE BUDDHAFIELD HOT TUB

BY RUPADARSHIN

The hot tub experience is an important – though totally optional - part of any Buddhafield retreat, being for many especially delightful after the evening puja, when all around is dark and one is sitting and soaking with friends under the open moonlit sky. It includes close contact with all four elements: the preparation of the ground in advance, then the careful – almost ritualised - combination of fire, water, and air necessary.

Rupadarshin has been for many years the acknowledged master of the hot tubs – and water in general at Buddhafield, and what follows are his 'how-to' notes for anyone interested, which have served generations of apprentices on many retreats. Warning – without actually having been introduced to 'the mysteries' on site and in person, it is likely to be trickier than it looks to get working for yourself at home in a timely, safe, and efficient manner...! Anyone interested in building their own hot tub is strongly advised to learn first-hand on a Buddhafield retreat, and to then use these notes as reminders.

Materials - The Kit.

Note: initials in what follows refer to the diagram below.

1. (T)1500 litre water/fruit juice container @ 1.5m diameter (a big black bottle of plastic)– cut down as detailed below.
2. (R) A water radiator: 1300x600mm single panel. A second (R) as arrowed on the Lay Out, can work when buried vertically long ways, as a solid wall to support the heating radiator over the fire – keep the joints open on this one though..
3. (C) 22mm extension (copper) in-pipes/out-pipes from the heating radiator. 2 of - 200mm long (You also need 2 joints from the radiator into this 22mm copper pipe, both at the same end)
4. (CM) Metal to plastic joints – 2 of. 22mm to 22mm HEP20 will do (ps Buy a spare:see Safety..)
5. 22mm inlets – 2 of. Usually cold water tank fittings, plastic or metal, to fit to HEP20.
6. Taps – 1 of, inline metal tap for 22mm plastic pipe. For the drain. Another on the hosepipe
7. (J) 22mm T joint – 1 of, plastic, HEP20 by Hepworth
8. (P) Hot water plastic pipe - HEP20, 22mm, 10 meters of. Plus (or including) drain pipe. (Must be capable of taking 120C temp)
9. 1 washing-up liquid bottle for the hot water inlet to the tub. Vital.
10. A Chimney – steel, flexible, central heating ducting is good. At least 150mm diam, 1.5metres tall min, pref 2.5. Could be iron drainpipe – or spot-welded tin cans!
11. WOOD – a good stack of <u>dry</u> firewood. A mix of pine and seasoned hardwood offcuts is great. Ash wood is brilliant:- try other free-range woods... Good pine burns fast but cool, the hardwood slower but hotter.
12. 1 rubber duck (well, I need one)
13. Canvas, plastic, even wood. A covered tub heats *much* faster; think 'am I heating air or water?' I use a weighted plastic or canvas sheet.
14. A metal sieve is useful for removing stray grass and insects.

15. WATER – about 1000 litres. Delivered by hose-pipe, clean mains.
16. The chimney and water piping will need support posts with <u>wire</u> ties. The water pipes shouldn't sag, but follow a steady gradient down to the heating radiator.
17. A lid for the tub.

Cutting the tub

The tub has to be cut to size. A wood saw cuts it fine. The height of the tub or depth of water is down to your inside leg measurement – literally how deep a tub can you climb into comfortably. With steps up the outside and a seat inside (wood or plastic, bolted to the tub side with rubber washers) the depth can go up.

The cut edge can be sharp so needs calming down before the tub can be comfortably used. The common method is to cut a length of 25mm plastic water pipe (thicker than hose pipe) *lengthways*, then push this cut down around the tubs' edge then gaffa tape it in place. Soft rubber pipe is rare but very nice. The clever way to solve this is to somehow melt the top edge and model it down to a smooth round, wide rim.

Layout Illustration (of the pre direct-feed system)

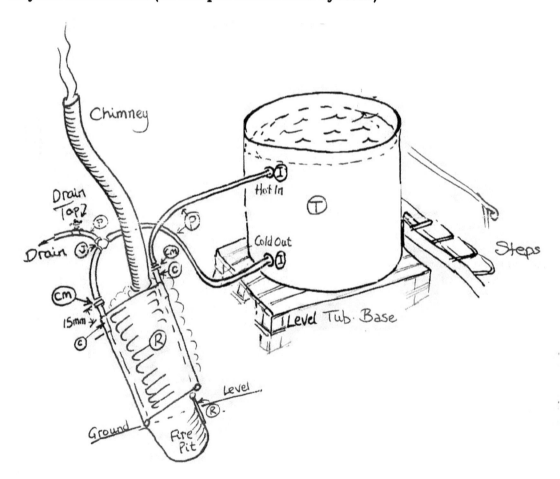

Place Tub on a level base, a pallet or two above the heating radiator – so gravity pulls cold water down into the radiator.

Hot tub construction details

Water Inlets (this sketch includes Top Inlet, bottom inlet and fire construction illustrations) Note: The hot inlet is around 350mm below the top of the tub, so that hot water flows into water, not air - while the tub is in use. Safer too.

The washing-up liquid bottle is topped and tailed, then a hole is cut in the side so that one wall of the bottle fits onto the inner end of the hot water inlet like a washer. Hot water coming into the tub hits the inner side of this bottle and shoots sideways around the tub, so protecting *delicate skin.*

Note: The cold inlet is cut as close to the bottom of the tub as the fitting will allow, for ease of emptying.

Radiator + Tub – angles and relative heights

Note: The radiator does need to be angled as shown, with the hot out-pipe above the cold in-pipe– but the jury is still out as to the ideal relation between the tub and the radiator. It **works** whether the tub is level with the radiator – or 3 feet below it! My preference is to have the fire at ground level, dug in, with the spoil sealing the chimney and insulating the tub. The platform for the tub is then 2 pallet heights above ground, carefully levelled. A non-slip surface on steps and platform top surface helps – as a well as a handrail. Extending the steps up the side of the tub is brilliant.

Fire Construction

See Illustration above.

Note 1: Fitting the chimney is tricky – I hammer a long metal stake into the ground beside the top of the radiator close to the hot out-pipe. The chimney is then slid down onto this stake. I then build a loose wall of stones or bricks to hold the chimney mouth high up (with a space for smoke to get into the chimney, of course.) – then complete the wall across/around the gap and seal it all in with wet clay/ soil. It's all meant to keep the heat on the radiator, not escaping too soon!

Note 2: ALSO note the radiator slopes both lengthways and sideways: The lowest point is by the fire entrance, the highest point is the hot out-pipe. The angle is critical – you are aiming for the hot outlet to be about 6" above the diagonally opposite (lowest) corner for a 4'6" radiator.

Enjoying a Buddhafield hot tub

Running and using the Hot Tub

1. Empty the tub and re-fill every day if using the tub for more than a day. There's a **definite** risk of bacteria breeding overnight as the radiator cools. Chlorine solution is good against bugs.

2. Always clean the tub with disinfectant, flush out the pipes and the radiator before filling – particularly if the tub has been unused for a period.

3. Don't light the fire when the radiator is empty.

4. Keep the water level above the hot in-pipe when the tub is in use, topping up the water if it falls below this level. This practice keeps the hot water flowing into the existing hot-tub water, which keeps the heat much better than the air.

5. Turn the drain tap OFF before filling the tub or starting to heat the water.

6. If the tub – or the pipes - gets too hot, add cold water and take wood out of the fire; do NOT throw water on the radiator. (It makes the fire hard to light afterwards)

7. Don't overload the fire with wood – leave a good air gap below the radiator to ensure a good burn – you are heating water, not burning wood!

8. The ideal fire is a long bed of coals with a couple of logs thrown on to keep it ticking over

9. Pine burns hot and fast – good to start with, then hardwood maintains the heat and lasts well

10. BE PATIENT. 7-800 litres of cold water takes 3 – 4 hours to get up to heat even if the wood is dry. A weird detail – heating water from 0C to 5C takes a lot of energy. 5C to 45C takes less effort 'they say'. If you can find a few buckets of hot for the first half of the tub to take it over this starting point, then fill the tub slowly, maintaining this initial heat, it can be done in under 2 hours. A tight cover for the tub is essential for this to work. A faster method of heating the water is offered in step 13.

11. *Strongly encourage all users to wash carefully before getting in*. A foot wash bowl to remove mud and grass as they enter helps too. This keeps the water clean and hygienic for later users.

12. Try to design in a removable metal door over the fire entrance. A wooden slab will work too – though it will burn through quickly. Reducing the air supply to a well-sealed fire pit improves the 'draw' – the fire blasts from 700C to over 1000C, I am told.

13. If you have a good water supply – and good drainage – consider 'direct hot filling'. It can be faster by 2 hours - particularly if the tub is covered. Feed the water supply, via a T-joint, straight in to the cold-in radiator inlet (into the bottom of the radiator). You fill the tub *while heating the water.* Blast the fire as hot as you can manage – the hot water is flowing straight through the pipe, so no pressure – it will not melt as long as the water is flowing. The tub fills up with hot water – or warm if it runs too fast. Once the tub is full, maintain the temperature by adjusting the fire and water flow so the right heat water comes in. **Leave the drain tap open to reduce overflowing. You *may* reconnect the cold out pipe from the tub to the radiator once it's hot and full and run it as usual. This is MUCH easier if you use extra taps here! This method is good for silent events – as the pipes do not rattle.

14. **Safety check.** Hot tubs have obvious risky points, so once it's built, but before it's used, look at the system as a whole and decide what safety measures you need – and do them. A fence around the fire pit (even a pallet fixed a foot or so above the radiator), a sober person in charge at all times, a handrail, straw bales packed on the ground around the tub, whatever you think it needs.

Burst Pipe Protection

To reduce danger of injury from bursting pipes, put a large tin can around the hot out-pipe by the radiator – over the joint where the metal joins the plastic HEP20. See illustration.

This is the only joint/section of pipe that I have ever seen burst (unless you put a tap on the hot pipe - very risky). When it does burst – and it will occasionally – there is a short-range spray of hot water/steam that is contained by the can and directed away from the tub.

EMERGENCY ACTION:

When the pipe bursts, remove all of the wood from the fire. (*Don't* throw water at it, the radiator won't like it.) Disconnect the plastic cold-in pipe from the radiator's copper pipe and lift the pipe as high as the tubs water level and fix it there (or ask an occupant to hold it for you – it's their water supply after all). Block the hot water in-pipe in the tub – a cork inside the washing up bottle hole will do. This isolates the radiator. Run the cold tap through the radiator's cold in-pipe until the water flowing out of the burst is manageable, then turn off the water. Remove the damaged fittings from the end of the radiators' hot-out copper pipe OR cut the burst section of pipe square and refit it to the joint with new fittings if required – and/or replace the burst joint. Fix it all back together again, reload the fire and fire it up again. 10 minutes if you are focused. Expect cheers.

1. Always have a bend in the hot water plastic pipe. If the fire gets too hot and the water turns to steam, it usually bursts the plastic pipe. The bend directs the spray away from the tub – via the tin can mentioned earlier.
2. Check all of the joints for leaks or looseness, particularly the radiator to plastic joints, before use.
3. Rattling or vibrating pipes are OK. It is hot water/steam trying to go up the down pipe. It is an 'open' system - quite normal. However, if the rattling speeds up and gets sharper, the water is getting too hot, risking a burst pipe. If this happens, take wood out of the fire.
4. If anything goes bang STAY IN THE WATER till it calms down – 10 secs or so. It is the safest place to be because it takes a long time to heat up that much water. Think about it. The view is better too of muggins fixing it – and you could hold a pipe/spanner for him/her...

And finally - Enjoy!

Rupadarshin - Buddhafield crew 08/12/01

Preparing the Hot Tub

BUDDHAFIELD PUJAS AND OTHER VERSES

Buddhafield has a long tradition of creative and beautiful rituals, including the performance of special and elaborate pujas using verses specially composed by one or another member of the Buddhafield team. Two of these are presented below: Dhiramati's much-loved 'Padmasambhava of Blazing Light' puja, and a less-known piece titled 'To the Ancestors'. They are followed by Akuppa's classic 'Shambhala Warrior Mind-Training' verses.

PADMASAMBHAVA OF BLAZING LIGHT PUJA
BY DHIRAMATI

1 The Radiant Guru
Padmasambhava of blazing light,
Padmasambhava of radiant appearance,
Padmasambhava of luminous vision.

Padmasambhava of blazing light,
Revealing jewels and treasures in our struggles.
Padmasambhava of blazing light,
Revealing the truth in each changing moment.
Padmasambhava of blazing light,
Revealing the heart of compassion in every action.

Padmasambhava!
Yogi-magician,
Moving between worlds.

Padmasambhava!
Vision seeker,
Finding the ways to freedom,

Padmasambhava!
Compassionate master,
Revealing the inner path.

Padmasambhava!
Mystic yogi,
Burning in the fires of transformation.

Padmasambhava!
Alchemist,
In the cauldron of the heart.

Padmasambhava!
Shaman,
Beating the drum of awakening.

Padmasambhava!
A blazing light,
On the primal plain.
Blazing light,
Before the first stars.
Blazing light,
Life-giving sun.
Blazing light,
Tide turning moon.
Blazing light,
Traveller of time.
Blazing light,
Shapeshifter.
Blazing light,
Rainbow bodied.
Blazing light,
Seasons turning.
Blazing light,
Darkness of night.
Blazing light,
Midnight's sun.
Blazing light,
Otherworld journey.

Blazing light,
Chaos and death.
Blazing light,
Of cremation fires.
Blazing light,
Of undying awareness.

2 Touching the Body of Enlightenment

Padmasambhava!
Ancient ancestor,
The keen-eyed hawk hovers,
In the deep blue skies.
The salmon of wisdom swims,
In the dazzling diamond river.
The black crow calls,
Shadow on the face of light.
The birds flock and gather,
Swirling patterns as moving as one.
The stream ripples in shimmering light,
The still pool mirrors the sky,
The rocks whisper in sunlight,
The moon climbs over the silver hills,
The golden harvest fills the field,
The crimson flower wavers in the breeze.
Padmasambhava,
In our hearts,
In the land,
Body of awakening
Inseparable.
OM AH HUM

Padmasambhava!
Master who is here and gone,
Illuminating everything as it arises and passes.
The impermanent, inconceivable, wonderful,
Flow of experience.
Before you I stand
Alive,
Aware,
And you are here,
In each moment,
With me always,
Padmasambhava!

OM AH HUM (slow)
Om Ah Hum Vajra Guru Padma Siddhi

The dragon holds the jewel,
Om Ah Hum Vajra Guru Padma Siddhi

Demons hold the energy,
Om Ah Hum Vajra Guru Padma Siddhi

Obstacles hold the path to our freedom,
Om Ah Hum Vajra Guru Padma Siddhi

Sensations are the pathways of inner wisdom.

Breathing in Om
My body is purified.
Holding the breath within Ah
My speech is purified.
Breathing out Hum
My mind is purified.
Body, speech and mind,
All qualities and acts,
Purified by the awareness of emptiness.

Om Ah Hum,
Blazing light.
Om Ah Hum,
Fierce light,
Om Ah Hum,
Light of fire.
Om Ah Hum,
Fire of change.
Om Ah Hum,
Path of love.
Om Ah Hum,
Inner heat rises.
Om Ah Hum,
Inner fire grows.
Om Ah Hum,
Melting hardness.
Om Ah Hum,
Loosening grasping.
Om Ah Hum,
Everything flows.

3 The Guru comes

Guru,
No growth without change,
No life without death,
No progress without obstacles!
Holding the vajra to our hearts!
Holding everything there in our hearts!
Dark and light both,
Our sorrow and joy,
Fear and strength,
Agitation and calm,
Pleasure and pain.

Happy and sad.
Everything there,
In the dance without centre,
Embodying all experiences,
Everything naturally self-liberated.

Radiant Buddha Padma!
He will come,
Two ravens at his shoulders
He will come,
Two wolves at his side.
He will come,
One vulture circling overhead.
He will come,
An eagle before the sun
He will come,
A serpent in the lake
He will come,
A tiger in the forest.
A god before the mountain
A shadow in the cave.
Mysterious guru Padma!

He comes,
Drinking from the skull.
He comes,
Staff rooted deep.
He comes,
Drum beating,
He comes,
Flames leaping.
He comes
Rainbow lights circling.

Fearless Yogi Padma!
Coming,
Out of death.
Coming,
Out of barren wastes
Coming,
Thunder crashing.
Coming,
The waters flowing.
Coming,
New life growing.
Coming,
Awakening unfolding,
Coming,
Joyful laughter ringing.

Dynamic knowledge holder Padma!
Dawn rising clear,

Mind expanded,
Face glowing in the fires,
Master of ecstasy,
Bringing release,
He comes!

Om Ah Hum Vajra Guru Padma Siddhi Hum

4 The Compassionate Guru
Out of fear,
He brings courage.
Out of madness,
He brings peace.
Out of hate,
He brings love.
Out of separation,
He brings wholeness.

Guru,
Going into darkness,
Going into fear,
Going into change,
Going into loss and grief,
Going beyond what is known,
Going beyond what is safe,
Going into that great space of freedom.

AH
AH
AH

With the Guru,
Secret thoughts revealed,
Let go.
Clinging to our selves,
Let go.
Nothing to possess,
Let go.
Breath of body free,
Let go.
Looking into that mirror,
Let go.
Sensing pain,
Let go.
Sensing pleasure,
Let go! Let go! Let go!

5 The dance of the great Yogi
Padmasambhava!
Yogi standing naked before the universe,
Yogi who stands everywhere,

Infinitely expanded.

Padmasambhava!
Guru within,
Guru without,
No separation,
Guru within,
Awakens.
Guru without,
Guides.

Dakini!
Sky dancer,
Dakini within,
Sings,
Dakini without,
Dances.
No separation,
Guru Dakini of my heart,
Speak!
Guru Dakini of my mind,
Sing!
Guru Dakini of my actions,
Dance!

Hrih Guru Padma Vajra Ah
Into the space of freedom,
I dance!
Naked before the ocean,
I dance!
Joyful in the Dharma,
I dance!
Steady, confident, serene,
I dance!
Vital, dynamic, bold,
I dance!
Open, spacious, liberated,
I dance!

Dance,
Dancer of Dharma,
Dance,
Clothed in light.
Dance,
Calling out your names.
Dance,
Moving in emptiness.
Dance,
In vastness of space.
Dance,
Dynamic joy.
Dance,

Energy in space.
Dance,
Drinking a cup of bliss.
Dance the earth,
Dance the sky,
Dance the elements,
Dance the mind.
Dance your magic,
Subduing.
Attracting.
Maturing.
Liberating.
Dance,
Holding everything in your dance,
Everything in your embrace,
Everything in your heart!

Om Ah Hum Maha Guru Sarva Siddhi Hum

6 Conclusion and Dedication
Look with attention
Feel with depth
Sense with clarity
Enter the palace of liberation

Now is the time
To pass into the land of mirror knowledge,
Where there is no hatred.

Now is the time
To pass into the land of serenity
Where there is no craving

Now is the time
To pass into the land of intuitive action,
Where there is no envy.

Now is the time
To pass into the land of the plane of essence,
Where there is no ignorance.

Now is the time
To pass into the land of impartiality,
Where there is no pride.

Now we go there,
To meet the Guru.
Now we go there,
To the Glorious Copper-Coloured

Mountain,
Now we go there,
To the Pure land of the Dharma,
Now we go there,
To the Realm of Dharma's infinite light!
It is time to go x3
We follow,
We follow,
We follow.

OM AH HUM VAJRA GURU PADMA SIDDHI HUM!

May the Guru always be with us.
Om Ah Hum Vajra Guru Padma Siddhi

May the Guru's blessings fill us.
Om Ah Hum Vajra Guru Padma Siddhi

May this suffering grow into compassion.
Om Ah Hum Vajra Guru Padma Siddhi

May these experiences flow freely.
Om Ah Hum Vajra Guru Padma Siddhi

May I dance in that freedom of change.
Om Ah Hum Vajra Guru Padma Siddhi

May my life be a prayer to the Guru.
Om Ah Hum Vajra Guru Padma Siddhi

May these actions be fruitful.
Om Ah Hum Vajra Guru Padma Siddhi

May this meditation be one of compassion.
Om Ah Hum Vajra Guru Padma Siddhi

May this reflection open into experience.
Om Ah Hum Vajra Guru Padma Siddhi

May all beings be happy
Om Ah Hum Vajra Guru Padma Siddhi

May all beings be free from suffering
Om Ah Hum Vajra Guru Padma Siddhi

May their joy never come to an end
Om Ah Hum Vajra Guru Padma Siddhi

May they dwell free of aversion and attraction
Om Ah Hum Vajra Guru Padma Siddhi

May all attain liberation of heart and mind
Om Ah Hum Vajra Guru Padma Siddhi

And may I and all beings become inseparable
From the compassionate Guru Padmasambhava.

TO THE ANCESTORS
BY DHIRAMATI

Life flows from the root,
Downward into the past and underworlds,
Down toward death.
Upward through the trunk and branches,
Toward the sky and sun,
Upward growing into life.

Life is a passage of transmigrations.
A birth that passes from one nature to
every other.
Only shared,
In many shapes,
Ever changing.

Remembering.
Bringing back together.
To everything we keep alive in memory,
Here we give,
Our song,
Our voice,
Our love,
Our heart.
Remembering.

The tree and heartwood,
This world of fruit,
This shifting veil of forms,
The deep layers of creation,
From which we come
We relive,
We re-enact,
We remember.

Holding the branch of that old tree,
Hanging upside down looking down,
We cry,
We reach out,
we journey deep.

History is in our bones,
As we walk the earth,
Every step with us,
Within us,
Ancestors,
Guides,
Memory.

They have gone before us,
Holders of the treasures of knowledge.
Bringing knowledge of the future,
Regaining what has been lost,

Singing that wisdom of ages,
Touching traditions across time,
Healing the broken heart vessel.

Here we are,
Sleeping with the ashes of the dead.
By the burial mound.
By the doorway.
Waiting in the cave.
Entrances through which you speak.
Tribe of spirits,
Faery ones,
Ancestors.
Timeless ones,
Dwellers at the wellspring,
You are with us.

Here we speak of your coming,
From stone and fire,
Heat and hard,
Father of fire,
Mother of water life.
Your dreams that waken in our bodies,
Plants and flowers our flesh,
Blood flowing in water, rivers, rain
Springs.
A layer of breath, vision, movement,
Layer of wind and animals,
Growing out of the earth.
All of us,
Come Into forms mirror,
Come into this time to remember,
With you spirits!

Old man,
Old woman,
Singing words out of the layers.
Repeated, revealing, giving names,
Sung into things,
Sacred and calling,
Their stories coming into life.
Their eyes watch us still.

Songs of places on their lips,
Songs of words in our bodies,
Songs of the earth's life,
The old ones pass us on,
Into song,
Welcoming us into life.

So we remember,
The spirits.
We know they are here.
So we remember,
The dead,
We know they are here.
So we live in memory,
That we know who we are,
So the sparkling spirit of life comes,
And we know to offer ourselves.

We feed the dead on our love.
We remember where we have come from.
How much we take,
How much we have to give.
The spirits,
The ancestors,
They feed on our remembering and our
care.

Those who have seen before us.
Know.
We seek their wisdom.
To become good gifts to life.
To take root.
To become ripe fruit.
To pass through all the pain and loss,
Passing through the world of becoming,
To the heart,
To the root,
All through the layers.
Dying, reborn,
Aging, learning,
Birth, childhood
Adolescence,
Adult,
Elder,
Death.
Cycles in cycles,
Death in growth,
Growth in death,
Shaded by the elder trees we grow.
We fall as leaves and rot,
A good dying.
A good song of passing.
A good giving.
The old ones words with us,
They echo long,
Spring into song.

Wrapped in all the layers of life,
Layers of creation,
We are taken apart.
We forget.
We come together.

Re-membered.
All we know,
Rests on that ground,
Of death,
Of the ancestors.

We re-learn,
On the long road of remembrance.
Recollecting,
Recognising,
All the signs.
In us,
In nature,
In others.
Seeing how we touch,
And are part of,
Everything.

Wind on sea.
Wave on ocean.
Clouds before sun.
Rain on hills.
Trees that grow.
Fruit that falls.
Roots that sink.
Into the bones of death.

I am green life,
Sung out of death-earth.
I am incantation on the winds.
I am the people's gatherings.
I am the memory of my people.
I carry time.
The fruit of my life for life,
I am covered in layers of memory,
I am feeding the world for future
generations.

Life does not come from us.
Life flows from the ancient root.
From there comes the sap of life.
Touching the earth,
Touching the heart,
We walk the land to remember,
We walk the land in beauty,
We walk the land together.

The worlds all around us,
They planted, grew, ripened.
As I sing,
Their words are on my lips,
Holy speech,
Name magic,
Family name,
Inherited name,
Given name,

Sacred names,
Seeds from the old tree of life.

There is a spring at the trees roots.
That's where we remember to make life
itself again.

So I will speak well,
Speak well,
All your names,
All my songs,
All my stories,
With you,
With you all.

Speak like one of those,
who passed before us,
Who lives in words,
Who lives in image,
Who lives in story,
Who lives in dream,
Music,
Poetry,
Song,
Craft,
In the land.

Coming from you,
Ancestors,
Deep well of memory,
Indigenous soul awakens.
Deep songs of ancestors in the bones.
Deep love of parents.
Deep love of family.
Deep love of tribe.
Deep love of community.

Oh dead.
Oh ancestors.
Remembering you,
We talk to you,
We feel you,
In the world around us.
Be with us
Share with us.

Whispering in leaves,
Song of birds,
The scent of rotting,
The sudden memory,
The singing tree,
You are here!

You are here in image rising.
A Pilgrim,
Travelling to the clear streams side.
Wanderer on the far hill.
The call out of silence at dusk.
The crow crossing the field.
The sun's path and gateway.

You are here for us!
We are here for you,
For the dead,
We have come.
For the ancestors we have come,
For the dying we speak,
For the grieving we speak,
For all the loss,
For all the parting,
We give voice,
We utter our hearts.

Under our feet,
About us,
Within us,
Walking the earth,
In memory.
Buried in the earth,
Deep within us,
The memories,
Ancestors,
Born and buried there,
Unfolding flowers,
In the soft white hands,
Of death,
Releasing the beautiful scent,
Of our remembering.

THE SHAMBHALA WARRIOR MIND-TRAINING
BY AKUPPA

Firmly establish your intention to live your life for the healing of the world. Be conscious of it, honour it, nurture it every day.

Be fully present in our time. Find the courage to breathe in the suffering of the world. Allow peace and healing to breathe out through you in return.

Do not meet power on its own terms. See through to its real nature - mind and heart made. Lead your response from that level.

Simplify. Clear away the dead wood in your life. Look for the heartwood and give it the first call on your time, the best of your energy.

Put down the leaden burden of saving the world alone. Join with others of like mind. Align yourself with the forces of resolution.

Hold in a single vision, in the same thought, the transformation of yourself and the transformation of the world. Live your life around that edge, always keeping it in sight.

As a bird flies on two wings, balance outer activity with inner sustenance.

Following your heart, realise your gifts. Cultivate them with diligence to offer knowledge and skill to the world.

Train in non-violence of body, speech and mind. With great patience to yourself, learn to make beautiful each action, word and thought.

In the crucible of meditation, bring forth day by day into your own heart the treasury of compassion, wisdom and courage for which the world longs.

Sit with hatred until you feel the fear beneath it. Sit with fear until you feel the compassion beneath that.

Do not set your heart on particular results. Enjoy positive action for its own sake and rest confident that it will bear fruit.

When you see violence, greed and narrow-mindedness in the fullness of its power, walk straight into the heart of it, remaining open to the sky and in touch with the earth.

Staying open, staying grounded, remember that you are the inheritor of the strengths of thousands of generations of life.

Staying open, staying grounded, recall that the thankful prayers of future generations are silently with you.

Staying open, staying grounded, be confident in the magic and power that arise when people come together in a great cause.

Staying open, staying grounded, know that the deep forces of Nature will emerge to the aid of those who defend the Earth.

Staying open, staying grounded, have faith that the higher forces of wisdom and compassion will manifest through our actions for the healing of the world.

When you see weapons of hate, disarm them with love.

When you see armies of greed, meet them in the spirit of sharing.

When you see fortresses of narrow-mindedness, breach them with truth.

When you find yourself enshrouded in dark clouds of dread, dispel them with fearlessness.

When forces of power seek to isolate us from each other, reach out with joy.

In it all and through it all, holding fast to your intention, let go into the music of life. Dance!

BUDDHAFIELD DHARMA QUOTES

Over the years Buddhafield has drawn on a huge range of Buddhist sources, both traditional and contemporary, for its Dharmic inspiration, though it is firmly anchored in the Triratna Buddhist Community. Sometimes these have been deliberately drawn together to help the Buddhafield community explore in more depth that year's theme, sometimes they have simply 'appeared' as if by magic. Be that as it may, here's a selection:

If you wish to visit Buddhafields,
Purify ordinary deluded attachment.
The perfect, excellent Buddhafield is near at hand.
Dudjom Rimpoche, from
'A prayer to recognise my own faults and keep in mind the objects of Refuge'

Without things,
There would be no appearance or disappearance;
Without which,
There would be no things.
from the 2012 Festival, Doorways to Freedom (Nagarjuna)

'Provided we remain mindful,
the process of transformation will continue
of its own accord'.
from the 2015 Festival, Awakened Awareness (Sangharakshita)

'The word 'mindfulness' can feel rather cool and cognitive.
It might be better to call it 'heartfulness'.
Our experience will not open up to us
unless we can bring kindness to it'.
from the 2015 Festival, Awakened Awareness (Maitreyabandhu, 'Life With Full Attention'.

What the Buddha taught was freedom –
freedom from the illusion of self,
and freedom to abide in the wordless mystery,
the ever-changing beauty
of the way things are.
from the 2012 Festival, Doorways to Freedom

A Reflection for Eating:
'In this food
I see clearly
the presence of the entire universe,
supporting my existence'
from the 2012 Festival, Doorways to Freedom (Thich Nhat Hanh).

'Deeper pleasures have a distinctive inner radiance and softness.
They feel different to superficial thrills.
Deeper pleasures feel deeper –
they have less 'self' in them.
from the 2015 Festival, Awakened Awareness (Maitreyabandhu)

'In mindfulness, we hold the secret of our own happiness.'
from from the 2015 Festival, Awakened Awareness

'If the doors of perception were cleansed,
everything would appear to man as it is,
infinite'.
from the 2015 Festival, Awakened Awareness (William Blake)

'To see the preciousness of all things,
we must bring our full attention to life'.
from the 2015 Festival, Awakened Awareness (Jack Kornfield)

'If we knew that tonight we were going to be blind,
we would take a longing last real look at every blade of grass,
every cloud formation,
every speck of dust,
every rainbow,
raindrop –
everything.'
from the 2015 Festival, Awakened Awareness (Pema Chodron)

'Not causing harm requires staying awake.
Part of being awake is slowing down
enough to notice what we say and do.
The more we witness our emotional chain reactions
and understand how they work,
the easier it is to refrain.
It becomes a way of life to stay awake,
slow down,
and notice.'
from the 2015 Festival, Awakened Awareness (Pema Chodron)

'When the mind is full of memories and preoccupied by the future, it misses the
freshness of the present moment. In this way, we fail to recognize the luminous
simplicity of mind that is always present behind the veils of thought.'
from the 2015 Festival, Awakened Awareness (Mathieu Ricard)

'Enemies such as craving and hatred are without arms or legs.
They are neither courageous nor wise.
How is it that they have enslaved me?'
from the 2015 Festival, Awakened Awareness (Shantideva)

Try to be mindful, and let things take their natural course.
Then your mind will become still in any surroundings,
like a clear forest pool.
All kinds of wonderful, rare animals
will come to drink at the pool,
and you will clearly see the nature of all things.
You will see many strange and wonderful things come and go,
but you will be still.
This is the happiness of the Buddha.
from the 2015 Festival, Awakened Awareness (Ajahn Chah)

Be Here Now
Be here. No need to move:
You are all that's needed.
Leave wealth to those who have nothing else.
Listen! The wind's dropped.
Stars overflow above your head.
These moments have taken billions of years to grow.
Don't drop them now. Here.
Take the key. It's all yours.
from the 2015 Festival, Awakened Awareness (Ananda)

'The more we try to squeeze enjoyment out of experience,
the more likely it is that what we end up with is pain.'
from the 2015 Festival, Awakened Awareness

It can be helpful to have a place in the body where we keep our awareness as
much as possible, and come back to. The lower belly works well. Keeping
awareness lower in the body conduces to being less lost in thought.
from the 2015 Festival, Awakened Awareness

Loving-kindness is not weak or passive,
but is the strength that comes from seeing
the true nature of suffering in the world,
enabling us to bear witness to that suffering without fear.
from the 2013 Festival - Fire in the Heart (Sharon Salzberg)

The point of cultivating metta is to bring you closer to reality.
from the 2013 Festival - Fire in the Heart (Sangharakshita)

It is a rare and beautiful quality to feel truly happy when others are happy.
from the 2013 Festival - Fire in the Heart (Sharon Salzberg)

There is in metta no desire to impress,
or to ingratiate oneself,
or to feather one's nest,
or to gain favours.
from the 2013 Festival - Fire in the Heart (Sangharakshita)

To be undivided and unfragmented,
to be completely present, is to love.
To pay attention is to love.
from the 2013 Festival - Fire in the Heart (Sharon Salzberg)

What unites us all as human beings is an urge for happiness,
which at heart is a yearning for union,
for overcoming our feelings of separateness.
We want to feel our identity with something larger than our small selves.
We long to be one with our own lives and with each other.
from the 2013 Festival - Fire in the Heart

By reconnecting to the little things,
we awaken again to a delightful kind of openness....
When we are touched by things,
moved by the actions of people,
we open to what is around us.
When we feel happy for others,
we feel happy and connected ourselves.
The separateness and dullness of boredom is dissolved.
from the 2013 Festival - Fire in the Heart

'Mindfulness harmonizes and unifies
every aspect of Buddhist practice
into a concentrated, responsive awareness...'
from the 2015 Festival, Awakened Awareness (Sangharakshita)

"Perfection of character is this:
to live each day as if it were your last,
without frenzy, without apathy, without pretence."
from the 2015 Festival, Awakened Awareness (Marcus Aurelius)

When we feel love,
our mind is expansive and open enough
to include the entirety of life in full awareness,
both its pleasures and its pains.
from the 2013 Festival - Fire in the Heart (Sharon Salzberg)

Looking at people and communicating that they can be loved,
and that they can love in return,
is giving them a tremendous gift.
It is also a gift to ourselves.
We see that we are one with the fabric of life.
from the 2013 Festival - Fire in the Heart (Sharon Salzberg)

It is only through seeing our fundamental connection with the world that a life of
true peace becomes possible.
from the 2013 Festival - Fire in the Heart (Sharon Salzberg)

217

THREE DOORWAYS

In the experience of the three lakshanas (impermanence; dukkha/unsatisfactoriness; and insubstantiality/no fixed self), we find the three vimokshas, the doorways: **mystery**, **letting-go**, and **limitlessness**. This way of looking at the lakshanas turns them into a practice rather than a statement 'this is how it is'.

The first doorway, arising from the laksana of impermanence, is **mystery:** seeing that the nature of life is change, or flow, and so cannot be pinned down and is totally beyond any ideas we might have about it.

The second doorway, arising from the laksana of unsatisfactoriness, is **letting-go,** or equanimity: when we let go of trying to control it all, we can find peace and stillness in the midst of the storm.

The third doorway, arising from the laksana of no fixed self, is **limitlessness**, or the discovery that we are not separate from the rest of life; this separation is an illusion and the root of all our suffering.

from the 2012 Festival, Doorways to Freedom

The Dharma Parlour, 2013

FURTHER INFORMATION

The Buddhafield website at www.buddhafield.com offers up-to-date information about Buddhafield's programme and a wealth of background information. It's also a portal for anyone interested in volunteering with Buddhafield - whether in the Café, the Festival, Retreats, or on the land, plus pages for FAQ, Fundraising, the new Buddhafield Arts Collective, and plenty more.

Listed below are some other Buddhafield-related links that are a little harder to find:

Buddhafield Dharma talks
go to www.freebuddhistaudio.com and search for 'Buddhafield'

Buddhafield Facebook
www.facebook.com/groups/buddhafield

Buddhafield in the City
search on Facebook or the Buddhafield website

Buddhafield Photos
www.flickr.com/photos/buddhafield

Buddhafield Videos
go to www.videosangha.net and search for 'buddhafield'

The Buddhafield Blog
blog.buddhafield.com

Buddhafield's several sister projects have their own websites, as does the Triratna Buddhist Community itself. Find them at:

Buddhafield East
www.buddhafieldeast.co.uk

Buddhafield North
www.buddhafieldnorth.org.uk

Buddhafield New Zealand
www.facebook.com/groups/BuddhafieldNZ

Buddhafield Sussex:
www.buddhafieldsoutheast.co.uk

Triratna's main website:
www.thebuddhistcentre.com

Triratna Retreats:
www.goingonretreat.com

EcoDharma
www.ecodharma.com

Published by Avalonia
www.avaloniabooks.co.uk

Ingram Content Group UK Ltd.
Milton Keynes UK
UKHW030400250523
422304UK00005B/36